The Way of the Eight Winds

"Nigel Pennick is one of Britain's living treasures. Like a latter-day Pythagoras, he reveals the unity behind existences, upholding the cosmos as animated, not as dead matter. This wonderful book of lore discerns the essential harmony connecting all things while exploring the geomantic art of placement that helps us make sense of the order of each place. An indispensable guide to understanding our dear world."

CAITLÍN MATTHEWS, AUTHOR OF
THE COMPLETE LENORMAND ORACLE HANDBOOK

"In a world yearning for a deeper spiritual connection, Nigel Pennick's *The Way of the Eight Winds* offers a timeless animistic approach to living in harmony with the natural world. Born out of a need to bring ancient wisdom to the pressing dynamics of modern life, Pennick guides readers toward a more harmonious relationship with nature, themselves, and their communities. This book is a must-read for anyone seeking to rekindle a land-based identity and interdependence with ecosystems."

S. KELLEY HARRELL, AUTHOR OF *RUNIC BOOK OF DAYS*

"Nigel Pennick has spent a lifetime as a multitalented artist and artisan, author, and pagan practitioner, and *The Way of the Eight Winds* brings together many branches of his verdant work. The resulting system—which illuminates everything from higher cosmic principles to the more modest cultural arts of craftsmanship—is rooted in the timeless lore of how humans interact meaningfully and reciprocally with their living landscape and its myriad inhabitants, seen and unseen."

MICHAEL MOYNIHAN, PH.D., COEDITOR OF
THE RUNE POEMS

"Employing his wide-ranging scholarship and years of experience, Nigel Pennick presents nature as numinous, imbued with subtle energies, a gateway to the unseen, reached through geomancy—the art, as the author puts it, of 'making ourselves right with the earth.'"

ANNA FRANKLIN, AUTHOR OF
THE HEARTH WITCH'S KITCHEN HERBAL

"Nigel Pennick has an encyclopedic knowledge of traditional magical practices, which is evident in the well-researched and clearly explained material in this book. Highly recommended."

IAN READ, EDITOR OF *CHAOS INTERNATIONAL* MAGAZINE

"The author writes about the spirit of place and pagan geomancy and magic from a traditional and pluralistic viewpoint, describing true principles that are universal and then detailing their expression in the European tradition from antiquity to the arts and crafts movement. For the first time, the material on the Way of the Eight Winds is brought together in one place. A long-awaited gem."

PATRICK MCFADZEAN, AUTHOR OF
THE GEOMANCERS GUIDE TO THE VASTUPURUSA MANDALA

"This beautifully illustrated compendium distills the wisdom of Pennick's lifetime of research and more than 50 published books. Across cultures and millennia, he describes the 'ever-changing and ever-flowing cosmos' and how uniquely human intelligence and creativity have evolved in relation to the complex immutability of the laws of nature. This book should be on university reading lists and essential for those who seek to restore balance and harmony in our relationship with the natural world."

LINDA KELSEY-JONES, RETIRED LECTURER, TEXAS STATE UNIVERSITY,
COLLEGE OF FINE ARTS AND COMMUNICATION, ART EDUCATION

"A complete compendium of symbolic and geomantic practices derived from the fourfold layout of the human body."

PRUDENCE JONES, COAUTHOR OF *A HISTORY OF PAGAN EUROPE*

The Way of the Eight Winds

Elemental Magic and Geomancy in the Pagan Tradition

Nigel Pennick

Destiny Books
Rochester, Vermont

Destiny Books
One Park Street
Rochester, Vermont 05767
www.DestinyBooks.com

Destiny Books is a division of Inner Traditions International

Copyright © 2025 by Nigel Pennick

All drawings and photographs are by Nigel Pennick unless otherwise noted. Archive illustrations courtesy of the Library of the European Tradition. Images credited to other sources and not old enough to be in the public domain are shared under CC-BY-SA.

All rights reserved. No part of this book may be reproduced or utilized in any form or by any means, electronic or mechanical, including photocopying, recording, or any information storage and retrieval system, without permission in writing from the publisher. No part of this book may be used or reproduced to train artificial intelligence technologies or systems.

Cataloging-in-Publication Data for this title is available from the Library of Congress

ISBN 979-8-88850-074-3 (print)
ISBN 979-8-88850-075-0 (ebook)

Printed and bound in China by Reliance Printing Co., Ltd.

10 9 8 7 6 5 4 3 2 1

Text design by Priscilla Harris Baker and layout by Debbie Glogover
This book was typeset in Garamond Premier Pro with Avenir LT Std, Gill Sans MT Pro, Skolar, and Spirits used as display typefaces

To send correspondence to the author of this book, mail a first-class letter to the author c/o Inner Traditions • Bear & Company, One Park Street, Rochester, VT 05767, and we will forward the communication.

Scan the QR code and save 25% at InnerTraditions.com. Browse over 2,000 titles on spirituality, the occult, ancient mysteries, new science, holistic health, and natural medicine.

Augurandi scientia nobilis erat et antiqua, apud gentes praesertim Hetruscos: quibus erat collegium et domicilium celeberrimum Augurum, quorum summa fuit authoritas et dignitas per totam Italiam, potissimum Romae.
—BEN JONSON,
THE MASQUE OF AUGURS (1622)

Contents

PREFACE
An Ever-Changing and Ever-Flowing Cosmos   xi

PROLOGOS
Origins of the Way of the Eight Winds   1

PART I
Philosophical Viewpoints

1   Points of View   20

2   The Recovery of Ancient Wisdom   27

3   Unity   32

4   The Eternal Tradition   39

5   A History of Authenticity   43

6   On Spectacle   51

7   Divination and Chance   53

8   Human Personifications of the Divine   57

9   The Naming of Names   65

10   Ørlög and History   69
     The Formation of the Modern World

11   The Eldritch World   75

PART II
Cosmic Principles

12	The Four Elements and the Cosmic Egg	80
13	The World, the Cosmos, and the Human Body	85
14	Temperament and the Divine Harmony	90
15	The Planetary Spheres and the Ogdoas	94
16	Myths of Coming into Being	98
17	At the Center of the World *The Omphalos and the Spindle of Necessity*	101
18	Time, Space, and Fate	108
19	Our Place on Earth	113
20	The Four Directions	119
21	The Eight Tides of the Day	126
22	The Winds	132
23	Specific Winds	143
24	The Right Place at the Right Time	153
25	Nature and the Eldritch	159
26	The Sacredness of Manifested Phenomena	169
27	Places of Spirit	176
28	Trees, *Temenoi*, and Places of the Ancestral Spirits	184
29	Numinous Places in the Land	192

30	Feng Shui	199
31	Crossing the Borderlines	205
32	The *Locus Terribilis* and the *Locus Amoenus*	219
33	The Sacred and the Profane *Archaeology*	225

PART III
Geomancy

34	Physical Elements of Geomancy	230
35	The Cosmic Axis	239
36	The Road Leads Us On	247
37	Stonehenge	250
38	The Crossroads	257
39	Labyrinths	261
40	Geomantic Protection	267

PART IV
Makings

41	The Spiritual Arts and Crafts	276
42	Sacred Geometry	284
43	Specific Geometric Forms	293
44	Spiritual Exercises	297
45	Tools and Techniques	306

PART V
Metaphorical Texts

46	The Labyrinth	324
	Ariadne's Dancing Ground	
47	Wayland's House	327
48	The Wayfarer's Legacy	335

EPILOGOS
Confluence   337

APPENDIX 1
Number Symbolism   341

APPENDIX 2
Musical Ratios   343

APPENDIX 3
The Tides of the Day   344

Glossary   346

Bibliography and Sources for Further Study   352

Index   375

PREFACE

An Ever-Changing and Ever-Flowing Cosmos

The Way of the Eight Winds is a spiritual path that recognizes and celebrates the plurality of the Cosmos and the creativity of Nature, of which we are part. The inner essence of all religions and spiritual ways is in the relationship of humans to the Cosmos. Usually, this takes the form of the adoration of some specific aspect of multivalent reality; this can be perceived in an infinite variety of different ways, described by different explanatory mythologies.

The Way of the Eight Winds recognizes the essentially false nature of all dogma and doctrine and the destructive results of literalism. The sad limits of fundamentalism—the insistence on there being one and only one way, a literal interpretation of some time-bound and culture-bound writing—stand exposed when we contemplate the grand diversity and plurality of existence.

Nature, on both her physical and spiritual levels, is infinitely diverse, ever-changing, flowing, never fixed. There is not just one sort of bird, one size of fruit, one cloud-form, one color of sunset, one type of soil, one crystalline shape, one form of wave, one size of star or galaxy. In the psychic realm of humanity, there is not just one language, one

xii Preface

Cover of an original Way of the Eight Winds publication

alphabet, one idea, one type of art, one form of music, one type of gameplay, one science, one spirituality. We live in a polytheistic, polyvalent, polycultural Cosmos, in eternal change and flow.

The Way of the Eight Winds brings a mindful approach to our environment, both seen and unseen. It practices the essence of the Indigenous European spiritual philosophy in contemporary form, taking it beyond the borders and limitations of dogmatism. Although it is expressed in the terminology and style of traditional spirituality from a temperate northern-hemisphere perspective, it also recognizes that these

Way of the Eight Winds banner,
designed and painted by Nigel Pennick, 1989

universal principles underlie comparable ancient practices from other lands and cultures, which are mentioned where applicable.

The essence of traditional ways, expressed mindfully in contemporary forms, brings wonderful possibilities for the spectacle-free experience of human life.

PROLOGOS

Origins of the Way of the Eight Winds

Occasionem qui sapis ne amiseris.
(Ye who are wise—do not lose the opportunity.)
—Seventeenth-century motto

My Early Influences

I was born in 1946 and brought up in postwar London amid the poisonous smog that swirled around the ruins of that monstrous conflict. As consciousness emerged, I saw the physical environment I lived in, the richness of a diverse culture that flourished despite the poverty that prevailed. Close to where I lived in the Bloomsbury district was the British Museum, where my mother would take me occasionally. I saw ancient artifacts that most children of that time never got to see; indeed, they had no means of seeing even pictures of them in an age when there were few televisions and no internet. The impressive larger-than-life images of ancient Egyptian deities, such as the awesome and terrifying lioness-headed goddess Sekhmet, made a great impression on me. They showed me that human culture and understanding was far more diverse and ancient than the things I saw around me every day.

It was clear to me that the culture I lived in was the successor of many earlier ones that had almost disappeared except in surviving fragments. They were rather like the burnt-out shells of buildings that still stood, forlorn and overgrown, in local bomb sites, relics of lost times. London's buildings that had survived the Blitz, though dirty and delapidated, still retained their period ornament, which ranged from eighteenth-century classical elegance through Victorian Gothic exuberance, to Arts and Crafts, Edwardian Baroque, and interwar Art Deco. Ancient churches, too, built in the seventeenth and eighteenth centuries, had forms and patterns that were redolent of a former age when the vastness of Creation was recognized and embodied in symbolic form. I could feel the numinous qualities of these venerable places whenever I entered them. I came to understand that there is a hidden landscape beneath the outer surface.

There was a cognitive dissonance between the religious teachings I received, which dealt with antiquity and occasionally the infinite, and the burgeoning modernity of a new era of jet aircraft, space rockets, atomic bombs, television, and modern brutalist concrete architecture. There was also the obvious poverty and ruined state of things in a country that supposedly had just been on the winning side of the war. I was living in the run-down ruins of the splendid future that world-improvers had promised long before. The official arts of the age, manifested in roughcast concrete and aluminium, seemed to me to be an atavistic cry of anguish in response to the horrors of war, a rejection of all that was good about the past in an attempt to expiate the bad. These new brutalisms were the beginning of a merciless onslaught of sociocide that destroyed at a deeper cultural level than ever the bombs could.

At the age of ten, I suffered a major infection that affected my brain. I was treated with antibiotic injections, but during the week or so the infection lasted, I underwent a terrifying ordeal of what would probably

Origins of the Way of the Eight Winds 3

THE BLOOMSBURY WONDER

SACRED GEOMETRY AND THE ETERNAL TRADITION
by
NIGEL PENNICK

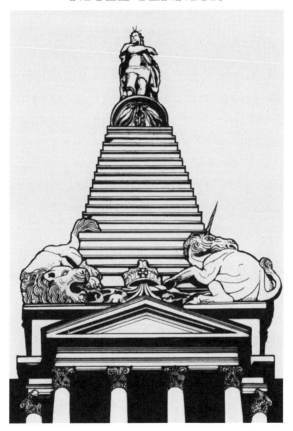

Cover of *The Bloomsbury Wonder* (2005) with the author's drawing of the steeple of St George's Church, Bloomsbury, London. Nicholas Hawksmoor's step-pyramid design derived from eighteenth-century ideas of the form of the mausoleum at Halicarnassus, one of the Seven Wonders of the World in antiquity.

now be called a "near-death experience." Deaf and almost blind with infection, I hallucinated terrifyingly bright, pulsating, colored spheres. I felt myself in the top corner of the room looking down on my body lying in the bed. Then I was taken upward, passing through the solid ceiling and roof, and upward above the streets and houses into the clouds. I descended again through the roof, the ceiling, and the bed, through the lower floors and cellars and deep into the earth and rocks below, where I was enclosed in a series of granite and metallic shells. There I stayed for aeons of time, so I experienced, until gradually I regained normal consciousness and finally was walking about again.

My hearing and sight had returned, and I was "back to normal." In actuality, I was not. I had no idea of what had happened to me, or whether there was any meaning at all to this harrowing ordeal. But I could remember everything that had happened to me in those other places. I never told anyone about it until years later, and nobody around me had any idea that I had experienced such a traumatic dislocation from "familiar reality." Events such as this are communicable in words, or I would not be able to write about them at all, but my actual firsthand experience is impossible to convey.

During the 1950s, I made regular visits to my maternal grandmother, who lived in Guildford, to the southwest of London. She was a southern English countrywoman from the laboring class, born in 1884, living on the edge of poverty and feeding herself with vegetables grown in her garden according to the traditional ways of "Old West Surrey." I helped to dig the garden, and on one occasion, I was told not to touch the vegetation of a triangular corner, where weeds grew. She told me that it should not be dug because "the fairies live there." Later I found out that this was not just a personal custom of my grandmother, but a folk tradition with venerable roots (the "Halyman's Rig"). The expression "Old West Surrey" was coined by the noted artist and gardener Gertrude Jekyll (1843–1932) to describe a traditional culture and way of life now totally destroyed by modernity in the interrelated forms of commuter suburbia and consumer society.

I have only outlined some of my formative childhood experiences here. I describe these and others in much greater detail in my autobiography, *Wyrd Times: Memoirs of a Pagan Renaissance Man* (Pennick 2023, 9–24).

The Spirit of London

I learned the structure and essences of places by walking, and I navigated the city from stations on the underground rail system, some of which appeared to have been designed by their architects to contain esoteric elements. The London Underground is an aspect of modernity that the ancients could never have dreamed of except in terms of the underworld—a liminal space beneath the city streets. There is a current or tradition in London, that expresses a sensibility of otherworldliness and can be perceived by those in the right frame of mind, lying just below the surface of the mundane, everyday existence of the city streets. The extraordinary may appear suddenly from the ordinary milieu as an *ostentum* or a revelation. The invisible and the symbolic are both dimensions of reality.

This is the cryptogeography that writers of both spiritual and fictional works on London have tapped into over many centuries. This London visionary tradition is informed by a particular sensibility that prioritizes the search for the miraculous. Arthur Machen (1863–1947) called it the "Ars Magna of London," and the essence of this art is that it must be an adventure into the unknown. It is achieved, if at all, through wandering. Wanderers in the city encounter many things when they exercise what Arthur Machen called the "art of wandering." This is not tourism, which is a visit focused upon "seeing the sights," often with a guide. This, while instructive to those who are receptive, is not a means of accessing the hidden levels.

Wandering is not a pilgrimage to a particular place, passing through fixed way stations of intellectual or spiritual interest. The surrealist André Breton (1896–1966) told of "wandering in search of everything."

6 Prologos

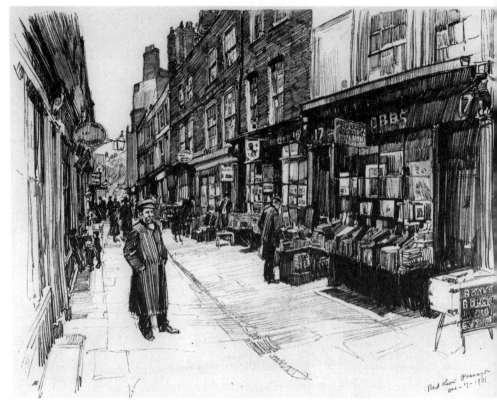

A 1901 drawing of Red Lion Passage in London, redolent of places where the Ars Magna of the city manifests amid the everyday to those who can see beyond the mundane

Trouvailles, "found objects," are part of this practice. Many Dada and Surrealist artists, most notably Joseph Cornell (1903–1972), worked with found objects. *Trouvailles* may just be seen as interesting items or as gifts from the gods or the otherworld, depending on one's worldview. According to East Anglian teachings, they contain *sprowl*, the essence of the place, which may be accessed once they are taken home and kept in a Sprowl Box. Pilgrimages and journeymen's travels, such as the *Tour de France* of members of the craftworkers' Compagnonnage,* are

---

*The name of the cycle race called *Le Tour de France* was appropriated from the much earlier handicraft tradition.

valuable exercises in their own right and have a transformative effect on their participants. But wandering is a form of divination, a random or serendipitous means of enabling us to consider life questions that do not lend themselves to linear thought. Sometimes we may encounter something that illuminates a particular dimension of the extraordinary in the world.

What we learn to feel in our wanderings is the "influence of surroundings" as Charles Webster Leadbeater (1854–1934) called it. According to his Theosophical interpretation, each thing has its own "temperamental characteristics" that express its elemental essence appropriate to its astral counterpart and thus determine the kind of nature-spirits it attracts. People who are sensitive can pick up these "vibrations" either consciously or unconsciously. Every philosophical system has its own worldview and a terminology that expresses it.

Charles Dickens's The Old Curiosity Shop, London

Leadbeater's "influence of surroundings" was expressed before him in various other traditions, notably the Provençal concept of *ambience*. It was not strictly materialist, as was, for example, the psychogeography expounded in the 1950s by Guy Debord (1931–1995) and his Situationist International followers. This principle was also hinted at in the many *Maigret* detective novels by Georges Simenon (1903–1989).

But psychogeography, emerging from twentieth-century militant secular materialism, had little understanding that, historically, towns and cities were divided up into quarters—and even specific streets—where particular trades and crafts were practiced. Today, the city of Birmingham in England still has districts called the Jewellery Quarter and the Gun Quarter. The character of different streets and districts was determined by the trade conducted there. For example, the traditional song "The Dublin Jack of All Trades" lists the various city streets of the Irish capital where the different trades were plied. One of the song's six verses tells:

> *In College Green a banker was,*
> *In Smithfield was a drover,*
> *In Britain Street a waiter, and*
> *In George's Street, a glover.*
> *On Ormond Quay, I sold old books;*
> *In King Street, was a nailer;*
> *In Townsend Street, a carpenter;*
> *And in Ringsend, a sailor.*

These streets of old cities had a human scale, where people could relate to one another, even in competition, for there was a wider common interest in their specific location. This close-knit human solidarity was engendered by common livelihoods contained in a specific location in the city. When I was young in London, there were still places associated with particular trades such as Fleet Street, where all the national newspapers had their offices, and Covent Garden, where wholesale vegetable merchants plied their trade. Even when these trades had gone—having either ceased to exist or moved elsewhere—some residual trace of them remained in the physical buildings or in a more subtle sense. André Malraux (1901–1976) called this phenomenon the persisting life of certain forms reemerging again and again like specters from the past (Malraux 1978, 13).

I learned that there were indeed numinous, special places in the city where one might glimpse visions of the Otherworld. I came upon these places by chance (or providence), and through my reading of rarely opened volumes in libraries and books I purchased from the incomparable Atlantis Bookshop (founded in 1922), I encountered the then-almost-forgotten art of geomancy. Geomancy is about being "right with the Earth," in harmony with the place we live, and is more than just geographical orientation, the management of subtle energies, or the placement of individual artifacts. It is an art that has existed in various forms across the world, including the ancient *Etruscan Discipline* and the medieval art of *Location* in Europe, *Vastu Vidya* in India, *Vintana* in Madagascar, *Feng Shui* in China, and *Taj al Maluk* in Malaysia and the related *Tajalmaluk* in Indonesia.

The "Ars Magna of London" had been the preserve of notable writers and mystics before Arthur Machen. William Blake (1757–1827) expounded visions of the spiritual New Jerusalem underlying the London of his day, waiting to break through the surface into "England's green and pleasant land." Other nineteenth-century writers who tapped into this current included the opium-eater Thomas de Quincey (1786–1859), Charles Dickens (1812–1870), Robert Louis Stevenson (1850–1894), and Arthur Conan Doyle (1859–1930). Their literary explorations of "the influence of surroundings" described the streets and hidden places of London as mysterious and dangerous. Twentieth-century exponents of the London Art as defined by Machen included the Druidic-inspired Elizabeth Oke Gordon (1837–1919), Lewis Spence (1874–1955), Ross Nichols (1902–1975), Anthony Roberts (1940–1990), and Colin Murray (1942–1986), as well as the current author, who knew the last

A glimpse of the Ars Magna of London

three personally. Visionaries all, they understood that every place could be experienced on levels other than the obvious surface of everyday life and that certain of them were gateways to the unseen. As Arthur Machen encapsulated these visions (1923, 127):

> Strangeness which is the essence of beauty is the essence of truth, and the essence of the world. I have often felt that, when the ascent of a long hill brought me to the summit of an undiscovered height in London; and I looked down on a new land.

Geomancy

As a student in Cambridge, I met old practitioners of the local rural tradition known as the *Nameless Art*. I learned from them that although Nature is treated as if it were a human possession, it is not. We are subject to Nature, no matter what we do, and it is to the earth that we must return when we die. They talked knowledgeably of various magical practices used by the farm laborers in the days when horses were used for plowing and transport, which was in living memory then (Pennick 2023, 61–63). I was made aware of special places and means of dealing with harmful influences, if necessary. My geomantic teaching emerged and developed through my extensive reading in the Cambridge University Library and participation in the alternative press paper *Cambridge Voice*, of which I was a cofounder in 1968. John Nicholson (1940–2021) was editor of *Cambridge Voice* and later opened the King Street Market shop, which sold occult publications as well as alternative press titles. It was the first shop in Cambridge to sell tarot cards. John Nicholson then set up a company called the Land of Cokaygne Ltd., and soon opened the Cokaygne Bookshop in better premises at Jesus Terrace in the Kite Area, much of which, being part of the town and not the university, was slated for demolition.

There was a building out the back where typesetting and printing equipment was installed, and Cokaygne Press came into existence. It produced *Arcana* magazine, subtitled "a magazine of Cambridge occult lore," and a series of other publications including my *Geomancy* (1973); a reprint of the Reverend J. Eitel's 1873 book *Feng-Shui, or the Rudiments of Natural Science in China* (1973); and my book *The Mysteries of King's College Chapel* (1974). Many years later I discovered that the part of Cambridge where the Land of Cokaygne operated was formerly called the "Garden of Eden," a series of market gardens before the area was built upon. In their mythos, the fraternal guild called the Free Gardeners had revered the Garden of Eden and referred to it in initiations into the first degree. Eden Street and Adam & Eve Street (whose name changes to Paradise Street at a bend in the road) still exist in this former garden area at the time of writing. Underlying the city streets today is the Blakean vision of an earthly paradise, of which Cokaygne (aka Cockaigne) was a medieval English version. The earthly paradise is a remarkable geomantic confluence that has been noted in many other places in different forms.

The Institute of Geomantic Research (IGR) was founded in 1975 by the current author, Prudence Jones, and Michael Behrend. We all had connections with *Arcana* magazine and formalized our investigations once Cokaygne and *Arcana* ceased existence (which was brought on by the rampant inflation and political turmoil of the time). The IGR produced many publications dealing with geomancy, archaeoastronomy, landscape lines, terrestrial zodiacs, and traditional understandings of the landscape. It also conducted field research and staged six geomancy symposia, meetings that attracted speakers from various parts of Britain and the United States. It was finally disbanded in late 1982.

The Society for Symbolic Studies (SSS) emerged from the IGR; it held meetings and published a journal, *The Symbol*. From the SSS, the Way of the Eight Winds emerged as a medium for symbolic teaching and practical geomantic work. The Way of the Eight Winds operated

Cokaygne Press cover of *Geomancy*
by Nigel Pennick, 1973

in the spirit of a sentiment ascribed to Heinrich Cornelius Agrippa von Nettesheim (1486–1535), which states:

> I do not give you these facts as truth, but as hypotheses that approach the truth. The lesson we need to learn is how to derive good from evil, and how to keep all things on the straight path.

It was never a polemic organization with a set of doctrinal tenets that were compulsory beliefs for all participants, but, like the Institute of Geomantic Research before it, a means of disseminating ideas about spiritual principles and practices that transcend particular belief systems. The Way of the Eight Winds sought to preserve and expound the Mysteries that may serve as gateways to the unseen.

In addition to numerous events, workshops, geomantic walks, and tours organized by the IGR, SSS, and the Way of the Eight Winds, I also gave talks to numerous geomantic and esoteric groups, spiritual orders and organizations in Britain, mainland Europe, and the United States. They included the Servants of the Light, the Wrekin Trust, the Odinic Rite, Hagia Chora, the Pagan Federation, Unlimited Futures, the Ojai Foundation, Tantra Galerie, the Rainbow Circle, Arkuna-Zentrum, the Research Into Lost Knowledge Organisation (RILKO), and others that must remain nameless. I also taught and led workshops at alternative fairs and gatherings that included the Festivals for Mind, Body, and Spirit at Olympia and Brixton Town Hall in London

Emblem of the Institute of Geomantic Research

and Bury St Edmunds in Suffolk; the Mercian Gathering in central England; the alternative fair at Polgooth; the Leicester May Fair; Lyng Faerie Fair; the Rougham Tree Fair; and the Strawberry Fair at Cambridge (of which I was a founder), where for several years I laid out the Green Area geomantically, which included temporary biodegradable labyrinths. I also presented lectures and multimedia shows there, as well as performed in mummers' plays.

I spoke in Britain at bookshops, including Atlantis in London and Libra Aries in Cambridge, as well as at Moots (gatherings) organized by *The Ley Hunter* magazine and other earth mysteries groups in London, Edinburgh, Oxford, Hereford, Ludlow, Machynlleth, Swansea, Bakewell, Nottingham, Northampton, Newcastle, York, Brighton, Leicester, Penzance, Harlow, Peterborough, Diss, Norwich, and numerous smaller places. At the beginning of the 2010s, I gave several lectures, presentations, and participated in a multimedia show at Wysing Arts at

Geomantic visit to the turf maze at Hilton (Huntingdonshire, England) by the Society for Symbolic Studies, 1993

Bourn in Cambridgeshire on subjects from the Way of the Eight Winds including geomantic mirrors, borderlines, and the wildwood.

Labyrinths were an important practical element of the Way of the Eight Winds, exploring their symbolic principles, and practical construction and use. The majority of labyrinths I have made over the years have been for practical events, not as permanent structures. Once constructed, they survived only for the period that they were needed. Then they were deliberately dismantled or allowed to disintegrate naturally. This is the natural way of labyrinths. Starting in the late 1970s, for particular events or teachings I laid out temporary labyrinths at various places in the British Isles: England, Wales, Cornwall, and the Republic of Ireland. I made a series of biodegradable sawdust labyrinths annually over a number of years in the green area at the Strawberry Fair on Midsummer Common in Cambridge.

In mainland Europe, I laid out temporary and permanent labyrinths in Germany between 1984 and the early twenty-first century; at

Strawberry Fair labyrinth, Cambridge, England, 1998

Linderhof in Zürich, Switzerland, in 1985 and 1988; and in Austria at Salzburg in 1988 and Baden bei Wien in 1994. The materials used have included wood blocks, stones, bricks, tree bark, fir cones, and sawdust. In 1986 I constructed a permanent stone labyrinth at the Ojai Foundation in California, one of the first of the new wave of spiritual labyrinths in North America. I had a number of subsequent private commissions in Great Britain and Germany, some of which were built while others never got off paper. In 1987, I was invited to participate in the traditional crafts section of the *Art in Action* festival at Waterperry House, Oxfordshire. Over a four-day period I used standard British house bricks to make a series of temporary labyrinths on the neatly mown lawn. I used all the common historic patterns, from the simplest three-circuit classical design to the larger Roman and medieval Christian forms. In 1991 I was one of the invited judges of a maze competition organized by the *Sunday Times* newspaper at Chenies Manor in Buckinghamshire. The prizewinning maze was built and is still there. The last labyrinth I made in Germany was near Cologne in 2003. In addition to walkable (and danceable) labyrinths, I painted various forms on wood and metal, and made stamps to press ceramic tiles with the pattern.

The End of My Traveling

Finally, I was forced to give up my Way of the Eight Winds teachings abroad. In August 2003, after an event at Cologne in Germany, I returned to England where I had a heart attack, though I did not get to hospital until sixteen hours later. There, in intensive care in Addenbrooke's Hospital, Cambridge, I endured my second near-death experience. I was aware that I was dying, and this was my last moment. I felt my body dissolving into a brilliant white light, which grew to blinding intensity as sharp shards of glass and gleaming metal emanated from within it. They tore through my body, and I was ripped apart from outside and inside as the shards ricocheted through my flesh and bones. I was physically cut to pieces, yet somehow my consciousness continued as my bodily fragments were transformed into forests, grasslands, wind and water, clouds in the sky. I was experiencing the primal event of dismemberment as told in the Norse myth of the cosmogonic giant, Ymir. As I lapsed into the void, I felt my ripped-apart body being reassembled. I survived, but my recovery spelled the end of my long-distance traveling. After 2003 I continued to write further on the themes explored by the Way of the Eight Winds, and to do occasional teachings and multimedia events in the United Kingdom. Subsequently, in October 2015, I suffered heart failure and collapsed. In the process of being resuscitated, I had a third near-death experience, in which I received the message: "Ask not the name of thy guardian angel."

PART I
Philosophical Viewpoints

Many who came before us explored unimagined realities emanating from the far depths of multiple vague terrains and left us accounts of their experiences, some incoherent and others terrifying in their clarity. As the Chaldaean Oracles of Zoroaster *tell us, we should "Seek Paradise," and it is through these delvings into what lies beneath and within that we may achieve this objective.*

1
Points of View

Alternative Viewpoints

There are two fundamental philosophical viewpoints of human existence, contradictory to one another. The viewpoint with the greatest currency at present in developed countries is that human life is a finite phenomenon hemmed in by time, essentially random and meaningless. As long ago as the seventeenth century, the English utilitarian philosopher Thomas Hobbes (1588–1679) saw human society as potentially the war of all against all. In this viewpoint, human life is no more than a constant struggle, "nasty, brutish, and short." Hobbes was writing at a time when traditional spirituality was questioned by the result of brutal, ruthless wars and new technical inventions, and the order of the world seemed to be disintegrating. It is clear that this grim and bleak view of existence underlies current materialist doctrines that promote the accumulation of power and wealth as the sole aim of human life.

Another way of living is the traditional spiritual view, that human life can be active and purposeful by being integrated with Nature's eternal return. Whether or not this has a religious dimension, the human being is integrated with Nature, not an alienated individual. Traditional rites and ceremonies—which are related to place, time, and

The Unity of All Existence, woodcut by Karel de Bazel (1869–1923)

the prevailing culture—link individuals into the wider community and through collective action to Nature and the Cosmos. As an expression of this eternal spiritual current, traditional rites and ceremonies across the world are concerned primarily with being in the right place at the right time.

The Power of Imagination

Nature itself would give us the impression of a work of art, if we could see the thought which is present at once in the whole and in every part.
—SAMUEL TAYLOR COLERIDGE
(1772–1834)

The imagination is a human ability of paramount importance. Creativity, the outward expression of the imagination, is the common property of all humans. Our mental power of image-making can liberate the human mind from the daily grind of conflict and survival, elevating us to another level beyond the material conditions with which we must cope. Early in the nineteenth century, the nature philosopher and poet Samuel Taylor Coleridge observed that the imagination is the living power and prime agent of all human perception. It is a reenactment of the eternal and transcendent act of creation in finite minds. As a "synthetic and magical power," Coleridge saw the imagination working through metaphor, which is "the perception of similitude in dissimilitude" (Coleridge 1920, 197).

Familiar reality generally obscures the eternal realities that exist just out of sight. The struggles of everyday life often mean that we must concentrate on surfaces, appearances. Those whose job it is to sell things create beautiful and beguiling artifacts that we must work to buy. They are presented to us by their shiny surfaces presented through highly skilled advertising. But there are glimpses through the cracks, for it is our imagination that unifies and shapes our relationship to the world, bringing us new meanings presented in a way they never were before. This is, according to Arthur Machen (1923, 48), "the magic touch that redeems and exults the dull mass of things, by tinging them with the soul of man." The incomplete reality that we experience is thereby given meaning. J. R. R. Tolkien (1892–1973) perceived that our imagination emerges from the same source of coming-into-being that gives the Cosmos its presence and allows us to remain alive. It has an infinitely plural and multiple expression of possibilities, always finding fresh forms expressive of the eternal. Johannes Ludovicus Mathieu Lauweriks (1864–1932) pointed out that the creative act is a transposition from the spiritual realm to the sensory, or the fixing of a visible form of something that previously did not exist (Lauweriks 1919, 5). Science, the law, divination, magic, and religion are not true reality—that is irreducible; they are only methods for investigating reality, more or less successful in their outcome, but nevertheless essentially flawed and incomplete. Only when the imagination is applied to any of them can deeper truths be glimpsed.

A Symbolic Worldview versus the Madness of Literalism

The psychologist Alfred Adler (1870–1937) observed that "In literalism lies madness." There are a number of ways of viewing the world, and today literalism is the predominant one. But the symbolic, upon which all spiritual systems depend, is an alternative to literalism. A symbol is not a sign, for literalism recognizes and uses signs. A sign represents being, or the world, but a true symbol denotes being-in-the-world. The sign exists in a fixed form, indicating a particular meaning that only requires human awareness; the symbol involves the participation of the individual. The symbol expresses or reveals the connection between the participant and itself thereby transforming or enlightening the individual. A living symbol is never received ready-made; it is re-created within the person. Religion and esoteric traditions are presented in symbolic form, though some institutions insist on a literal rather than a metaphorical interpretation. Symbols are doorways leading toward the invisible—they are a means of transcendence, not mere information. Existence is multilayered and our understanding of this tends to be limited because everyday experience requires us to concentrate upon the necessities of living. However, symbols do not exist to be deconstructed or decoded.

The traditional presentation of symbols and the worlds used to describe them vary from culture to culture. The Way of the Eight Winds presents them in the terminology of the ancient European Tradition while recognizing that in other cultures and at other times, these features have other descriptions. But the essential core remains the same. So, within the basic framework, there is always the freedom of personal experience. This is the epitome of the creative force, a personal exploration of a system that emerges from the deepest structure and meaning of existence. Any observation that can aid this vital flow of creativity and prevent it falling into the trap of claiming to possess absolute exclusive truth is of great value. There is no religion higher than the truth, and truth can never be the exclusive preserve of blinkered, dogmatic people.

The same mythic forms and symbols exist in many different cultures. They differ only in their cultural expression and historical context. They emerge from our shared experience of the human condition and our being in the world. Because symbols appear less real than physical objects, their reality is often dismissed as metaphysical constructs that have no place in the "real world" of science, medicine, technology, politics, and war. However, all of these spheres of human wisdom and folly can be viewed through the lens of symbol, and their structural and spiritual meanings seen in a deeper, nonliteral, way.

It is a human trait to seek the simplest solution to understanding the world. The medieval English philosopher William of Occam (1270–1347), known by the epithet of "Unique and Invincible Teacher," is best remembered for his Latin razor, *"Entia non sunt multiplicanda,"* literally: "Entities are not to be multiplied." This means, that when we are seeking the cause of a problem, we must be as sharp as a razor, slashing through the temptation to complicate matters, and first look at the simplest, the most obvious answer to our question. If we fail to do this, then we will be led away from a proper sequential process of investigation and fail to get to the roots of the matter. It does not mean, of course that simplification of complex matters is the right way to approach them. Later, in industrial times, an ironic engineer devised the acronym KISS—"Keep it simple, stupid!" In practice, however, engineering rarely adheres to this maxim, consistently producing exceedingly complex and overengineered products that are destined to be rapidly superseded by even more complex ones.

The propensity of modern engineers, politicians, and students of the esoteric to ignore the simple, basic roots of things and to make them more complicated than they need be is one of the greatest failings of contemporary society. Often it is driven by hubris and encouraged by the profit motive. Looking at the history of human institutions—whether religious, military, political, economic, or technical—we can see recurrent refusals to go for the obvious, simple solutions. Time and again, such institutions have chosen routes that led to catastrophic failure through following unfounded beliefs even when the evidence demonstrates unquestionably that they are going in the wrong direction. It is a very human tendency to be unaware of what has been done already in the past, and so to repeat the same mistakes. Even those who do study history and recognize mistakes that occurred often feel immune from the way of the world and act as though "this time" the failings of the past will not happen because the present is somehow materially different from the past. But it is not, and the "way of the world" has not changed, for it is innate.

Those who understand the inner meaning of myths and symbols can perceive in the present day the same processes and sequences of events that occurred in the past. The temptation to do the same failed and disastrous things again is prevented by an awareness that if we repeat things that did not work in the past, they will not work now. Spectacular failures have passed into history as symbolic instances of human hubris, and a warning to us all. The mythic downfall of Atlantis and the Tower of Babel are metaphors of overstretched hubristic human attempts to go beyond the limits of nature. The more extravagant the attempts, the greater the downfall appears to be. If we are to be aware of ourselves, our place in the Cosmos, and the transient events of wider human society, viewing the world symbolically is important.

Religious mystics have asserted that there are four aspects to the human experience of a text or physical artifact. It possesses, they maintain, an exoteric meaning and an esoteric meaning, and in addition a literal interpretation and a symbolic, spiritual interpretation. But however different they may appear, these four approaches are similar in that they all still perceive the artifact as a neutral object, whose essence is circumscribed within its perceived meaning and the interpretation thereof, rather than its existence as a physical thing that may be ensouled in its own right. As the artist Georges Braque (1882–1963), the originator of Cubism, noted: "I do not believe in things; I believe only in their relationship."

2

The Recovery of Ancient Wisdom

Metaphors of Primal Speech

Ancient traditions tell of a primal state of humans, when we were much closer to nature than most people are today. This is expressed in the legend of the Garden of Eden, a primal state of paradise from which humans were expelled. According to the esoteric interpretation, this paradise was a psychocosmic state where being coincided with knowing and words were the things they described. The ancient Greek treatise *On Style* (II, 71), conventionally ascribed to Demetrius of Phalerum (ca. 360–280 BCE), tells us: "In Egypt the priests, when singing hymns in praise of the gods, employ the seven vowels, which they utter in due succession; and the sound of these letters is so euphonious that men listen to it in place of flute and lyre" (Demetrius 1932, 347). Through the sound of the vowels, intoned under the correct liturgical conditions, material existence would be transformed to spirit. Loss of this state involved loss of this linguistic connection.

The ancients also spoke of the "language of the birds," which attests to an integration of human consciousness with the other living beings of nature. Zeus was attended by eagles, and Odin by ravens. The prophet Orpheus was said to charm the birds and animals with his song, just as much later Saint Francis of Assisi communed with the birds. In the eighteenth century, Wolfgang Amadeus Mozart (1756–1791) wrote music from the song of birds, as did the twentieth-century composer Olivier Messiaen (1908–1992), who asserted: "Among the artistic hierarchy, the birds are probably the greatest musicians to inhabit our planet."

There are opportunities for us to rediscover forgotten things that once were created, then lost. Various currents of esoteric study postulate that in archaic times, humans possessed an early language—sometimes called the "lost speech." This was a language in perfect harmony with the Cosmos, where being concurred with knowing and the words and names of things expressed the essential inner nature of the things they described. The unity of speech and being expressed the unity of the visible and invisible. The numinous nature of the name survives in ancient scriptures that insist that in magical or religious rites one must use the correct name, or one's work will be in vain.

The *Chaldaean Oracles of Zoroaster* tell us: "Change not the barbarous Names of Evocation for these are sacred Names in every language which are given by God, having in the Sacred Rites a Power Ineffable" (Westcott 1895, 46). They are the most important remnants of a general language, now lost, of which only the names of spiritual beings survive. From this "lost speech" derive ancient forms of writing such as hieroglyphics and, later, alphabets, such as Hebrew, Greek, and the runes, whose characters refer to natural objects, human artifacts, and operative principles. In magical usage, letters and names are not only signs for things, but manifestations of their very essence.

In various extant cultures, totemic animals are a reflection of this concept, as are the runes. Words that are one with the things and aspects of the world contain the innate power of their being. Poetry, song, and literature can express this inner power; magic, through spells and incantations, seeks to use it. Some esoteric traditions seek to recover or restore this "lost speech," as creativity is a returning to the origin,

The Recovery of Ancient Wisdom

Ancient wisdom teaches that if our will is in conformity with Nature (the will of the Fates), we will fulfill our purpose in life.

and when the origin is re-created, then everything will be transformed. Unlike modern literalists, whose institutions are structured to prevent the cultivation of inner understanding, the ancients deliberately elucidated wisdom in poetic language.

Whether or not there was actually a form of primal speech, what it symbolizes is a profound truth. All things have a literal (exoteric) meaning, with a literal interpretation, but if we can only understand, they also contain a symbolic (esoteric) meaning that allows for a spiritual interpretation. In a text, exactly the same form of words can have both a literal and a symbolic meaning, if we can but comprehend this seeming paradox. These twin meanings operate together, and it is primarily with the esoteric meaning that this book is concerned.

William Shakespeare (1564–1616) wrote in *Romeo and Juliet*: "What's in a name? That which we call a rose by any other word would smell as sweet" (Act 2, Scene 2). But although words indeed are in some sense arbitrary (though some believe in the primal speech) the words we use embed within themselves many historical resonances, connections, allusions, and allegories. The language I learned and spoke as a boy in London was Cockney, the vernacular English of working-class Londoners. I was told that the Cockneys were called that because London had once been an earthly paradise—the Land of Cockaigne whose streets were paved with gold (Spence 1937, 265–66; 1947, 61). In 1901 the noted composer Edward Elgar (1857–1934) wrote an overture titled *Cockaigne (In London Town)* (Op. 40). The Cockney vernacular includes words derived from "rhyming slang" and Yiddish, which were used as alternatives for standard English words. There was a class element to this. Standard English—the "King's English" or "Oxford English"—was used in contexts where such words were deemed impolite.

Using these alternative words creates a consciousness based on analogy, sometimes with deeper connections, but at other times humorous or ironic. When I went to look at something I would "take a butchers" at it (butcher's hook—look), or perhaps "take a gander at it." Someone who chattered a lot would be rabbiting about something, from "rabbit and pork"—talk, rabbit and pork pie being a popular food in former times in London. Someone's hair was called their "barnet," a rhyme from Barnet Fair, a major trading place for cattle drovers in former days. When someone died (not a friend or relative), we would say they had "kicked the bucket" or "popped their clogs." The first came from a person having to stand on a bucket when being hanged, the bucket being kicked from under them, leaving them dangling in the noose, and the second was that one's clogs were valuable and were taken to the pawn shop ("popped") when someone died to get some money for them. Thus, memories of the harsh and impoverished world of our forbears were embedded in the linguistic and historic references of our everyday language.

I also encountered the "hip" language of jazz musicians (my grandfather was a professional drummer), especially the "Vout-o-Reeny" of Buleo "Slim" Gaillard (1911–1991), which had parallelisms such as *germ transport* for a fly, and *H Twenty* for water (a reference to its chemical composition, H_2O)—"*H Nineteen*" meant damp. These, like some Cockney words, were poetic kennings. Later I learned of the ancient Norse use of kennings, poetic descriptions of things such as *sea-plow* for a ship, or *whales' bath* for the sea. Cockney partook of a similar analogous worldview. Even an underground tube line in London had the portmanteau name Bakerloo as a version of the Baker Street and Waterloo Railway. So, not even knowing foreign languages (later I learned Latin, French, and German), it was clear to me that the way we view the world can be described in many alternative ways, most of them impenetrable to those not "in the know."

The traditional presentation of symbols and the worlds used to describe them vary from culture to culture. This vision is not unitary; different people have their own, personal connection. But the essential core remains the same. So, within the basic framework, there is always the freedom of personal experience. This is the epitome of the creative force, a personal exploration of a system that emerges from the deepest structure and meaning of existence.

3

Unity

In One Is All

In order to gain understanding, it is essential first to remove all preconceptions and prejudices, especially the postmodern worldview that simultaneously disenchants and desacralizes the Cosmos thereby disempowering those very spiritual faculties that enable us to achieve higher levels of consciousness. In the unimaginable plurality of the vast Cosmos, there are the natural things we know: these are those things that our systems of awareness, perception, and consciousness can deal with. But there are also unknowable things that are equally natural. Elements of these can be glimpsed when we recognize the boundaries that are inherent in our perceptive faculties, and endeavour to understand them and their implications. Only then can we fully acknowledge our own position in the Cosmos, as conscious living beings that are not separated, but one with all life.

There is an old English adage, "In One is All." This describes the primal, eternal oneness that emanates the many through whose aspects the One can only be defined. Numberless qualities emanate from the One, but only these can be described and named, for the One is ineffable and unknowable. Human beings are both an expression and a

Ab Uno (From One)

reflection of the Cosmos, which is an aspect of the One. The Cosmos is a single, living substance; mind and matter are one. In One is All, emanating from but still part of the primordial oneness of the Cosmos. This holistic unity of being, of space, time, matter, and life was expressed by William Blake in his "Auguries of Innocence":

> *To see a World in a Grain of Sand*
> *And a Heaven in a Wild Flower—*
> *Hold Infinity in the palm of your hand*
> *And Eternity in an hour.*

Although one or other state of existence may appear to be present at any one time, and others absent, all are present simultaneously. The Cosmos, of which we are all part, is structured according to recurring patterns of self-similarity, in space, time, and event. Any differences we can perceive are in scale, ranging from the smallest particle to the largest galaxy. The differences are not in character. This interconnectedness is encapsulated in the maxim ascribed to the ancient Egyptian founder of alchemy, whom we know as Hermes Trismegistus. This is the *Hermetic Maxim* "As above, so below," in which the lesser, or smaller, microcosm, is seen as a reflection of the greater, or larger, macrocosm. Human beings partake of the nature of the microcosm, and in so doing, reflect the entire Cosmos, which is the macrocosm.

The Greek philosopher Anaxagoras (ca. 500–428 BCE) noted that "Nothing exists apart: everything has a share of everything else," and in the Judeo-Christian tradition, Psalm 121 of the Vulgate expresses this concept of unity: "Jerusalem is builded as a city whose parts are united in one." The alchemist Zosimos of Panopolis (fl. 300 CE) stated: "Everything caused by Nature is one, not in form, but in system." Outward appearances thereby embed principles and functions that may not be obvious at first. The functions continue, though the form in which they manifest changes over time. I was once given the example by a Hong Kong feng-shui master that the domain of killing people unexpectedly was once the preserve of the tiger, but once tigers were exterminated, cars took over that function. Similarly, barbwire took over the function of hedges growing thorny plants.

The seminal occultist Heinrich Cornelius Agrippa von Nettesheim (1486–1535) noted that a kind of natural link exists that allows all parts of the world to communicate with one another and form a whole. In his *Religio Medici*, the Norwich philosopher Thomas Browne (1605–1682) used the example of the seasons and the Earth to explain this principle (1909–1914, 49):

> whatsoever Sign the Sun possesseth, those four Seasons are actually present. It is the nature of this Luminary to distinguish the several Seasons of the year; all which it makes at one time in the whole Earth, and successive in any part thereof.

Thus, all possible parts are inextricable components of the whole. And, in the twentieth century, Henri Bergson (1859–1941) stated that any division of matter into independent bodies with determined outlines is artificial. It is an integral teaching of many esoteric orders and societies. For example, in his memoir *Far Off Things*, Arthur Machen noted (1922, 25–26):

> I am reminded of one of the secret societies with which I have had the pleasure of being connected. This particular society issued a little manuscript volume with the note "remember that nothing exists which is not God."

Everything that exists is integral with its context, part of "something else," while being viewable also as an individual entity within its own presence. This is not an existential paradox, but the inevitable result of the human viewpoint. Only in modern thought do the parts become separated in a reductionist and fragmental way, and are used in isolation from one another without consideration for their place in the totality. When any phenomenon can be verified by well-tried and objective tests, it can be said to exist. This is the criterion of reality in both science and the law. But the principle that everything can be subjected to the same criteria of verification does not work with all things we may encounter. But not everything we experience in the world of reality behaves identically, so that if any particular phenomenon is not verifiable in the same way, that does not mean that it does *not* exist. The assertion that everything without question must conform to the criterion of verifiability excludes other areas of experience, limiting its usefulness to those specific cases where it works. The belief that absence of evidence is evidence of absence is a fallacy.

Existence is not totally random, nor is it chaotic, for the Cosmos works according to certain principles. Science and technology are grounded in verifiable phenomena that emanate from these principles. Observers over thousands of years have looked at how the world works

and found that in many cases what happens can be explained by the principle of "cause and effect" or that it conforms to the supposed principle of "the law of causation." The predictable behavior of objects and measurable forces gave rise to the human description of what happens as the "laws" of nature. But the word *law* is not a true description of the behavior innate in matter and energy. There is no external power policing the inner workings of physics.

The principles that underlie disciplines such as geomancy, sacred geometry, mechanics, magic, or electronics are all linked fundamentally with the nature of the Cosmos. Variations in external form may be dictated by the varying tenets of scientific or religious worldviews or the "rules of the game," which are only human stories told about the irreducible, but the operative fundamentals remain the same. Technicians throughout the world must adhere to these fundamentals or their work will fail. Because certain objects behave in a particular predictable way, an anthropomorphic view of nature views them as "obeying" ultimate "laws" like a subservient inhabitant of a nation-state. The behavior that scientists detect is not imposed upon intransigent matter, which otherwise would deviate, as is the case with human laws. Laws are viewed as objective powers that rule their respective domains of Nature, compelling things to obey them. But they are not so, stemming only from human observations that things always take the same definite course. They do so not because they are forced to by external power, but through their inherent nature and relationships with other things. The concept of *laws* infers a *lawgiver* who forces physics to conform to some kind of cosmic jurisprudence, which is a projection onto the Cosmos of ideas that originated in the human mind.

This idea of *laws* originated in prescientific civilizations whose winning warlords crowned themselves kings and issued edicts that their subjects were forced to obey whether they liked it or not. To enforce the arbitrary laws they had thought up, conquering warlords claimed that the laws did not originate in their whims and prejudices, but that they had been received by revelation from their god or gods. To those who do believe that human laws have come directly from a divine source, then they are impossible to question. There can be no means to develop or change them, and they must remain fixed for all time at the moment of their invention, even when times have changed beyond all recognition.

When chemists and physicists described the workings of material existence in a usable way, they called the principles they discovered by the name "law," for example: Boyle's Law, Fick's Law, Avogadro's Law, and Newton's Laws of Motion. Religiously inclined scientists still view these literally as aspects of God's "laws." But they are not laws in a human sense, as people with free will can disobey laws, even when the consequences may be fatal. Laws are imposed on other humans by people in power and enforced by legal systems. They can be beneficial, harmful, or oppressive. The "laws" of the Cosmos cannot be broken, for they are innate in the ways things are. They are neither beneficial nor harmful, nor are they oppressive. They are impersonal and subject to no appeal. So, it is better to understand the inherent structure of matter and energy in terms of symbols. These symbols may be expressed as words, as mathematical formulae, or, most traditionally, as personifications. Through these symbols, we can get a better glimpse of an almost infinitely complex reality that we can scarcely comprehend. Science, the law, and religion are not reality; they are human constructs that provide a language to describe reality. Inevitably, they work well in only limited areas, though they claim that their deterministic theories are applicable to everything in all of space and time. Clearly, they are not.

4

The Eternal Tradition

The Eternal Tradition is a living creativity that underlies and prefigures the unfolding genesis of history and our present actions in the here and now. The insights, teachings, and acts of the sages, prophets, seers, spiritual teachers, and grand masters of the past are signposts and landmarks in this present journey. Wise people who lived in former days gave us the means to ascend to a pure intellect conjoined to the powers of the gods, thereby acquiring perfect knowledge of all things knowable. If understood properly, they give us the true principles of how to live and act in the world. If we are to practice these ancient skills and wisdom, we require an understanding of our personal place in the continuing culture, based upon place and the accumulated understanding of countless ancestral generations. The matter of our work is everywhere.

These ancient skills and wisdom are timeless because the basic true principles of existence do not change. These are a means, and they work in their own right. It is necessary for the seeker to go through such skills and wisdom, ultimately reinvigorating and transcending them. There may be many other ways of achieving this aim, but this is the way that has been perfected over many generations and so it is our path. But one must not expect immediate success without hard work, and even then, there are many areas of human experience to which all people are not granted access.

> *Nothing comes free-cost here; Jove will not let*
> *His gifts go from him, if not bought with sweat.*
>   ROBERT HERRICK (1591–1674),
>   *HESPERIDES*

Underlying all human activities is the principle of *Transvolution*, the way things progress. There are stages in this process: *Inception*, which is an exploration of the possible ways forward, conditioned by previous experience and within a particular cultural milieu; *Crystallization* of the form, which comes from the decision made of what to do; *Expression and development* of the form, changes that take place over time as the work progresses; *Stabilization* of the form as particular characteristics emerge to the exclusion of others; *Transition*, the exploration of variations emergent from the stabilized form in accordance with experience of what is possible within the already established parameters; then the end of the project either through failure to complete the work, abandonment of it for other reasons, or its successful *Completion*. But as the Stoic philosopher Epictetus (ca. 50–135 CE) said (2008, 11): "We do not abandon any discipline merely for despair of ever being the best in it." The perfect should not be the enemy of the good.

The task of every manifestation of creation is to fulfill its existence. This is its purpose; its meaning lies in the spiritual manifestation of its being. Nothing comes into being fully formed; all things progress by degrees. Most living organisms pass through stages of growth and development. So it is with understanding. The neophyte who has just entered the portals of knowledge cannot expect to comprehend any but the most basic, coarse elements of the system. Only by means of progressive steps upward, through the successive stages, can the intellect become enlightened, finally to be enmixed with the divine light itself.

The seeker experiences transformation by coming into direct contact with the cosmic order. The passage from the visible to the invisible is thereby made accessible. But none can behold the inner nature of creation who has not purified the mind. The Jewish creation myth tells how God uttered the words (in the lost speech!) "Let there be light"— and there *was* light. In Latin, the phrase is rendered as *"fiat lux"*—*Lux* is the primal light, the unpolluted light of knowledge, spiritual illumination. The light we see from the Sun is *Lumen*, which, however, is one step removed from the ineffable primal light, *Lux*. The fire of the Sun, pure though it is, is numbered among the lights of heavenly objects, the Luminaria, which were created as manifestations of *Lux*. They emanate *Lumen*, the secondary light. *Lux* is a substance in itself, and *Lumen* is what flows from *Lux*, illumination: the Light behind the Light.

Tradition teaches that there are seven stages of progression in this process. It also expresses the stages of initiation, transformation, and spiritual progress among the living. In ascending, the soul first abandons the power of growth and decay. Secondly, all disruptive principles are de-energized, and thirdly, illusions of desire fade away. The fourth stage sees the arrogance of power neutralized; in the fifth, impious daring and presumption is abandoned. The sixth stage reached means that all striving for wealth by unethical means is past; and the seventh, that ensnaring falsehood is negated. This process is possible during life, if we take the opportunity and have the courage to attempt it.

Unlike modern literalists, whose institutions typically prevent the cultivation of inner understanding in favor of instrumental functions, the ancients deliberately concealed wisdom within poetic language. The early stages of progress are of no less worth than the higher ones. Every seemingly distinct stage is nevertheless an essential component of the Whole; the structure of each phase corresponding with the form and structure of the Whole. That which is revealed is related through unseen correspondences with that which is concealed. It is important not to commence the work with preconceptions about its purpose or meaning. If we only seek to reach a particular objective we have decided upon in advance, then we must follow a path dependent upon our original concept of what that objective must be. What we will find is limited by our preconceptions at the outset, and we may never gain creative insights into realms far beyond our original understanding.

We must also remember that success is never guaranteed. Even if we do everything correctly, to the best of our abilities, things may still go wrong. For the world is uncertain and although luck, serendipity, and providence operate within it, we can do no more than our best. As an ancient craft motto (from Sextus Propertius, *Elegies*, II, X, 5) tells us:

Quod si deficiant vires, audacia certe
Laus erit: in magnis et voluisse sat est.

("Even if strength fails, at least boldness will deserve praise; in great endeavors it is enough just to have possessed the will.")

5

A History of Authenticity

To be ignorant of what happened before you were born is to remain always a child. For what is human life worth, unless it is woven into the life of our ancestors by the records of history?
—CICERO (106–43 BCE)

The Way of the Eight Winds is one modern expression of the Tradition of ancient Europe. Naturally, the expression of Tradition without practical re-creation is barren. Tradition is handed down not just from a nostalgic intention of exhibiting continuity, but of having a practical value in the accomplishment of necessary tasks. Tradition is in no way an attempt to return to the past, which in any case is impossible, but is a creative force in the present. It may be viewed as the reenactment of the original act of creation; actualization of the instant of creation as an eternally present event. This is the metaphysical basis of Tradition.

Tradition is expressed through a metaphysical understanding of cosmology. The hierarchical structure of the Cosmos is analogous to the relationship between Macrocosm and Microcosm. It is expressed through the language of symbols. This eternal Tradition is the reflection and expression of the perceived structure of the Cosmos. We humans interpret them as essential principles, which we see as the laws that govern the way things are and the means to make things happen. These essential principles are timeless: they are the essentials of Creation, seen in some religious ideas as the mind of God. The tools we use to achieve our aims are derived solely from an understanding of these essential principles. But, of course, a tool without the user's skill and inspiration is useless. Things that are made that respect these essential principles are in themselves also timeless.

The traditional view of the world that we follow was the basis of ancient European civilization. While the actual forms used now will inevitably differ, the principles were laid down over 3,000 years ago. This careful relationship to the Earth is attested to historically in the ancient Roman College of Augurs who were masters of this ancient practice. Related to them were the *agrimensores*, practical field surveyors who were schooled in the arts of reading the landscape for its numinous as well as its physical characteristics. Every Roman temple and town was thus located according to the spiritual geomantic principles of the Etruscan Discipline, the ancient spiritual art of the Augurs of Etruria from the early years of the first millennium BCE, rather than according to the price of land or the other considerations that are universal today.

After the collapse of the Roman Empire in the West, geomantic practices were maintained in the placement and orientation of churches, and in various building traditions maintained by guilds of craftsmen. During the Renaissance, Roman techniques were reinvigorated and served as the basis for town layout, which included straight avenues punctuated by churches, fountains, and monuments. From Rome, this tradition spread to the north, where it appeared in town planning as well as parkland around cities and great country palaces such as Versailles (1671) and Kassel (1688). There are examples of this type of placement in early eighteenth-century London in the work of British architects James Gibbs (1682–1754) and Nicholas Hawksmoor (ca. 1661–1736). The new city of Karlsruhe in Baden, Germany, is the most perfect manifestation of the system, founded on the site of a hunting lodge in a forest in January 1715. It had thirty-two straight roads radiating from the ducal palace tower at its center, and churches on insular sites, with some of the lines as parkland avenues. The layout remains to this day.

In so-called developed nation-states today, the majority of people live in cities. Their ancestors were rural, but later moved to live in cities either by choice or necessity. In some places, this process began centuries ago. It continues apace throughout the world. In the nineteenth century, deracination of society caused by removal of people from the land into vast conurbations was praised by "progressives" as heralding the dawn of a new classless age that would bring a brighter, better future. Tradition became truncated and only certain elements of it were able to survive in a radically changed world. Some visionaries saw and warned against the destructiveness of industrial life to both nature and humanity, with the consequent loss of social cohesion and individuals and communities relating to place in an increasingly materialist way. Urban modernity served to abolish cyclic time in favor of linear time. The cyclic variations inherent in the repeated rounds of the seasons, the weather, and even day and night were minimized as far as was possible and effectively removed from relevance. The human constructs of the calendar and the clock became the measure of existence. Only the measurable was valued. The rural was marginalized and forgotten by the descendents of those whose ancestors had left the land for work in cities. The development of mass media focused interest away from the importance of happenings in one's local place to the reportage of selected—usually violent and spectacular—events from all parts of the world not too dangerous to report upon. It also eroded local difference, taking various marketable elements of culture from different lands and melding them into genres that had commercial potential.

As the cities sprawled outward over once-productive farmland or felled primal forests, diverse ecosystems that had been conserved over the generations were degraded and destroyed. Ancient skills and wisdom were discounted as worthless, and traditional ways of life embedded in the landscape were largely degraded or erased by industrial power. In the

Philosophical Viewpoints

The Appearance of Modernity—Starr Gate, Blackpool, England

early twentieth century Max Weber (1864-1920) characterized modernism as the progressive secularization, disenchantment, and demagicalization of life—a disjunctive view of reality substituted for a holistic one, and postmodern theories have taken this a step further. The process continues today with the oxymoronic "green industrial revolution" that seeks to cover the fields with manufactured solar panels and metal wind farms with the parts that still produce (genetically modified) crops, plowed and harvested by autonomous vehicles and robots built in urban factories by other robots—all of it using immense amounts of energy. However power is generated, even methods that avoid using fossil fuels, all energy use puts heat into the environment. In this dystopian scenario of a "green industrial revoltion" the depopulated landscape filled with machines becomes just another zone of urban industry. There is no place in this for living signs that symbolize the cycle of the seasons and articulate the inner world of humans. Humans have been rendered almost superfluous except as alienated technicians who ensure the continued operation of the system. But nature, at a deeper level than just the ravaged and depleted ecosystem, has not been conquered. It has not gone away.

Apart from the impoverished regions of the world, modern life is mediated by images and largely dominated by them. We are subjected to a nonstop series of mediated images that range from the design of automobiles, advertising, and general media imagery on both broadcast and social media. These images appear more vivid and cogent than what we see off-screen, for they are engineered to be so in order to promote conformity and sell products. They have become not only a re-presentation of visible reality, but a spectacular substitute for it. Viewers see themselves mimetically reflected in images skilfully contrived to sell products to their particular demographic. Sensibility, an emotional response to actual reality is thereby diminished or never has the chance to develop. Engagement with the actual environment around us becomes almost impossible without the mediation of the electronic screen. Even actual events take on an unreal feeling unless they have been recorded by photography or video. Experience of the moment, as it happens to us as living individuals, is not enough in the society of the image. Instead, it must be theatricalized, and interpreted as a representation, a secondhand image. So often people who witness some catastrophic event cannot understand what they have experienced, and can only describe it as "like in a movie." The electronic media have inflicted sensory damage upon the experience of everyday life.

But life is not a performance—we are not actors. What happens, what we experience, does not exist in order merely to be posted on social media. The consciousness of the Way of the Eight Winds de-theatricalizes life. Of course, many events are created with the sole purpose of appearing on the media, social or otherwise. These events are part of a commercial system of mediated and monetized imagery, the entertainment industry, which includes such items as news broadcasts and so-called documentaries that seek to manipulate the viewer into holding particular views on life and being. The theory of the

Zeitgeist—the supposed "spirit of the age," in which certain things are more appropriate to "the time" than others—is frequently used as a recommendation and justification for many of the destructive tendencies in modernism. By being aware of the constructed artificiality inherent in what we view, and understanding its embedded agenda, we can experience the world directly without its mediation. We do not need to be actors in a show, to react to each and every fad, fashion, and fancy thrown at us by commerce, that "system of reckless waste" as William Morris (1834–1896) described it.

Of course, we all tell stories. Stories are perhaps the origin of culture and every variety of human civilization. All ancient knowledge was preserved in the form of an orally transmitted epic or story-complex whose episodes were re-created at appropriate instances by storytellers, poetesses, and poets. These tales were versions of "the story" from their point of view; different storytellers told alternative viewpoints of the story-complex according to the necessities and requirements of teller and participators ("audience"). Millennia may have passed between the time a story complex came into being and when it was written down.

The ancient Druidic tradition of the Celts, for example, forbade writing things down—it dulled the memory and removed the dynamic power to re-create the myths each time they were told. But later, under the influence of so-called Religions of the Book that revere the written word, often literalistically, only written material was considered of value by those in power. Priests, who obviously knew by heart the texts they were reciting, nevertheless read them from books, emphasizing the primacy of the written word and demonstrating their literacy to the illiterate. The fixity of the written word, in important ways contrary to the flow of *manred** in the Cosmos that is Nature's way, led inevitably to the impoverishment of mythology.

When any story was written down, it was the specific oral version circulating among the men who recorded it. The text written down,

---

*The "matrix of being" in Welsh Bardo-Druidic teachings; see chapter 34.

held as immutably sacred by some, is just a version. Chance might have meant that another, variant version became the definitive text instead. In his famous avant-garde poem "Un coup de dés jamais n'abolira le hazard" (A Throw of the Dice Will Never Abolish Chance), written in 1897, Stéphane Mallarmé (1842–1898) noted this fixity of the written word produces inflexible certainty. This is usually taken as ultimately definitive, but definitions themselves are fragments of unbroken irreducible continuous reality, and "to define is to kill." As Gottfried Wilhelm Leibniz (1646–1716) pointed out, every system is true in the reality it affirms, and false in the reality it excludes. In any work, there will always be more excluded than included.

Writing at a period when patriarchal religion was in the ascendancy, the male priests and monks who committed the stories to writing invested them with their own worldview, to the exclusion of others. Pluralism was killed. Other versions were either unknown to the writers, or were ignored or censored according to their prejudices, dogmas, and doctrines. In general, the viewpoint of women was ignored or suppressed. It is still the case in patriarchal theocratic nation-states. Later, with universal education based on the same belief system, the fixed written version of the legend was assumed without question to be the correct one.

Now the written version, essentially a fragmental selection of a multivalent whole, was taken as the standard of correctness and authenticity by which the alternative oral versions that still circulated should be judged. Appropriate knowledge as an agent of transformation was thereby truncated, forced into a specific mould, and forged in an inflexible, unchanging form that reinforced the patriarchal status quo of knowledge. It still has the negative effect of producing in the individual an inability to change life in a meaningful way, preventing direct human experience of a larger realm. Intuition, imagination, memory, vision, and foresight became secondary to studying the authorized text. Universal education, sponsored by the state with national curricula intended to promote certain worldviews, drove down alternative viewpoints, including the orally transmitted storytelling that once was the core culture of society.

Highly developed human technical expertise today contrasts markedly with contemporary human spiritual barbarity, only different in outward appearance from the atrocities of warlords of the preindustrial age. In the long spread of time, these contemporary transgressions, terrible as they are, and catastrophic though their consequences may be, are just more of those things against Nature that the Pythagorean sage Apollonius of Tyana (ca. 15 CE–100 CE) noted will "quickly pass to destruction" (Conybeare 1912, I:65), for existence is but a process of transformation. The Renaissance architect Leon Battista Alberti (1404–1472) observed (1986, 23): "How many of the mighty Works of Men do we read of, and know ourselves to have been destroy'd by no other Cause than that they contended against Nature?" Ecological imbalances created by overuse of industrial technology and the detritus of consumerism will certainly be resolved by the consequent disasters that ensue. It is clear that climate change will either destroy or radically transform the civilization that triggered it. But this dissolution is also a natural process, the inevitable consequence of what has been done for the last three centuries. It is not an external punishment decreed by the fates or the gods. A few hundred years is rapid compared with aeons of geological time. The most permanent things that we make are but transient and temporary.

6

On Spectacle

Spectacle is inherent in all perception; essentially it is the focusing-in of the consciousness upon a single aspect of reality, removing awareness of all connections between that aspect of reality and everything else of which it is part. While focusing-in is often necessary, it contains within itself the danger of misperception wither by ignoring the surroundings/environment, and/or giving an imbalanced emphasis upon the relevance of what is beling viewed. In spectacle, the wider context of something is ignored. This denies the real nature of the "object" within its environment. When spectacle arises in its full-blown form, it involves the creation in the mind of the beholder of a fiction she or he is seeing, which is (a) something special, (b) perhaps unique, or (c) characteristic of all other "examples."

Spectacle is perhaps the major force in modern civilization; through selective, edited representation, the process of spectacle serves to reduce the vibrant, living richness of existence to a lifeless image that is then presented as reality. Spectacle serves to remove the "object" or "specimen" from its state of being itself into a state of separation. It is extracted from reality to be represented as external to its own being. It is *re*-presented, not presented, for it is not present. Only an image is present, not the reality. This image is displayed as though it exists outside reality. This is the "disease view" of normality, which is no longer understood as a continuum, but represented as a collection of discrete objects.

Essentially, spectacle is a secondhand experience, in which reality is viewed through a series of lenses, tubes, and screens, each of which operates according to parameters that filter and modify the "image" in their own characteristic way. In addition, these images (and I also mean those conveyed through the printed word) are filtered, censored, rationalized, judged, and chanelled, deliberately and accidentally, by the operators of the system, both commandants and technicians. Inherently, there is an attempt to subvert *ørlög*—both that of the "object" and the "observer."* But each time the image is represented, it is a new one, generated specifically for the representation. Thereby ørlög is not bypassed; instead, the ørlög of spectacle is reinforced.

Ultimately, the Cosmos is represented as dead matter, parts of which are "examples" or "specimens" of the absolute face of order, regimented, exhaustively known, and therefore psychically dead images. The pale shadow of reality that is spectacle is inevitably soul-destroying. Reality is negated by the image that purports to represent it. It denies ørlög, representing a fixed, unchanging image that has no reference to time, location, or history. Spectacle propagates the fiction that there is an actual, objective, complete, eternal, and circumscribed reality "out there," which can be isolated, dissected, and viewed meaningfully.

Spectacle is a self-referencing fiction. It is a closed loop that has, by accident and intention, created a specific modus operandi that is self-perpetuating. Only those objects that fit into the framework of the spectacle-mentality can appear within it. Elements that lie too far away, do not fit the time slot, or otherwise transgress the "moral code" of spectacle have no place within it. To the consumer of spectacle, it is as if these "examples" do not exist. Indeed, in the spectacle-mentality, they really have no existence.

---

*Ørlög can be defined as "the concatenation of events and influences that have resulted in our place in the present." See chapter 10, "*Ørlög* and History."

7

Divination and Chance

The world we experience is perplexingly multidimensional, and so, whatever techniques we may use to gain extrasensory knowledge can augment our understanding. Divination appears to access the inner workings of causality. Many traditional techniques of divination relied upon choosing a particular sign from among a series of signs, such as an individual number generated by dice, or a combination of tarot cards. They were seen as means to predict what was going to happen in the future, for the future was believed to be predetermined by extrahuman powers. But during the Renaissance, mathematicians devised statistical techniques that led to the discovery of randomness and probability. The mathematical "laws" of probability that emerged gave a means of describing what percentage of occurrences an event is likely to take place over the long run. Once the concept of mathematical probability had been discovered, the occurrence of these signs, formerly believed to access the will of the Fates, or God, was now seen as subject to statistical "laws," and thus of no value being merely subject to random chance. *Chance* is defined as the happening of events and the way in which things "turn out": a happening or occurrence of things in a particular way, perceived as a casual or fortuitous circumstance without conscious manipulation or a deterministic end.

But although we know that divination, like many other events, is subject to the mathematical "laws" of probability, divination enables us to transfer decision-making from the realm of the rational and the emotional into another, extraordinary level of cognition. There are many well-established means of divination in use today: tarot cards, runes, dice, divinatory geomancy, and oracle books such as the *I Ching* and Napoleon's *Book of Fate*. Although divination operates according to randomness, the *purpose* of any divination is not random, for it is seeks an answer to a question put by a person. Divination is thus personal, and its outcome is eminently practical, providing the querent the means to think about and understand their problems in another way. This is the unique value and promise of divination. Divination, which is non-rational, enables us to disconnect ourselves from the everyday world until a flash of illumination bursts forth from the darkness. Through its use, we may gain new unthought-of and unexpected insights into our condition.

Whatever chance is, things are not determinate in a literal way. For a very long time, certain people have asserted that the world will end on a determinate date. But this is impossible, for calendars are not a reality like day-length. They are arbitrary human constructs, operative fictions devised to enable events to be documented, or future actions planned. The present author has lived through several much-heralded "end of the world" prophecies in 1954, 1960, 1975, 1999, 2000, and 2012. But the world did not end then, as we can plainly see. All of these putative years of doom were dates in the Christian calendar, many of them "round figures." But the Christian way of dating years is only one of many calendars used in the world, past and present. If these "significant" dates are translated into other calendars, then the round-figures fade away. For example, in the Roman calendar (AUC), these dates are 2707, 2713, 2728, 2752, 2753, and 2765, none of them particularly meaningful numbers. Translating year dates into other calendars is an antidote to "date-based" prophecies, demonstrating their arbitrary nature.

The process of events emerges from a state of temporary liminality. We make decisions that may be either deliberate or accidental. The outcome is imminent, but it is not yet determined. Once the decision is made, and the action taken, then the outcome is present and cannot be altered. The uncertain becomes determinate. There is a spiritual side to these instants of liminality. The old Emblem Books of the seventeenth century gave a motto of the crossroads as *"omnes praeter unam praeclusae,"* which means: "When we choose to take one way, we close off the possibility of taking any other." When we reach a crossroads, we are not lost but are forced to choose.

The moment of choosing—"Crossroads"

The immutable actuality of physical forces such as gravity, energy, weather, and climate, and the physical structure of the world we live in, are not a matter of opinion, though they may be of interpretation. But for almost everything else, there is enormous diversity of theory and opinion. Often, we are forced by circumstance or necessity to choose one over another. Many people have no choice because either they are born in particular families, societies, or nations that demand unwavering loyalty to their belief system, or because they never encounter any alternatives to the way they have been taught by schoolteachers and clerics.

8

Human Personifications of the Divine

The ancient Poets animated all sensible objects with Gods or Geniuses, calling them by the names and adorning them with the properties of woods, rivers, mountains, lakes, cities, nations, and whatever their enlarged and numerous senses could perceive. And particularly they studied the genius of each city and country, placing it under its mental deity. Till a system was formed, which some took advantage of & enslaved the vulgar by attempting to realize or abstract the mental deities from their objects: thus began Priesthood. Choosing forms of worship from poetic tales. And at length they pronounced that the Gods had ordered such things. Thus men forgot that All deities reside in the human breast.
—WILLIAM BLAKE,
THE MARRIAGE OF HEAVEN AND HELL (1790)

Spiritual truths are embedded in mythological tales. Things in nature were given human identities whose personalities and assemblages of attributes reflected the qualities and effects of the corresponding natural

Frau Percht, personification of winter and the care of souls awaiting rebirth

phenomenon. Hence there were gods who produced thunder; the individual weathers brought by winds from particular directions were given personal names, and described as wearing garlands, robes, and so forth, which signified the nature of the weather the winds brought. They exist in a way that is not approachable through literalistic, analytical methods, and so the everyday techniques of verification are useless in these cases. These personifications are also not a primitive superstition that we are ruled by literal beings in human form. Although largely ignored and forgotten by modernity, their symbolic value remains. It is an alternative way of viewing the world, not a literalistic belief in the objective existence of these personifications, but a means of gaining access to a symbolic understanding.

Religious traditions embody the attributes of human trades and crafts in appropriate gods, demigods, and saints. These beings personify particular functions in a way comprehensible to human understanding. So, Hermes (the Roman Mercury) oversaw travel, transport, and communication. In Greek mythology, he invented the alphabet after seeing the shapes of cranes flying in the sky, just as his Norse parallel, Odin, discovered the runes. Communication was seen as an art of divine origin; hence, Hermes, Mercury, and Odin are the gods of writers. Hephaistos (Vulcan) was venerated by blacksmiths as founder of the craft of ironworking, as was Tubal Cain in the biblical tradition and the Celtic Gobniu. Sucellos was god of vineyards and winery workers; Rosmerta, a Gaulish goddess of fruitfulness and financial gain. In the Christian religion, saints parallel the demigods and heroes of earlier Paganism. The Mediterranean god of the sea, Poseidon or Neptune, was paralleled in Celtic tradition by the god called Manannán (Irish) or Manawydden (Welsh). In many cases, saints took over from their

Personification of Cambridge University as the Alma Mater (entrance to the New Museums Site, Downing Street)

pre-Christian forerunners as patrons of trades and crafts. Saint Nicholas became patron of seafarers, taking over from Neptune, and Saint Clement became the patron saint of blacksmiths, assimilating the attributes of Vulcan, and so on. Whether or not they are "true" in the absolute, all of these concepts work as operative systems that give us some insight into the workings of the ineffable.

The Way of the Eight Winds is based upon ancient traditional ways of understanding, but it is not a belief system that asserts that any one interpretation of the world is true to the exclusion of others. It is nonsectarian in recognizing that all interpretations of the world are culturally determined and are symbols of ineffable realities, which cannot be truly grasped or described. Human culture has existed in all its diversity and complexity for thousands of years. It would be presumptuous to suggest either that any particular example is the pure truth or that any culture does not embody within itself previously existing elements from many sources. Syncretism and equivalence dates back at least to the Roman Empire's *Interpretatio Romana*, where deities of non-Roman tribes and nations were lumped in with the nearest parallel Roman deity. Thus, in Imperial times, the ancient British goddess Sulis at Bath was assimilated to Minerva as Sulis Minerva; Lugos became Mercury; Teutates, Mars; Ogmios, Hercules; and the sun-god Grannos, Apollo. Later, in medieval times, the name of the Welsh god of thunder, Daronwy, became an epithet of the biblical God.

At the time of Plato, classical European religion did not give a very important role to the sun-god. But as the years went by, under Egyptian and Persian influence, where the solar god reigned supreme, Helios (the Roman Sol) increased in importance, and by Hellenistic times he was seen as the ruling deity, Helios Pantokrator. A Hellenistic prayer to Helios calls him "All-ruler, spirit of the world, power of the world, light of the world" (Cumont 1919, 322). The physical sun was seen to possess a spiritual dimension, the "Intelligible Helios." In the third century CE, Elagabalus, a Syrian sun-worshipper, became emperor of Rome and renamed himself Heliogabalus (reigned

Human Personifications of the Divine 61

Saint Sidwell, patron saint of Exeter, Devon, England
(image on a building reconstructed after the destruction
of the city in World War II)

222–226 CE). He instituted the worship at Rome of the Syrian solar deity El Gabal.

In 274 CE, after an epiphany of the sun-god appeared to his army, the emperor Aurelian (ca. 215–275; reigned 270–275) proclaimed

Sol Invictus, the unvanquished sun, as the supreme god of the empire. Images of Sol Invictus show him with his right hand raised in benediction and with an orb, whip, or thunderbolt in his left. The Christian Church took over the Pagan view of the sun-god as spiritual light of the world. In place of the unconquered sun, Sol Invictus, Jesus Christ was declared the sun of righteousness, *Sol Iustitiae*, the judge of mankind. Jesus took on the judgmental attribute of Babylonian sun-god Shamash, with a biblical justification taken from the prophet Malachi (4:2): "Unto you that fear my Name shall the sun of righteousness arise."

The biblical sun became the new interpretation of the old supreme Imperial god, Sol Invictus. The solar attribute of Jesus was reinforced because his birth was celebrated on December 25, the birthday of the son of Helios, Mithras. In his *Repertorium morale*, published in Nuremberg in 1489, Pierre Bersuire (aka Petrus Berchorius; 1290–1362) made a heliocentric analogy:

> Further I say of this Sun that He shall be inflamed . . . when He sits in judgment. . . . For as the sun, when in the center of his orbit, that is to say, at the midday point, is hottest so shall Christ be when He shall appear in the center of Heaven and Earth, that is to say, in Judgment.

So, in Christian art, Jesus, Sol Iustitiae, is depicted at the central point between heaven and earth—*medium coeli et terrae*—the omphalos location of the Throne of Majesty on which Christians believe he will sit at the Last Judgment.

Unlike many ancient cultures and numerous more recent manifestations of holistic sacred praxis, the Abrahamic religious view is a dualistic, exclusive one. It asserts that all spirits, forces, and gods are creatures and rivals of the creator God and hence are identified with or under the control of their Devil (paradoxically also created by the Creator!), whom they see in Manichaean terms as their God's opponent. However, this dualistic view of the Cosmos that most of creation

Human Personifications of the Divine 63

Saint Cecilia, patron saint (personification)
of musical harmony

is evil is contrary to many worthy philosophies that recognize the unity of opposites. The Daoist symbol of yin and yang is the best-known example of this principle. It is not absent from the Judeo-Christian canon, for the apocryphal biblical book of Ecclesiasticus also states it (42:24–25):

> All things are double one against another: and he hath made nothing imperfect. One thing establisheth the good of another, and who shall be filled with beholding his glory?

9

The Naming of Names

Our experience of place is fundamental to our sense of being. Traditional society in each locality has a particular local way of looking at the world, which is not reproducible or transferable. History is site-specific; placeless events are impossible except in myth and fiction. In traditional societies, place-names are all descriptive in some way. Features in the land such as the shape of mountains and hills, bends in rivers, ravines, isolated rocks, fertile meadows, types of tree and animal, and the abodes of eldritch beings all appear as elements in traditional place-names. Ancient languages have words that express the subtle gradations of slope, water flow, the shape of hills, the color of rocks, places where deer graze, the local names of plants and where they grow, places where snow remains longest after the winter, and the *locus terribilis* where humans ought not to trespass.* The individual's being in his or her "home ground" is grounded in local culture as the repository of local knowledge. Place, language, and everyday life are enmeshed in landwisdom, a spiritual linkage that must be nurtured or lost. To recognize this is to acknowledge the *genius loci*, the spirit of the place. This is spirit in either sense of the world, both physical and intangible.

---

*For a discussion of the *locus terribilis* and *locus amoenus*, see chapter 32.

Ancient sacred places always had their human guardians, usually a hereditary role. The divinely enthused *derilans*, who kept the holy wells of Scotland, and the *harrowwardens*, who dwelt in tumbledown cottages among the stones of power in England, ministered to any passing pilgrim seeking an oracle or healing. These unpaid keepers assured that the hallowed wood, well, or stone would not be profaned, misused, or destroyed. There are those today who, unobserved, tend these ancient places of the land, where they still exist. They may not be hereditary guardians in the traditional sense, but they too are true *dewars*, spiritual gardeners who commune with the eldritch world. Theirs is the sacred stewardship of their spiritual forebears, bearing authentic testimony to their history, assuring the continuance of positive traditional values.

Many people are living in landscapes that retain the names of places in ancient and native languages that they cannot understand. Local names have been adopted by conquerors, colonists, and immigrants, but have no more meaning than a name of a place even when in the original language they are often richly descriptive. Language also changes and new languages are laid upon older ones until the literal meanings of place-names are unintelligible. Many English village and town names are descriptive and indicative of a different sensibility than is commonplace now. For instance, Golborne means a "stream where marsh marigolds grow"; Roundthwaite, a "clearing with Mountain Ash growing there"; Everdon and Everden mean "wild boar hill," and the Mersey, Old English *Mæres-ēa*, means "boundary river." It was the border between the Anglo-Saxon kingdoms of Mercia and Northumbria 1,200 years ago (Ekwall 1980, 170, 200, 343, 394). Howgrave means "grove on a *hah*, the spur of a hill," and Over, in Cambridgeshire, on the Great Ouse River, means a "riverbank" from Old English *ōfer* (Ekwall 1980, 254, 354). Although many things have changed in 1,500 years, some place-names of Old England still describe the characteristics of the place today.

Names that actually meant something in their original places were reused for settlements in the far-off lands of European empires.

So, Boston, Massachusetts, was named from the original Boston in Lincolnshire, England. But in North America that name had no meaning other than a recollection of the English port from which some emigrants had set out. In England, however, the earlier name Botolfston described a stone where an Anglo-Saxon clergyman called Botulf or Botolph once preached and where a church dedicated to him still stands (Ekwall 1980, 54). Other churches dedicated to Saint Botolph, named for the original, stand guard at the sites of gates in town walls of several English cities to this day. In England, names were changed sometimes by an onlay (onlaying of a new name and significance) from a basic landscape description to a religious one. Christchurch in Hampshire was once called Twinham, the "place between two streams" (Ekwall 1980, 483), and later a settlement in New Zealand was named Christchurch after it. New York City was founded in 1625 by Dutch colonists as Nieuw Amsterdam. The name of the city in the Netherlands, Amsterdam, is descriptive, meaning the "dam on the River Amstel," which Nieuw Amsterdam / New York City is not; and York in England, in its earliest known form was recorded by the Greco-Egyptian geographer Ptolemy in the year 150. Then, York was called Ebórakon, a name derived probably from the Celtic word *eburos*, a yew tree. To the Romans, it was Eboracum; under the Anglo-Saxons it became Eoforwic and under Scandinavian rule, Jorvik, from which the modern names York and New York derive (Ekwall 1980, 545). New York City is far removed from that original yew tree.

Founded in 1781, El Pueblo de Nuestra Señora la Reina de los Ángeles del Rio Porciúncula, a settlement dedicated to "Our Lady of the Angels," one of the Catholic attributes of the Virgin Mary, is now called Los Angeles or just L.A. This, of course, was an onlay upon the original sacred place of the Indigenous inhabitants in the land that became known as California. It is yet another instance of the axiom that things that began as sacred are inevitably profaned and secularized. The modernist reduction of precision and simplification accelerates this process. Many cities bear names of heroes or founders, such as Alexandria, Egypt;

Louisville, Kentucky; Austin, Texas; and Washington, D.C. But with the ever-turning wheel of time and fortune, founders and heroes fall from grace and their names are removed from the map and often from memory. Cape Kennedy reverted to its earlier name, Cape Canaveral, after a few decades, as did Karl-Marx-Stadt, which reverted to Chemnitz when East Germany collapsed. Hughesovka, Ukraine, named for its Welsh founder, was renamed Stalino under the Soviet dictator, and in 1961 was again renamed Donetsk. St. Petersburg spent many decades under the name of Leningrad before it was changed back. On a local level, many people can remember once-familiar street names in their neighborhoods altered because of the authorities' need to commemorate someone or expunge the memory of another. But as the Austrian artist and architect Friedensreich Hundertwasser (1928–2000) sagely noted: "If we do not honor our past, we lose our future. If we destroy our roots, we cannot grow."

10

Ørlög and History

The Formation of the Modern World

History is a story that people tell about events of the past, and the future has no existence except in the imagination. History is not the past, and the future is not inevitable, only conditioned by what has gone before. For each individual, *ørlög* is the concatenation of events and influences that have resulted in our place in the present. Our lives, for good or ill, are the result of everything that has gone before. History sets apart particular things that remain from the past and weaves them into a narrative. Inevitably selective, history tells of things that are of interest to the historian's particular theme. They help to explain the present by recalling past happenings that preceded the present condition of things; events that explain the present and indicate its potential.

One of the most significant historical processes that has brought us to where we are now is the process called Modernization. Modernization is epitomized by discontinuous alterations in well-established ways of life: it has always resulted in the destruction of human livelihoods and even lives. New techniques that those in power saw as being advantageous to them have always been introduced without consultation of the people who would be affected. The consequent suffering, if acknowledged at all, was dismissed as a necessary evil that must be endured if progress were to take place. It is the excuse of revolutionary regimes the world over, whatever their political or religious agendas, and it is a process that shows no sign of abating.

In Great Britain, the Highland Clearances of Scotland between 1750 and 1860 were a ferocious example of this disregard for human lives in the pursuit of efficiency and financial gain. Betrayed by their own kith and kin, the highlanders, peasant and artisan alike, were expelled from their homes in the Scottish Highlands so that sheep could graze where Scots people once lived. The dispossessed, livelihoods destroyed, were driven from their burning crofts and villages and forced to trudge southward, carrying their few possessions in search of somewhere to go. Many were forced to find work in towns and cities wherever they could. Others managed to emigrate to Canada and the United States, where they became settlers.

These Scottish refugees were compelled to abandon their native country, contrary to their wishes. But these poor people who went to other lands were no privileged imperialists bent on the subjugation of Indigenous peoples, as simplistic moralists would describe them today. They were homeless, displaced families, who had to rebuild their lives as refugees in an alien land, having been expelled by their own fellow countrymen as worth less to their lords and masters than the sheep that replaced them. Today this crime aganist humanity would be described as "ethnic cleansing"—except for the fact that the clearers and the cleansed were of the same ethnicity. It was not genocide because people were not actively killed, though many died as a result of being expelled. It was *sociocide*, in which a whole community and its entire culture was wiped out, and the people were left sad and uprooted. An honest, traditional way of life had been eradicated by the forces of Progress. The little they had was taken from them without pity and without compensation. Something similar happened south of the border in England and Wales, not with the same inhuman ferocity but with similar results.

Parliament's Inclosure Acts of England and Wales, signed into law by the monarch, enabled lords to appropriate common land that had existed since before feudal times. The land that once fed and clothed local people was now a privatized "estate," the sole property of the owner. They surveyed it, fenced it, evicted anyone who was living on it, drove off the animals, and turned it over to arable land or pasture for the lords' livestock. Parts of estates were reserved for game birds raised only to be killed for sport during shooting parties of rich and fashionable guests of the lord—what was then called "society." For "society" did not include the servants or the peasant classes. It meant the relatively few families who comprised the aristocracy and the hangers-on they deemed to be amusing at the time. Those driven into poverty were hounded if they dared to try to feed their families by entering the now-forbidden estates to hunt something to eat. Even wildlife living on the land, rabbits and hares, were now claimed as estate property. The new crime of "poaching" was invented, and if caught by the gamekeeper, a perpetrator could be shot on sight, or if captured, later hanged or transported to Australia as an indented slave.

In England, whole villages were demolished and their inhabitants evicted so that the lords could extend their estates over the inclosed fields that once were the livelihood of the now-dispossessed villagers. Sometimes, as at Madingley Hall near Cambridge, the houses were demolished merely to form a picturesque vista for the aesthetic pleasure of the aristocrats. At Madingley, they wanted to have a romantic view of Cambridge's King's College Chapel in the distance. So out went the people and down came their cottages. The poet Oliver Goldsmith (1728–1774), in "The Deserted Village," encapsulates the horror and sadness of the fate of so many who lost their homes and livelihoods:

The man of wealth and pride
Takes up a space than many poor supplied;
Space for his lake, his park's extended bounds,
Space for his horses, equipage, and hounds . . .

Paradoxically, many of the more cultured landowners laid out their newly acquired countryside as fine parks that took account of the subtle topography. The Villa Adriano, the estate of the Roman emperor Hadrian (76–138 CE; reigned 117–138) at Tivoli in Italy, which still stood as a ruin, was their model. The poet Alexander Pope (1683–1744), in his *Epistle to Burlington* (1731), gave geomantic advice to would-be "landscape gardeners" to recognize the genius loci:

> *Consult the genius of the place in all*
> *That tells the waters to rise, or fall,*
> *Or helps th'ambitious hill the heavens to scal*
> *Or scoops in circling theatres the vale;*
> *Calls in the country, catches opening glades,*
> *Joins willing woods, and varies shades from shades;*
> *Now breaks, now directs th'intending lines,*
> *Paints as you plant, and as you work, designs.*

"Landscape Gardening" also included picturesque temples, some of which, dedicated to the Roman gods and goddesses, actually acquired numinous qualities.

The arbitrary power of control that created these estates was soon exercised for the expansion of industries and transportation. Country people, driven off their land by inclosures, clearances, and fen drainages, were compelled by their lords and masters to uproot themselves from their ancestral homeplaces. Their livelihood destroyed, some escaped by joining the army or navy or by emigrating to settle in distant colonies. Others who did not leave were forced to travel with their families to the cities to eke out impoverished lives in squalid tenements, working long hours in relentless urban factories and service industries. The inclosures facilitated an all-out attack on those who made their livelihood without land or masters, including cattle and sheep drovers, yeomen farmers, inland fisherfolk and fowlers, basketmakers, woodturners, charcoal-burners, Gypsies, itinerant tinkers, stallion-leaders, and other freelance trades. As they were expelled from their own land, their land-wisdom was rendered useless, and, unless it was "collected" and documented by folklorists, lost.

In the ever-expanding towns and cities, Nature—or rather the human-altered remnants of it—was progressively destroyed. Inexorably, the expanding urban realm covered the land with roads and buildings until only a few trees and a few green spaces were permitted to remain as parks, but not even that in some places. The relationship between urban and urbanized people and nature was severed gradually but irreversibly. Horses, once the ubiquitous draft animal for all forms of transport, were progressively replaced by mechanically powered vehicles. Stables, horse hospitals, blacksmiths' services, and depots for the provision of fodder all disappeared from the urban scene. Knowledge of how to handle and manage animals was lost in the city, as was an understanding of the numinous. Only some churches and other places of worship still retained numinosity.

Industrialization enabled manufacturers to produce identical multiple items in almost unlimited quantities. This had the effect of destroying local identity, which until then had manifested through the traditional arts and crafts. Mass-produced goods flooded the world, replacing handcrafted artifacts that were made by individuals using sustainable local materials. Traditional cups, bowls, plates, jars, containers, baskets, woven fabrics, and larger items of everyday use were fitted to local conditions and embodied local cultural values and spiritual symbolism. Manufactured items made elsewhere possessed none of these subtle virtues, only a cheapness that undermined and extinguished local traditional craftsmanship. The rise of consumerism led to the manufacture of disposable objects that had to be replaced by new ones after a short existence—the "throwaway society." The result was an exponential increase in waste and pollution of the environment that only recently, after more than a century and a half, has become a political issue.

Traditional skills were rendered uneconomic and denigrated as anachronistic by progressive "world improvers" who sought to annihilate tradition as a hindrance to Progress. Clock time—including "daylight saving time"—became the driving force of daily work; the position of the sun in the sky no longer mattered, and noon was defined by what the clock said, not when the sun was at its highest in the day. Traditionally constructed buildings in cities, designed in harmony with local conditions, were torn down as "old-fashioned." As cities grew, they engulfed smaller settlements and replaced their buildings with standardized products. The *Système Hennebique* of reinforced concrete, invented by François Hennebique (1842–1921), which appeared in France in 1879, became the standard for all new buildings worldwide. The components of reinforced concrete were not natural or local, but manufactured in factories elsewhere and then transported to the site for use.

Reinforced concrete spread across the whole world in the following decades, displacing traditional buildings. Hence the collapsed and flattened apartment blocks the media shows every time an earthquake is reported. Traditional architecture and systems of placement such as feng shui, Taj al Maluk, and Vastu Vidya, which knew how to build in earthquake zones, have been abandoned as old fashioned or superstitious. Once they had been overwhelmed by industrial production, characteristic local artifacts were called "folk art" and collected as relics of a vanishing world. By the early twentieth century, their symbolism disappeared from industrial design as ideas of efficiency and the appearance of modernity condemned ornament as morally wrong and a hindrance to the creation of a New World. But the eldritch existed before the human race came into being and will continue to exist when we are gone.

It is a primary aim of the Way of the Eight Winds to spread and explain knowledge of how geomancy was once a worldwide practice that enabled people to live in harmony with their local conditions. It is based upon concepts and principles that modernity has rejected and destroys—either accidentally or deliberately—almost everywhere it exists.

11
The Eldritch World

The eldritch world is a place redolent of the quality of strangeness and wonder. J. R. R. Tolkien wrote about the quality of "arresting strangeness" that is present in his descriptions of ancient lands. In geomantic walks and visits, we seek the weird and wonderful in order to illuminate the dimension of the extraordinary in the world—those things that can be spoken of truly only in the lost speech but are accessible in parts in near-forgotten ancient words.

We may glimpse the shadows of things emanating from the remote past of human experience, seemingly immune to the passing of time. There are things that we do not realize consciously, but which we perceive nevertheless and know them to be realities, though not of this everyday material world. We may encounter that supernormal, eerie state, which is described by the ancient meanings of the words *Wyrd* and *Faërie*. This is the eldritch world. To enter it requires an altered state of consciousness in which we experience an eager longing for lost things, where every word evokes half-forgotten, archaic meanings, hinting at an uncertain range of possibilities that bridges the barrier between past and present. It is a place filled with beings in that state of timeless continuity, which is ever-present within us and also manifests as an external presence. It is a place where the passage of time has a different

The magic light emanating from the eldritch world

dimension than our usual experience of the everyday bustle of life. We have glimpsed this hidden realm when we witnessed those insubstantial beings that appear briefly in the corner of an eye; the shadowy sprites in the corner that flee when we look in their direction; the spectral bird of no known species that flits overhead just behind our field of vision.

Some gain entry to the eldritch world through various states of receptivity: dreams, trance, meditation, delerium, reverie, or from dire disorders on the borderline of life and death. Some may briefly glimpse it in a blurred, distorted form through drunkenness or the effects of drugs. This is a state of being in which there is no separation between human and nature, a place where we may gain understanding of the languages of bird and beast. It is the vague terrain that some call Elfame or Elfland. Scottish legend tells how Thomas de Ercildoun aka Thomas the Rhymer (ca. 1220–1298) was led there by the Queen of Elfland via the third road that is neither the difficult straight and narrow path "beset with thorns and briars" that leads to heaven, nor the broad road to Hell, but that nigh-imperceptible and little-trodden third path that winds across the ferny brae. We may encounter this world on an autumn afternoon dappled with oak-leaf shadows somewhere in old woodland; at a windy fen-dyke corner; on an ancient bridge; or even in some strange place in the city.

Almost two centuries of psychical and parapsychological research, and later Fortean and psychogeographical investigations, have proved unable to describe adequately the nondeterministic experiences of people. Their methods resemble those of science, attempting to list and categorize observable phenomena and devise theories based upon pre-existing ideas. Their attempts to produce verifiable results have always been doomed to failure, like trying to see the stars on a sunny day.

PART II
Cosmic Principles

We are all part of Nature: our living bodies exist because conditions on this planet are conducive to life. Cosmic principles embody the possibility of life and consciousness emerging everywhere that conditions permit.

12

The Four Elements and the Cosmic Egg

The traditional way of viewing the world describes the principles that rule it in simple terms. Process is usually described as having a threefold nature, most simply apparent in the sequence: beginning–continuance–end. Existent realities such as matter and planar space are understood in a fourfold way. The four directions divide the plane of the Earth's surface, while the four seasons divide the year. They are aspects of being, a symbolic worldview that is totally different from reductionist science, which nevertheless is also another truth that views the Cosmos from a different angle.

The individual natures of things, both nonliving and living, can be described by means of the four symbolic principles: Earth, Water, Air, and Fire. These four elements are an ancient philosophical description of the nature of the material world. They are the symbolic qualities that combine to make particulars. The same word *element* is used in modern chemistry to describe the basic characteristic elements in the periodic table. But the two are quite distinct, and the ancient meaning is not, as is often viewed, a primitive forerunner of the modern, but part of a quite different symbolic system that describes principles, not substances.

The four elements are thus a description of the nature of how the material world operates. They have their being within the physical structure of the world, the dimensions, which Pythagoras (ca. 570–ca. 495 BCE) classified into four parts: (1) the Seed or starting point, (2) height, (3) depth, and (4) thickness or solidity. This tetrad is the pattern inherent in all growing things and, equally, artifacts are made through the autonomy of the individual and by means of the human arts and crafts. Pythagoras emphasized the importance of the divine numerical series 1, 2, 3, 4 as the creative power of the Cosmos. Existence was symbolized by the *Tetractys* (Greek τετρακτύς), put in visible form as a triangle composed of ten points, arranged from the top down, 1, 2, 3, 4. Of the various forms of Tetractys, one represents the four elements,

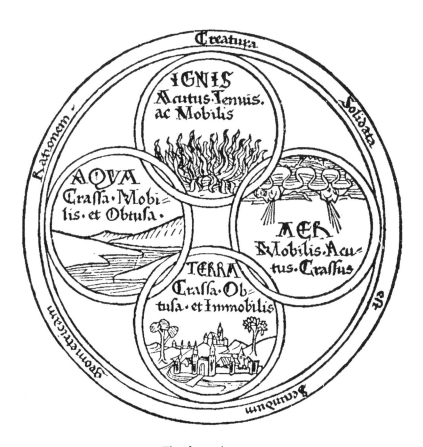

The four elements

while another, the *Intelligible Tetractys*, represents the four faculties of the human being: (1) intelligence and mind, (2) knowledge, (3) opinion, and (4) sensation.

The oldest surviving description of the symbolic tetrad of principles known as the four elements comes from Empedocles of Acragas (ca. 494–434 BCE) in his text *On Nature* (ca. 445 BCE). They are the four roots of all things, personified as the deities Zeus, Hera, Aidoneus, and Nestis, eternal and equally balanced:

> *For these are all equal and of like age in their birth,*
> *but each rules over a different prerogative and each has*
>   *its own character,*
> *and they dominate in turn as time circles around.*
> (trans. Inwood 1992, 89)

Believers in a single creator deity saw these four forces or elements as emanating from the earliest time, the act of Creation, the act of will of a preexistent deity. Another view is that the emanation of the four roots was a natural event, comparable with the "Big Bang" postulated by modern cosmology, where the universe originated in an event described as a "singularity."

The division of the matter of the world into four symbolic roots or elements is the basis for the traditional Western understanding of the subtle nature of the human body. The ancient Greek author of the alchemical text *Anonymus*, expressing ideas current in the third and fourth centuries CE, places the origin of the four elements in the Cosmic Egg, in which the potential seeds of all things was contained. This conception also appeared in the play *The Birds* by Aristophanes (ca. 460–388 BCE).*

According to the followers of the prophet Orpheus (460–380 BCE),

---

*For more details on the Cosmic Egg, see my book *Creating Places of Power: Geomancy, Builders' Rites, and Electional Astrology in the Hermetic Tradition* (Inner Traditions, 2022), 96, 98–101.

The Four Elements and the Cosmic Egg 83

The emanation of the Cosmic Egg

Cosmic Egg, carving on Little Trinity, Cambridge, England, 1714

the Cosmic Egg, symbol of all potential, was was born out of the Womb of Erebus in the formative age of existence when no distinct thing existed, except Æther, the empty brightness; Chaos, the void; and Erebus, the empty darkness. The ancient poetic skalds of the Northern Tradition also recognized these primal regions, calling them respectively, Muspellheim, Ginnungagap, and Niflheim. The concept of the Cosmic Egg may be viewed as an ancient poetic description of the current scientific "Big Bang Theory."

13

The World, the Cosmos, and the Human Body

Our being in the world is predicated upon the form of the human body. We are bilaterally symmetrical, having a face at the front where our eyes are situated, and a back, which is the part we cannot see. We have a left side and a right side, with corresponding arms and legs. Because we stand and walk erect, we are conscious also of up and down: the earth below, on which we walk, and the space above us. This physical structure is fundamental to our being and is the foundation of our cultural understanding of place in physical action, language, and in myth and symbol.

European alchemical thought proposes that we live in two worlds, the visible and invisible. Underlying them are two universal natures, out of which both those worlds proceeded. The passive universal Nature was made in the image of the active universal one, and the conformity of both worlds. This concept maintains that Nature has two extremes and between them a middle substance; we call this the Middle Nature. To each of us, with our awareness centered in our bodies, we are at the center of our world. The place where we are at any given time is *the* place, *our* place. The observed world originates here. As each person

86 Cosmic Principles

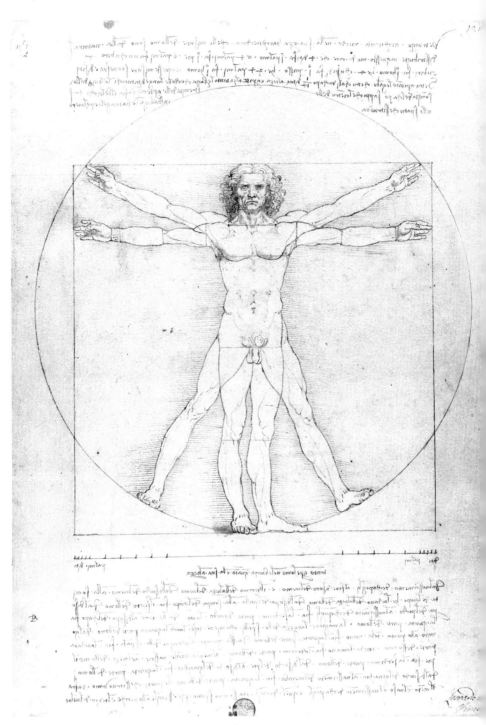

The Vitruvian Man by Leonardo da Vinci, ca. 1490

is centered upon themself, so the world can be viewed as centered at a particular place.

An ancient Jewish legend of the creation of humans involves the winds, which are an outward manifestation of the breath of life that sustains our physical being. In the Garden of Eden, the soul entered the first man as a result of the coming together of the Four Winds. The breath forming the soul was occasioned by the conjunction of the winds at the instant that the four elements composing the physical body were assembled at the center from the four corners of the world. Gathering together the Four Winds, God breathed into Adam's nostrils the Breath of Life. The human being was thus formed at and as the point of coincidence of the physical elements, the particulate matter of the Earthly Sphere, and the winds, the particulate matter of the Aetheric Sphere. Thus, the human being is composed of the substances of two worlds that came together at the center in the act of coming-into-being instigated at the Creation—the Middle Nature.

We perceive our bodies in a fourfold way—front, back, left, right—related to the vertical axis: head–feet, up–down. The natural world, too, is perceived in this way, the four directions of north, east, south, and west being related to our perception as beings existing on the surface of the planet. Our bipedal locomotion underlies our consciousness of verticality, which reflects a significant element in our perception of the planet upon which we live. As we perceive it, the earth appears as a generally flat surface, bounded by a circular horizon. Below us lies the earth, and above us the bright sky of day and the starry heavens of night. The Earth appears to be fixed and still, and the heavens above apparently rotate above us. Now we know this to be an illusion, the earth being a nearly spherical planet that rotates on its own axis, and additionally in motion in orbit around the sun. But for the greater part of human history—and embedded in many significant religious scriptures—the Earth was stationary, and this remains as our physical perception of our presence in the world.

The orientated cross-shaped church with the crucified Christ superimposed is a traditional interpretation of its meaning.

Human beings are both an expression and a reflection of the Cosmos, which is an aspect of the One. Our physical bodily being is determined by the structure and rhythms of material substance. Tradition expresses this symbolically as being composed of four elements existing within the matrix of time: Fire, Air, Water, and Earth. We begin life in the world as independent beings when we are expelled from the womb and draw our first breath. For the rest of our lives, our existence is measured by our breaths, in and out. When we die, we exhale our final breath. That final exhaled breath is a symmetry with our first inhaled one. With the last breath, the spirit, or bodily Fire, departs from us when air is expelled from the body for the final time. Then our bodily fluids leak and evaporate, losing the element of Water after Fire and Air have gone. Finally, the flesh, which is of the element of Earth, remains, and when that dissipates, the bones and teeth are the last to disintegrate. At death, the human soul breaks forth from the bonds of matter, ascending the ladder to the firmament, through the stages of the planetary spheres, mounting upward toward the roof of the Cosmos. There the soul becomes dignified, purified, and exalted, just as in astrology a planet may be dignified in its puissance by its favorable placement and aspects.

According to the traditional viewpoint, the four elements are all part of the Sphere of Earth. There is sometimes confusion over the use of the word *earth* to describe both the plane on which we live and one of the four elements whose virtues compose this place. When I refer to Earth as one of the four elements, this means the densest form of material existence. When Earth refers to the plane or planet upon which we live, which in the Northern Tradition is called Midgard, it is composed of all four forms of matter: solid Earth; liquid Water; gaseous Air; and plasmatic Fire. Within them, wholly part of all four and transcendent of them is the Quintessence. The Quintessence is sometimes called the Æther, which, however, is not the same as the primal Æther of the formative age of existence, in which the Cosmic Egg emerged.

14

Temperament and the Divine Harmony

Related to the symbolic four elements are the four humors, the subtle components of the human body. Traditionally, these are: blood, phlegm, black bile, and yellow bile. As symbolic, rather than the physical bodily fluids of modern medicine, they correspond with the four elements. Thus, blood corresponds with air; phlegm, water; black bile, earth; and yellow bile, fire. This tetrad of humors is a metaphorical way to describe the active qualities present in the bodies of all living beings. The four humors are produced by combinations of the quaternary of hot, cold, wet, and dry, which are related to the four elements. These combine in various ways, to produce four distinct physical natures. As Aristotle (384–322 BCE) described them, fire is the result of heat combined with dryness; air, heat and wetness; water, cold and wetness; and earth, cold and dryness.

According to the ancient Greek concept of the *perisomata* (sg. *perisoma*), the proportions of each of the four humors in any one being produces or describes that individual's personal temperament. The word *temperament* literally describes the outcome of the combination of humors tempering one another. The principle of Temperance, one of

Temperament and the Divine Harmony 91

Traditional zodiacal correspondence of the parts of the human body

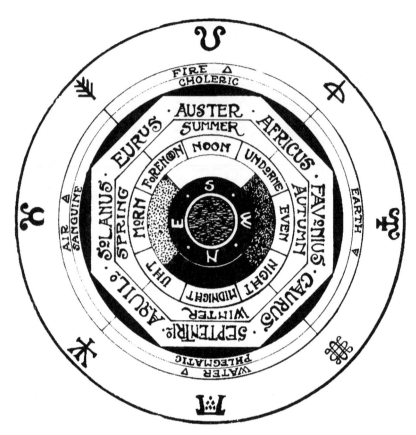

Wheel of the winds and the humors

the Four Cardinal Virtues, denotes this sort of tempering. Polybius (ca. 200–ca. 117 BCE), in his *The Nature of Man*, defines health as being the state in which the four humors stand in the correct proportion to one another, both in strength and quantity. They must also be mixed together properly. Whenever there is deficiency or excess of one or more of the humors, or the mixing of them is insufficient, then a particular disorder results. When the humors are in harmony with one another, according to the basic nature of the individual's constitution, then there is balance, and the person is healthy. Temperance, the art of balancing the humors properly, brings health. The commonplace expression of "being in a good humor" references this ancient concept.

Imbalances of the humors produce not only bodily disorders, but particular psychological states. Traditionally, music is a means of rectifying imbalances of the humors; rhythm and harmony impart grace to the inner parts of the soul. The human soul, being one with the Cosmos, responds to the music that drives the spheres. Aristotle asserted that music has the power to lead the soul back from states of unrest to that of harmony, relieving mental illnesses and stabilizing the character. In the twentieth century CE, the American bluesman John Lee Hooker (1920–2001) taught that "blues is the healer." Music that heals thus brings the hearer into confluence with the harmony of the spheres, aligning soul with the workings of the Cosmos, thereby purifying the emotions.

15

The Planetary Spheres and the Ogdoas

The concept of the planetary spheres, so significant in European symbolism, appears to have originated in the speculations of the Greek philosopher Anaximander (ca. 610–546 BCE), who suggested that the heavenly bodies are carried around the Earth on a series of concentric spheres. Although 2,000 years later, European scientists, most notably Copernicus, determined that the Earth is a planet in orbit around the Sun, and not the center of the Cosmos, the model created by Anaximander is still a valid spiritual metaphor. Credited to Pythagoras, who elaborated the ideas of Anaximander, the system of the octave was worked upon by later Gnostic researchers who used the concept known as the *Ogdoas*. In this eightfold system, the Cosmos is ruled by seven deities, who in turn were under the rulership of the Supreme One.

The Neopythagorean philosopher Nichomachus of Gerasa (ca. 60–120 CE) reinforced this concept when he commented that the planetary spheres each produce their own particular tones, each of which is reflected in a corresponding vowel in the Greek language. According to Nichomachus, the vowel α reflects the sphere of the Moon, and the mode called *Nete*. The sphere of Mercury is expressed by the vowel ε, that sound the tone *Paranete*. The vowel η sounds the sphere of Venus, the tone *Trite synemmenon*. The vowel ι reflects the sphere of the Sun, with the tone of *Mese*. The vowel o relates to the planetery sphere of Mars, and the tone of *Lichanos*. The vowel υ recalls Jupiter and *Parhypate*, while ω signifies Saturn and *Hypate*.

In ancient Greek culture, there were no separate characters for numbers, and the letters of the alphabet also represented numbers. Everyone who learned to read knew these numbers along with the meaning of the letters. Thus, Greek culture—unlike ours, in which Roman letters and Arabic numerals have no connection—had an integral symbolic understanding of the relationship of word and name to number. The assertions that the Creator had brought matter into being by the utterance of a word and that number is also the underlying structure of existence—which to modern culture seem separate and irreconcilable—were obvious and compatible in ancient Greek culture.

The Greek Magical Papyri contain numerous incantations that begin or end with the seven Greek vowels in differing combinations. One text (PGM XIII) gives an invocation that encapsulates the magical theory:

> . . . your seven-lettered name is established for the harmony of the seven sounds [of the planets which] utter their voices according to the twenty-eight forms of the moon, SAR APHARA APHARA I ABRAARM ARAPHA ABRAACH PERTAŌMĒCH / AKMĒCH IAŌ OYE Ē IAŌ OYE EIOY AEŌ EĒOY IAŌ. (Betz 1986, 190)

The numbers 7 and 8 are an integral part of this Greek spiritual current. The Greek alphabet, having twenty-four characters, is divided into three ogdoads, each of which has a ruling letter and is thus structured 1 + 7. Following Greek practice, the runes of the Common Germanic Futhark are divided into three ogdoads, usually called by their Norse name, *ættir* (sg. *ætt*). Identically, each *ætt* is ruled by the first rune of the group, a 1 + 7 structure. This cosmology is also reflected in

96 Cosmic Principles

The ascending planetary spheres with their corresponding heraldic tinctures and metals

the Pentecontad Calendar used in ancient agricultural cultures in the Middle East and among the Essenes and Nestorians.

The Greek Magical Papyrus text known as "Moses' Book of the Great Name" (in the ms. Papyrus Magicus Leyden W) tells of the godly power contained in the name of the Ogdoas: "For in it there is the name of the lord, which is Ogdoas, the god who commands and directs all things, since to him angels, archangels, he-daimons, / she-daimons, and all things under the creation have been subjected" (Betz 1986, 1989–90). The use of the musical modes in initiation is recorded in this papyrus. Apotropaic and invocational music based upon the octaval system operates by re-creating the vibrations of the divine name, that is, the Music of the Spheres.

16

Myths of Coming into Being

Lux e tenebris
(From the shadows, light)

Everything that comes into being emerges from a condition of pre-being into actual being. The arc of light on the horizon before the dawn presages the rising of the sun and the arrival of day. The dawn is symbolically a visible recapitulation of the act or process of Creation, when the material world emerged out of the primal cloud or darkness that was the invisible chaos. From out of this darkness all things that are in this world came into being. According to a hymn of the followers of Orpheus, "O Night, thou black nurse of the golden stars," for the act of Creation is signified in biblical terms by the words *fiat lux*: "Let there be light." Because all things were brought forth out of night, just as we gestated in the darkness of our mother's womb in a preconscious state before experiencing first light at birth, it is a concept that we, as existent conscious beings, find difficult to comprehend. Illumination can only be brought to those who dwell in darkness. And which of us can say truthfully that they have *not* dwelt in darkness?

The Northern Tradition coming-into-being myth, in common with many such myths elsewhere that do not tell of a god creating everything out of nothing, tells of a primal void, Ginnungagap, parallel to the Chaos in the Greek beginning-myth. The myth is recounted in the *Prose Edda* text *Gylfaginning* (4–7), which tells that in the southern part of the void Ginnungagap was Muspell, a burning and flaming realm. In the north part was Niflheim, place of cold and ice. The gap was formless, but not without a north–south orientation. Thus, the polarity of fire and ice, motion and stasis, was predicated upon a north–south axis within the yawning void. The vapor and sparks resulting from the coming together of ice and fire generated a primordial being called Aurgelmir or Ymir. Ymir was slain and dismembered by the Sons of Bor, who took his remains to the middle of Ginnungagap, and there formed the Earth from his body parts. From his blood the waters of the Earth were formed; his bones became the rocks; his brains, the clouds; and from his hair, the trees were made (*Gylfaginning* 8). Ymir's skull became the dome of the sky, and four dwarfs were commanded to support it at the four cardinal directions: Austri in the east, Sudri in the south, Vestri in the west, and Nordri in the north.*

This is just one of the creation myths that link the human body with the greater whole of which we are a part. Ymir's blood becomes the sea—the ebb and flow of the tides recalls the ebb and flow of blood in the body, the prescientific way of viewing the pulse. The sea's tides are related to the waxing and waning of the Moon, which parallels the heart as the origin of the bodily blood-tides. The penetrated body bleeds, just as springs of water emerge from within the body of the Earth. The spiritual principle of "As above, so below" links the bodily blood to the tides and the bodily breath to the winds. The myth is symbolic of the composition of the human body from the materials of the world, and the function of its various aspects. We are all Ymir reassembled for a while, composed of the *prima materia* from which the Earth was made.

The myth of Ymir is a typical "founding event"—these are the stories

---

*The names have been anglicized here; the original Norse designations for the southern and northern dwarfs are Suðri and Norðri, respectively.

that define the nature of spiritual cultures, organizations, and religions. Jesus's crucifixion and resurrection is the Christian founding myth, just as Odin's ordeal on the "windy tree" is the founding myth for the runes. The death of Hiram for Freemasons and that of Maître Jacques for certain crafts of the French *Devoir* are founding myths. The founding myths of nation-states are often battles, revolutions, and declarations of independence. Rituals of these organizations on the supposed anniversaries of the founding event are ceremonial evocations of a legendary past.

The traditional view of the Cosmos is that it is infinitely pluralistic and cyclic in nature. The Cosmos, of which we are part, has recurring patterns of self-similarity in space, time, and event. No part of it is the same as any other part, though all things share the commonality of interconnectedness. The maxim ascribed to the ancient sage Hermes Trismegistus (Thrice-great Hermes) is, in its most simple form, *As above, so below*. This means that the Cosmos has a holistic structure in which the largest is reflected in the smallest and vice versa. As living beings, we are subject to what artist-philosopher Wassily Kandinsky (1866–1964) called the "universal laws of the cosmic world." From the smallest particle to the largest galaxy, the same basic principles apply. Expressing "As above, so below," the human bodily form embodies in its parts the structure of the overall Cosmos, not literally but analogously. Other organic forms—indeed, the minerals of the Earth and other planets—are similarly analogous of the Cosmos. This applies also to human consciousness, the relation of the self to the nonself or other, and that of both to the Cosmos around us. The same structural principles exist both in molecules and galaxies. Human beings are part of the nature of the *Microcosm*, and our physical and spiritual nature reflects the entire Cosmos, the *Macrocosm*. All things are linked together in one great chain of being, an interconnected sympathetic system operating at all levels of existence. We are the image of the All—not literally, for a microscopic alga, an oak tree, a shark, a bee, or an ostrich, for example, are also images of the All. The cells and organs within organic life are the microcosm to the macrocosm of the body. In One is All.

17

At the Center of the World

The Omphalos and the Spindle of Necessity

Although we know the Earth is a sphere—and this was known thousands of years ago by knowledgeable people—the land around us appears to be generally flat. Taking mountains into account, the horizon around us can be seen as a circle, and the idea of a flat Earth is experiential. The philosphers who knew otherwise would not have been believed by the majority of people, and sometimes religious dogma asserted, as in the early Christian church, that it was heretical to deny the flatness of the Earth.

On a conceptually flat Earth, the center of the world is of great importance. In geomantic parlance, this central point is called the *omphalos*, from the ancient Greek ὀμφαλός. William Richard Lethaby (1857–1931) explained in his *Architecture, Mysticism and Myth* (1891, 72):

> When the earth was a plane surface with boundaries which were certain in form, if unknown in extent, "the centre is with us" would be a claim advanced in a much more definite form by different countries or rival cities. On an Arab fountain in Sicily was the inscription "I am in the centre of the garden; this garden is in the centre of Sicily, and Sicily of the whole world."

The ancient omphalos on the via sacra at Delphi, Greece
(photo by TimeTravelRome)

In ancient times, Lethaby tells us (1891, 72, 78):

For the Egyptians the centre was Thebes; for the Assyrians, Babylon; for the Hindus, Mount Meru; for the Jews, Jerusalem; for the Greeks, Olympus or the Temple of Delphi, and later, in the time of Herodotus [434–425 BCE], Rhodes. . . .

The Greeks seem to have attached great mystic and ritual importance to the centre. Delphi was the navel of all Greece, but Crete had an omphalos. . . . In Sicily the modern Castro Giovanni occupies the site of Enna, *Umbilicus Siciliæ*, and this was the place where Persephone was carried away to the upperworld. . . .

On the floor of the Temple of Delphi was a stone "called by the Delphians the Navel, according to their tradition, the centre of the world" (Pausanias [ca. 110–180 CE]).

According to tradition, Delphi was found to be the true center of the Earth when Zeus sent out two eagles, one from the east, and the

Omphalion in the Aachen Cathedral, Germany

other from the west, and they met at that place. The stone omphalos at Delphi was once flanked by two eagles made of gold, in commemoration of Zeus's divination. Stone omphaloi took various forms, from an egg-shaped stone to a dome-shape or a flattened sphere. Pavements inside buildings also had circular stones of porphyry or marble set in them to mark the omphalos. Called omphalia, they exist to this day in some ancient churches, such as the Chapel Palatine at Aachen in Germany (illustrated here) and Westminster Abbey in London. It was on the omphalion at Westminster that King Charles III was crowned in 2023.

The *Axis Mundi*, or Spindle of Necessity

In book 10 of *The Republic*, Plato (ca. 428–347 BCE) gives a narrative that may be considered an ancient European *Book of the Dead*. He tells how Er, son of Armenius, after his death in battle came back to life twelve days later and recounted his experiences. After death, he recalled, he arrived with other souls at a strange place where there were two pairs of mouths. One pair led up to heaven, and the others down into the earth. Between these entrances and exits sat judges who directed the righteous to take the right-hand road leading up into heaven and sent evildoers down the left-hand road into the earth. During the process of judgment, Er witnessed some souls coming back up out of the earth, and others coming back down from heaven. The returning souls met and told each other of their experiences in the upper and lower worlds. Those who had been in the underworld were weary and worn after a thousand years' journeying beneath the earth, while those who had been in the upperworld had been purified by the experience.

On the eighth day after their return from the upper and lower worlds, Er joined the gathered souls on a journey. After four days' travel, they reached a place where they beheld a pillar of light, like a rainbow, but brighter and more intense. It was the column of light, the Cosmic Axis holding together the whole revolving firmament. The traveling souls were privileged to behold this Spindle of Necessity by which all the revolutions of the Cosmos are maintained. Just like the spindle used in spinning, the Cosmic Axis they witnessed ran through a whorl. But this whorl is a multiple structure by which the heavenly spheres are kept in motion, strangely resembling the rings of Saturn (which were not discovered until two millennia after Plato).

The circle of its rim of the first and outermost of Plato's whorl is the broadest, that of the sixth is second in breadth, that of the fourth is third, that of the eighth is fourth, that of the seventh is fifth, that of the fifth is sixth, that of the third is seventh, and that of the second is eighth. The "circle of the greatest" is of many colors: that of the seventh is brightest, that of the eighth receives its color from the seventh, which shines upon it. That of the second and fifth are similar to each other and yellower than the previous ones. The third is the whitest in color, the fourth is pale red, and the sixth is the second in whiteness. The Spindle turns round as a whole with one motion, and within the whole as it revolves the seven inner circles revolve slowly in an opposite direction to the whole. The eighth goes the most swiftly; second in speed and all together go the seventh and sixth and fifth; third in the speed of its counter-revolution the fourth appears to move; fourth in speed comes the third; and fifth in speed is the second.

Plato depicts the whole spindle turning in the lap of Necessity. Each of the circles has a Siren, carried around with it. She sings one single note, and from each of the Sirens' notes, eight in number, comes the harmony of the spheres. Around the rotating spindle, at equal distances, sit the daughters of Necessity, enthroned. They are the three Fates— Clotho, Lachesis, and Atropos—clothed in white raiment and with garlands on their heads. They chant to the choir of the Sirens: Clotho sings of the things that have been; Lachesis of the things that are; and Atropos of the things that shall be.

Symbolically, the spindle is analogous to the *Axis Mundi*, the Cosmic Axis. The Etruscan Discipline projects its sixteen sectors of the Cosmos upward along the Axis Mundi into four spiritual planes, vertically situated, interpenetrating the planetary spheres. The lowest plane is the Earth, where dwell long-lived spirits of the elements and Nature, including fauns, satyrs, dryads, hamadryads, naiads, and meliae. Above the plane of Earth is the Air, which itself has two divisions: *Aer* and *Æther*. The lower part of the plane of Air is the Aer. This region is inhabited by apotheosized heroes under the rulership of Vejovis, whom the Romans called Pluto. Dwellers in this region are both benevolent and malevolent spirits. Above this, the plane of Æther is situated, occupied by the Semones, the demigods. Together, these two planes, Aer and Æther, are reckoned by the Augurs to be the realm of the element Air. The Etruscan Discipline teaches that inside a temple as far as the ceiling is the Aer and directly above it, the Æther. Hence circular temples have an aperture in the domed roof at the meeting point of the internal Aer with the Æther above and outside it. In Rome, the Temple of Vesta and the Pantheon are examples of this. Above the plane of Air, situated between the spheres of the Sun and the Moon, is a plane under the rulership of the Dei Manes, who are known by mortals as daemons of the underworld.

The uppermost plane is situated between the sphere of the Sun and the Empyrean. This is the plane of the gods, ruled by the supreme deity. In his *Hymn of Ascension*, Synesius of Cyrene (ca. 373–ca. 414 CE) celebrates Christ's ascension up this axis through the spheres, at which the resident aerial daemons trembled at his passing, and the choir of deathless stars was silenced in amazement while the Æther played a melody of triumph on its seven-stringed lyre. Oswald Croll (1560–1609) likens this link between the spheres as like a golden chain let down from Heaven, up which the rational soul climbs through the orders of creatures from the lowest to the highest. The symbol of the Cosmic Axis is a vision of the Cosmos that enables the human consciousness to penetrate the boundaries of the apparent visible world into higher levels of existence. It informs us that the sustaining power of Creation embodied in the ascent of the soul also empowers the essential harmony of the invisible world.

These potential modes and states may become actualized in the physical. The rotation of the Earth causing us to perceive the apparent rotation of the sky, is centered in the north close to a particular star whose position appears to be fixed. This is the star that stays close to the hub of the northern hemisphere night sky as it appears to rotate during the night. In modern astronomy, it is called Polaris (from *Stella Polaris*, the Pole Star or North Star). The North Star has many alternative names: Tir, Stella Maris, the Lodestar (German *Leitstern*), the Nave, the Leading Light, the (or God's) Nail or the Nowl. The latter name likens the star to a nail around which the heavens rotate like the hub of a wheel. The North Star was a guiding light for those navigating at sea and on land. It symbolizes constancy and reliability, the unwavering guiding light that leads us unfailingly to our destination. Its connection with maritime travel gives it the name *Stella Maris* (the Star of the Sea), which in Christian tradition is an epithet of the Virgin Mary. The *Old English Rune Poem* describes it as the rune *Tir*, "which keeps faith well, always on course in the dark of night." A medieval Latin epithet for the North Star is "*Stella non erratica*," the "unerring star," and as an emblem it bears the motto "*Qui me non aspicet errat*"—"He who does not look at me goes astray."

At the Center of the World   107

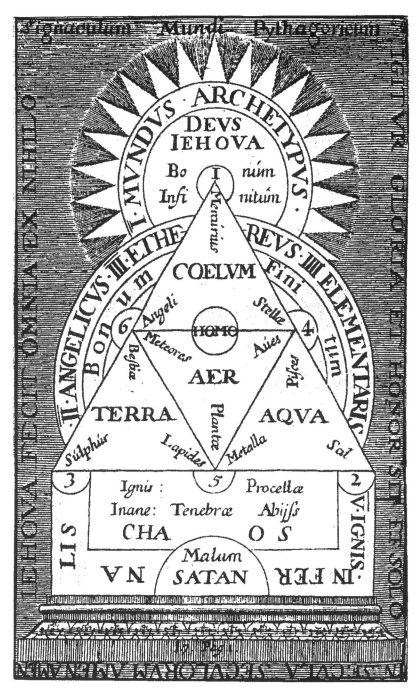

Schematic diagram of the Cosmos devised by the
English alchemist Thomas Norton (1436–1513)

18

Time, Space, and Fate

There are certain patterns that all things make, and which humans perceive as the Cosmic Order. They appear everywhere we care to look, and human craft by necessity exists according to these patterns, which are described symbolically in the myths and legends of coming-into-being. The most ancient crafts of humankind are weaving and potting, and both are metaphors for the human condition. The ancient philosophers viewed the multiple strands of human life interwoven like a piece of fabric, woven by hidden powers that we call fate. Our individual existence is envisaged as part of a great woven pattern, known in the Northern Tradition as the Web of Wyrd (see below). The otherworldly custodians of this weaving are personified as the Three Fates. Each Fate signifies one of the three stages in life's progression. There are three because this process can be divided into three stages: formation, becoming, and dissolution. The earliest awareness of these three shapers of becoming was in ancient Greece, where they were the Moirai or Fates, daughters born of the darkness of Night. Writing around 850 BCE, Hesiod named them as Clotho, Lachesis, and Atropos, "who give people at their birth both ill and good." The prophet Orpheus told of "the Moirai in white raiment." His disciples likened them to three phases of the Moon: waxing, full, and waning.

Clotho spins the thread of life, Lachesis measures it, and Atropos cuts it. The thread symbolizes human life, which sometimes hangs by a thread. How it is spun, what colors and textures it possesses, determines the individual's character. It is measured out in time, and at a certain point, ends. Our parentage, our genetics, our birth environment, is the character of the thread spun by the first Fate, Clotho. Composed of many fibers, the complex nature of the thread determines in great measure how life progresses. She spins the thread on a rotating spindle whose motion parallels the rotating heavens that appear to spin the nights and days of our existence. To understand this thread, spun and existing within a limited time, and to use it in the creative acceptance of life, was the ideal of the ancient philosophers. The Roman emperor Marcus Aurelius Antoninus (121–180 CE), himself a Stoic philosopher, recommended in his *Meditations* (IV, 36) that one "Gladly surrender yourself to Clotho, let her spin your thread into whatever web she wills" (trans. Hammond). This is the "creative pagan acceptance of life."

The second Fate, Lachesis, symbolizes the interweaving of one's personal thread with all the other strands of life and the world. To the Greeks, she was primarily the measurer of the span of life, but in the Northern Tradition, she is named Verdandi, who weaves the many threads into the fabric of life—the Web of Wyrd. The warp of the weaving expresses the passing of time and the appearance of events, while the weft symbolizes the actions of the individual who interacts with them. The final Fate wields the shears that cut the thread of life. Atropos signifies the inevitable end of all things, the dissolution of present existence and its return to the inchoate. The Northern Tradition also has three fatal sisters who preside over human existence. They are the *sceffarin*, (female) "shapers" who, as the three Nornir, determine the shape of things to come. The three Nornir, the Norns or Weird Sisters, are the northern version of the the Greek Moirai. Urda is the equivalent of Clotho; Verdandi, of Lachesis; and Skuld, of Atropos.* They spin, weave, and cut the Web of Wyrd.

---

*The names of the first two Norns, Urda and Verdandi, have been anglicized here from their Old Norse forms of Urðr and Verðandi, respectively.

110 Cosmic Principles

The three Wyrd Sisters (Moirae, Fates, Nornir)

The Web of Wyrd is the metaphor of existence. The word *wyrd* is from Old English and meant "fate, destiny," similarly to its counterparts such as Old High German *wurt* and Old Norse *urðr* (which is identical with the name of the first Norn, Urðr). These nouns are in turn related to verbs such as Old English *weorþan*, Old High German *werdan*, and Old Norse *verða*, all of which mean "to become," or "to come to pass." The Germanic verbs are more distantly related to the Latin verb *vertere*, "to turn."

Another Old High German word related to *wurt* is *wirtel*, a "spindle," which is the implement used in spinning thread as wielded by Clotho and Urda. Fortune and destiny are also likened to weaving in an Old English word *gewæf*, as in the phrase "*Me þæt wyrd gewæf,*" "Wyrd wove me that," in other words: that is my fate in life. Our culture sees fate as inevitable, as, indeed all that live are born to die. The sages of Old England taught that we are subject to *metodsceaft*, the "decree of fate" or the "shaping of destiny" by the Fates. Within the time and place we occupy in the Web of Wyrd, every moment we live, we still have the ability to influence the shape of our being. The Web of Wyrd is often visualized as an intricate fabric woven on a loom. But equally it can be visualized as a series of threads knitted or knotted together, for it is a metaphor and not a physical object. A rare Renaissance-era painting of the Virgin Mary exists in the Church of Sankt Peter am Perlach in Augsburg, Bavaria. (The church stands on the site of a pagan temple dedicated to the Swabian goddess Zisa.) Titled *Maria Knotenlöserin*, the painting depicts angels handing Mary a knotted thread, which she undoes. Said to symbolize the forgiveness of sins, Maria Knotenlöserin is a kind of reverse Lachesis. Knots are the means to tie things up magically as well as physically; undoing them either releases the magic or negates it. In the days of sail, wise women in ports sold strings with knots that were said to contain the winds. Becalmed sailors would undo a knot in the belief that this would release more wind at sea (see chap. 23).

The web is not a reality, but a powerful metaphor. The metaphor of the Web of Wyrd gives us some limited understanding of the way things happen, and an incentive to use what we have well. Existence is not composed of an assemblage of separate moments, but it is a seamless flow of process, the threads of which are as but currents in a river, tides in a sea or the blowing of the winds. Although we have beginnings and endings within our lives and actions, there is no fixed time; each moment that we may call separate actually is not. It leads on to the next, and the next, and the next, in an ever-flowing continuum. The present is not a fixed thing, but a condition of process, ever flowing and never static and determinable only in terms of the possibilities inherent within it. Mastery is thus a means of seizing the ungraspable instant. As with all events, all records and information are no more than individual statements of data available at some time in the past, only available because they are here in the present. They are expressions of the instant that the record was made—no more, no less. Of necessity they are partial and incomplete. Thus, no fixed views are possible, only a succession of subsequent interpretations, reassessments, and re-viewings, colored by previous interpretations and attempts at explanation and understanding.

19

Our Place on Earth

In the northern hemisphere, when we face southward, to our left is the east, the quarter of the rising sun, morning, the principle of increase. In front of us is the south, the high point of the sun, midday. Right of us is west, the quarter where the sun goes down, evening, the principle of decline. Behind us is the darkness of night, where the sun is behind and beneath us. Facing south, we actually face toward the equator; the north pole and the North Star are behind us. This is physical reality. Above us are the heavens; below us, the earth. The sun, moon, planets, and stars of the sky appear to move "clockwise." This is the meaning of being in place, being in the world. For we perceive our bodies to have a fourfold structure, left–right; front–back. Our bodies are bilaterally symmetrical, the left and right sides being more or less "mirror images" of one another. Wherever we are, this is our center of the world. So, wherever we are, we experience being *here* in a fourfold way.

In the Northern Tradition, the four corners of the heavens are supported by four dwarfs named Nordri, Sudri, Austri, and Vestri. In European high magic, the four corners of the heavens are ruled over by the four archangels, Gabriel, north; Uriel (or Nariel), south; Michael, east; and Raphael, west. There are also the four corners of the heavens: rising, falling, the middle of the heaven, and the bottom of it

(Agrippa 2021, I, 3). In Amsterdam in 1913, stone images of the four northern dwarfs were set in the ceiling of the main entrance of the archetypal "Amsterdamse School" building, the shipping companies' office called Het Scheepvaarthuis, designed by Johan Melchior van der Mey (1878–1949). Supporting the heavens, they surround a metal image of the Great Bear constellation with the stars, including the mariners' guiding light, the North Star, represented by electric lightbulbs. The building is now an exclusive hotel.

The center is where we begin, facing south. Round us, the horizon is divided by visible and invisible phenomena, which we analyze in a fourfold way. Facing south, we face the position of the sun at noon, the *meridian*, the middle of the day, when it is at its highest point in the sky for that day. This is one of four points we call the Four Corners of the Heavens, which are the positions of the sun at equinoctial sunrise, noon, equinoctial sunset, and midnight. These four corners are otherwise known as rising; zenith or midheaven; falling; and nadir and to the medieval Locators by their Latin names: Oriens, Meridies, Occidens, and Septentrio.

The Four Corners of the Heavens are also the Cardinal Points of the compass, known from their likeness to the hinges of ancient Etruscan and Roman doors. This was the *Cardo*, supported by two pegs or tenons on the top and bottom of the door on one side, which fitted into sockets in the upper and lower sections of the doorframe. Modern hinges came later. By analogy, in the landscape, the *Cardo* between the upper and lower sockets denotes a north–south line, with the "hinges" as the revolving points on the Cosmic Axis. For while the ancient sages knew and taught that the Earth is a sphere and Eratosthenes accurately measured its circumference, to us it appears that we stand in the midst of a circular horizon, which appears flat.

The oldest record of this tradition is from the ancient Etruscan Augurs of central Italy, who practiced the *Disciplina Etrusca*, the Etruscan Discipline. This is a series of practical ritual techniques that deals with the spiritual nature of the land and the placement of

Divisions of the horizon and the heavens in the Etruscan Discipline, with the eight winds at the center

buildings upon it. Their guiding books—such as the *Libri Tagetici* (Tagetic Books), otherwise called *The Ostentarian*—were the repository of the teachings and practices that continued within the medieval tradition of *Location*.* The *Disciplina Etrusca*, upon which Western geomancy is based, divided the horizon into sixteen.

The Etruscan *templum* is a division of space whose directions are ascribed certain spiritual qualities. It is the earliest example of geomancy recorded in Europe, though the much earlier megalithic era, which left no written records, appears to have had a similar system. The Etruscan Discipline first divides the surface of the Earth into four quarters, the

---

*Location comes from the title of the *Locator Civitatis*, a specialist used by the Zähringers when founding new towns such as Nuremburg am Rhein, Fribourg, and Freiburg-im-Breisgau. He found the sites, laid out the plots, and recruited inhabitants.

dividing lines being meridional (north–south) and equinoctial (east–west). The two lines cross at right angles at the center, which has been divined beforehand. They are by no means arbitrary, but indeed direct manifestations of the structure of our planet. Where these lines cross, *there* is the center. The land and the sky are divided by the meridional line, the *Cardo*, which divides the circle into eastern and western parts. Because the Augur faces south, to the left is the eastern half. This is called the *Pars Familiaris*, the friendly part. To the right side of the Augur is the west, the *Pars Hostilis*, the hostile part. At right angles to the *Cardo*, running due east–west, is the *Decumanus*, which divides the land and sky into north and south regions. The northern half, the *Pars Postica*, lies behind the Augur. It denotes the dark half of the day and the year. In front of the Augur lies the southern half, the *Pars Antica*, which denotes the light half of the day and year. The land and sky are further subdivided by lines toward the four intercardinal directions, southeast, southwest, northwest, and northeast. Between these lines are four quadrants, each of which is then subdivided further into four regions, each ruled by a specific deity. Thus, the Etruscan Discipline divides land and sky into sixteen regions.

The southeast quadrant denoted good fortune and is called *Felicitas*. Progressing sunwise, the four deities ruling the regions are Catha, Nethuns, Fufluns, and Selvans. Catha, the Sun's daughter, is ruler of sudden dawnings and rapid starts. Nethuns, is identical with the Greek Poseidon and the Roman Neptune, ruler of the seas. Fufluns, whom the Greeks called Dionysus, and the Romans, Bacchus, is god of wine and drunkenness, ruler of all bodily ecstasies. Finally, the fourth region of the southeast quadrant is Selvans, the Roman Sylvanus, god of the forests. This last god of the quadrant is called the *Tutor Finium*, guardian of boundaries, who thereby terminates it at the Cardo in the south.

The southwest quadrant contains the *Regiones Diræ*, the Fearful Regions. The first region of this quadrant is ruled by Letham, a deity of protection who has the character of Mars but has an underworldly character. The next region is ruled by two deities, Tellus and Tellumo.

Together called the Tluscva, they are the Earth Mother and the Earth Father. The following region is ruled by Cel, equated with Gaia, the fruitful Earth. The final region of the quadrant is ruled jointly by the female *daemon*, Culsu, spirit-ruler of doors and entrances; and Alpan, handmaiden of Turan, the Etruscan Venus, goddess of love. Alpan is equivalent to the Roman goddess Concordia. The *Tutor Finium* of the *Regiones Diræ* is Culsu, who terminates the quadrant at the *Decumanus* in the west.

The northwest quadrant comprises the Most Fearful Regions, the *Regiones Maxime Diræ*. Vetis, also called Vejovis, deity of destruction and death, rules the first region of the *Maxime Diræ*. The next region is ruled by Cilens, goddess of fortune, known to the Greeks as Tyche and the Romans as Fortuna. She brings fortune or loss, victory or failure, as chance would have it. The third region is under the joint rulership of Tin, who is the Greek Zeus and the Roman Jupiter, and again Cilens. This is the region from which comes destructive lightning. The next region contains the Fury called Tins Thulftha, punisher of wrongdoers, who is the daughter of the thunder-god, Tin. Tin is active in this region, too, for from here comes lightning that does good as well as harm. Tin is *Tutor Finium* of the *Regiones Maxime Diræ* of the northwest, which terminates at the Cardo in the north.

The northeast quadrant is the *Summa Felicitas*, the greatest of good fortune. Tin again influences the first region of this quadrant through the agency of Nethuns. The lightning that comes from this quadrant, called *Tinsth Nethuns*, is an omen to Augurs and those who can read it as a warning from the gods. The next region is that of the goddess Uni, the Etruscan Juno, and Mae or Maius. Uni is ruler of fertility and protector of the nation and its rulers. Mae is her consort. The third region is ruled by Tecum, also called Tikamne Iuvie, god of the ruling classes. Finally, the region of the *Tutor Finium* of the northeast quadrant is ruled by Lusa, goddess of fields and woodlands. She terminates the quadrant at the *Decumanus* in the east.

Directly related to the *Disciplina Etrusca* is the system of eight winds and sixteen breezes that became disseminated widely through the writings of the Roman architect Vitruvius (ca. 70 BCE–15 CE), who wrote his *Ten Books of Architecture* between 33 and 14 BCE. The most influential representation of these eight winds exists in Athens. It is the octagonal Tower of the Winds, designed around 50 BCE by the Macedonian architect Andronicus of Cyrrhus (see chap. 22).

20

The Four Directions

The cardinal points are fundamental, as ancient Greek teachings tell of four winds that correspond with the four directions: Boreas, Euros, Notos, and Zephyros. More about the winds below. Each of the four directions has its own quality that manifests symbolically as spiritual beings. As we noted in the preceding chapter, in the Jewish spiritual tradition and later magical practice, the four archangels—Michael, Uriel, Raphael, and Gabriel—reign over these four directions, respectively. In the Northern Tradition, we find the Corners of the Heavens are supported by four dwarfs called Austri, Sudri, Vestri, and Nordri.

The tradition of medieval European guilds associated with location ascribes the four Cardinal Virtues to the four cardinal directions. In this system, north signifies darkness; east, wisdom; south, beauty; and the west, strength. These qualities correspond with the four Cardinal Virtues: Prudence, Temperance, Justice, and Fortitude.

In the north, Prudentia, the personification of Prudence, is symbolized by a female figure whose head bears a golden helmet crowned with mulberry leaves. Mulberry was deemed the most prudent tree because it puts out its leaves very late in the spring, when all danger of frost is past. In her left hand Prudentia holds a mirror, and in her right, she holds an arrow around which a Remora is twined. Although

Cosmic Principles

Roman dedication stone from a crossroads,
depicting the Quadrivium goddesses of the four directions,
Bad Cannstatt, Germany (photo by Vexillum)

Prudentia looks forward in time, she holds a mirror in which she can view things that are behind. The prudent person is thus aware of past events, which give a guide to present decisions that must be made, and their consequences. The Remora is a legendary giant eel that Pliny the Elder (23–79 CE) described as attaching itself to the hulls of ships and dragging them to a stop by its sheer weight and size. The arrow symbolizes speed, but the Remora brings a slowing-down, warning us not to make hasty decisions.

In the east is Temperance, personified as Temperantia, who is depicted as a woman clad in purple. Purple is a compound color, made from red and blue in just measure, for neither dominates, but makes a harmonious third color, symbolizing a joyous balance between desire and reason. Temperantia is shown holding in her left hand a horse-bit and reins, and in her right the balance-wheel of a clock. The bridle signifies restraint, for the power of temperance holds our appetites under control. The balance wheel advances step by step, by regular units, for Temperance knows when it is time for action and time for quiescence.

In the south, Justice is symbolized by Iustitia, who stands at the balance point of the meridian where the Sun is at its zenith. Justice is the pillar of society, for without justice, manifested through the rule of law, universal violence and anarchy break out. This image of Justice depicts a white-clad woman, wearing a crown and blindfold. The white clothing signifies that the judge must have no moral blemish, which could impair the proper dispensation of justice. The crown signifies that Justice is a noble and sovereign virtue, and the blindfold tells us that only the evidence of reason, not the potentially misleading impressions of the senses, must be employed in making judgments. In her left hand, Iustitia holds a pair of scales, and in her right hand, an unsheathed sword. Because scales are used to measure out material things fairly in due measure, according to universally agreed-upon principles, they signify that Justice metes out what is due to each and every one, no more and no less. Her sword symbolizes the rigor of Justice, which will in full measure punish the convicted wrongdoer.

In the west is Fortitudo, fortitude, the power of resistance against and triumph over difficult, adverse forces. Fortitudo is depicted as an armored and helmeted woman with a shield and a club of oak. The shield is primarily a defense yet can be used as a weapon in combat should the necessity arise. The oaken club is the main weapon of the demigod Hercules; it represents strength in both Ogham and runic symbolism. A lion—fearsome symbol of potential power—accompanies Fortitudo. Fortitude is that inner strength expressed in courageous endurance and perseverance against all odds, no matter what. But it is also the outward show of strength that wards off would-be adversaries. Fortitudo is not an aggressive figure—she threatens no one but waits patiently for anything that may occur.

The oriental, meridional, occidental, and septentrional directions have intrinsic qualities that are described in various spiritual traditions according to their doctrinal principles. Jewish rabbinical tradition teaches that Adam was created by God with his face toward the east. Thus, the right and left directions were symbolic of good and evil. Jesus's parable of the Sheep and the Goats tells that the sheep, the elect, are sorted to the right, which is the south, and the goats, the damned, to the left, which is the north. But the south-facing Etruscan Discipline, upon which European classical architecture and agriculture is based, has the left to the east, the quarter of Oriens, the region of the rising light, which is thus a favorable direction. The eastern quarter, the "House of the Rising Sun," witnesses the ascent of the sun in the morning. As with Adam, it represents life, whose birth is symbolized by the dawn. As we see the sun rising, we also see the world turning round. The southern quarter, Meridies, signifies the high point of the Sun in the south, the midheaven. In human terms, this signifies maturity in the midday of life. Decline to old age and death is Occidens, the west, the region of sunset. In the north, the direction Septentrio, Nox, signifies the cold and darkness of night.

There are particular Greco-Roman deities that also rule the directions. The House of the Rising Sun is under the rulership of the

The House of the Rising Sun

goddess Aurora Pallantias, who opens the vermilion gates of dawn, enabling daybreak to fill the land with the illuminating rays of the Sun. She is depicted as a dark-skinned young woman with black wings. She wears a saffron-colored robe with a veil gathered up behind her head, signifying the darkness of night. Garlanded with flowers, she scatters roses upon the earth with her right hand. In her left hand she holds a downward-pointing flaming torch, signifying her role as Phosphor, the Morning Star, also known with the title Lucifer, the light-bearer. (The name Lucifer was later attached by Christians to a quite different and demonic figure.)

In the southern quarter, Meridies, the eponymous Meridies is a blonde, white-winged boy clad in flame-colored robes. He flies through clouds above the ground and in his right hand he holds aloft the planetary sigil of Jupiter, and in his left a lotus blossom. Pliny noted that the lotus is emblematical of the cycle of the day, for it rises from beneath the surface of the waters at dawn, attains its full height and flowering at noon, and then, closing as the sun declines toward evening, it sinks again below the waters as darkness falls.

The western quarter of Occidens is signified by Hesperus or Vesper, the Evening Star, depicted as a winged boy hastily flying westward, close to the ground, as the shadows lengthen. He bears a seven-pointed star upon his brow, and in his left hand holds an owl. In his right hand he holds a single arrow, having already thrown others to the ground. The arrows signify the vapors of the Earth, which, having been drawn upward during the day into the aer, return at nightfall into the ground.

The quarter of Septentrio in the north is signified by Nox, the personification of night. She is depicted as an old woman clothed darkly in the colors of the night. She wears a garland of poppies and their seed heads, signifying sleep, on her head. She is barefoot and strikes a flint against steel to make fire. On either side of her stands a child, one black and one white, emblematic of the continuity and oneness of night and day. Behind her are the stars of night, a waxing

Moon, and an owl about to take flight into the darkling sky where bats are flying. Nox is the daughter of Chaos, one of the primal forces that gave birth to the material world. Certain ancient bards said she was the mother of all things, and so an image of Nox stood in the temple of Diana at Ephesus.

21

The Eight Tides of the Day

The four directions are the fundamental structure of our being in the world, being directly experienced from the structure of the planet upon which we live. Because planet Earth rotates, the star around which it orbits, the Sun, appears to rise, move through the sky, and set. Night comes when the part of the Earth on which we are located has rotated so that it no longer faces the Sun. Although we know that we are not on a still, flat surface with the Sun moving from side to side above us through the sky, that is our experience. Ancient societies that had not discovered the reality of the rotating, spherical Earth described the motion of the Sun in literal, personified ways. Carried in a ship, or borne on a chariot, the Solar deity traveled across the sky during daytime, then, at sunset, plunged beneath the Earth to travel underneath us to the other side appearing again at sunrise. Sometimes other deities of light accounted for the predawn light, for the Sun had not yet arrived to pass through the gates of dawn. These include goddesses such as Eos or Aurora, or the Morning Star, and the male light-bearer Phosphor or Luciferos. The natural event of the Earth rotating toward the Sun, creating the dawning light, was not understood. During the day, the perceived position of the Sun with regard to the directions marks the time of day, as its perceived height marks the time of year. In the northern hemisphere, when the sun is in the south, it is noon, the middle of the day, the zenith. In this position, it attains its greatest height at the midsummer solstice, and its lowest at the midwinter solstice. At the equinoxes, the sun is seen to rise due east and set due west; at the Winter Solstice it rises and sets at its most southerly points, while at the summer solstice it rises and sets at its most northerly. The actual azimuths of rising and setting depend upon the latitude of the observer. Taken from a center, the rising and setting points at the solstices are opposite one another. Thus, a straight line through any viewing point links midwinter sunrise with midsummer sunset, and vice versa.

Although the twenty-four-hour clock is now used all over the world, this is not the only way of dividing the cycle of day and night. There are many possible ways of marking the passing of time, but all are based upon the division of the circle into regular segments, either a fourfold or sixfold division with corresponding subdivisions. The ancient Romans divided the day into twelve parts ("hours") from sunrise to sunset, which meant that the length of an "hour" varied through the year. The Roman system works better the nearer to the Equator one gets, because the difference between day length in summer and winter is not as great as it is closer to the poles. Coming from a much higher latitude than Rome, the northern European day-division is based on a totally different principle, being determined by solar position with regard to the horizon, divided eightfold. These are the eight tides of the day. Tides here should not be confused with the tides of the sea, which have cycles unrelated to the times of day. These tides tell the place the sun appears to be in an eightfold division of the horizon, known as the eight *airts*. It recognizes that even at night when the Sun is "beneath" the Earth, it is still at a certain position. So, at midnight, the Sun, though invisible, is standing due north. This is the nadir. But the phenomenon of the midnight sun, visible north of the Arctic Circle at midsummer, sees the Sun standing due north, rendering the concept of the nadir irrelevant in that place at that time. In that location, the sun's course through the eight tides of the day can be observed in its entirety.

Conceptually, the horizon is divided into eight equal divisions, which can be depicted as an octagon. The four cardinal directions define the centerline of four of an octagon's sides. The centerline of each face is at the middle of each tide, and the corners of the octagon are the cusps between the airts. Unlike the twenty-four-hour division, which ends and begins at midnight, that is, when the Sun is due north, the tides begin one-sixteenth part of the circle before the cardinal points. The tides are called: Morntide; Daytide or Undernoon; Midday or Noontide; Undorne or Afternoon; Eventide; Nighttide; Midnight; and Uht, otherwise the Small Hours.* In sundial and clock time, Morntide begins at half past four; Daytide begins at half past seven; Midday at half past ten; Undorne at half past one, *post meridiem*; Eventide, half past four; Nighttide, half past seven; Midnight, half past ten; and Uht, half past one, *ante meridiem*. Each Tide thus lasts three hours by the clock.

Certain parts of the world have distinct seasons that come in regular cycles each year. These cycles have affected the development of culture, religion, and magic. The seasons dealt with in this book are those of the temperate northern hemisphere, covering Europe, Asia, and North America. The cycles of natural magic follow the cycle of the year. This exists because of the form of the Earth and its orbit around the Sun. The year is divided naturally into two halves, which are further subdivided into four quarters. The two halves are the dark and light halves of the year. In the dark half, the nights are longer than the days. In the light half, the days are longer than the nights. At the transition points between the two halves are the equinoxes, when day and night are of equal duration. At the Spring Equinox, the light half begins, and at the Autumnal Equinox, the dark half.

The quarters of the year are defined by the solstices, or turning points of the Sun. At the middle of the dark half of the year is the

---

*A list of the corresponding names from medieval Anglo-Saxon England can be found in Appendix 3, "The Tides of the Day."

The eight tides of the day with clock and runic correspondences

130 Cosmic Principles

Winter Solstice. From the Summer Solstice, the middle of the light half of the year, the length of daylight each day has been steadily declining, and the length of the night increasing. At the Winter Solstice, the longest night of the year passes, and, afterward, the length of daylight each day increases. This increase continues through the Spring Equinox, when both day and night are of equal length, and the light half of the year is entered. The proportion of light to darkness continues to increase until the Summer Solstice, when daylight is at its maximum, and the night is the shortest. At this point, the length of day begins to decline, and the length of night to increase.

The interrelationship of light and dark in the twenty-four-hour cycle of the day is essentially the same as the cycle of the year, having

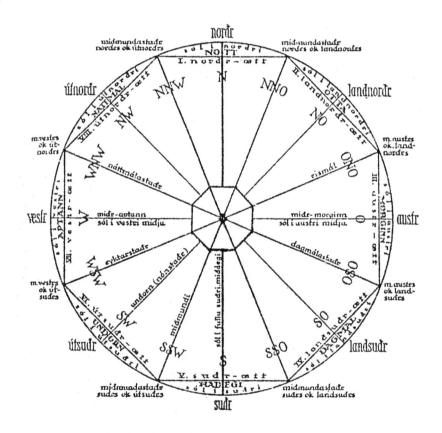

Icelandic wheel of time, early twentieth century

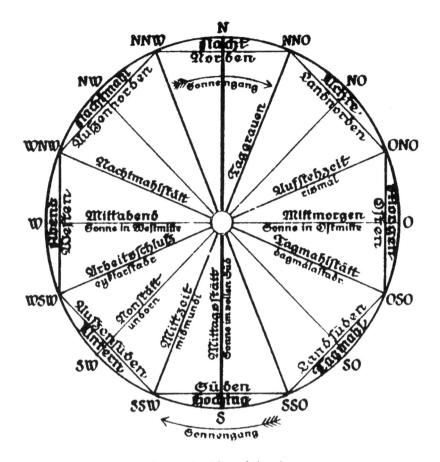

Germanic tides of the day
by Otto Siegfried Reuter (1876–1945)

the same fourfold structure. But, except at the equinoxes, the relative length of the quarters is not equal. Whether we find it in the light/dark cycles of the day, the year, or the Moon, this is a natural principle that underlies the existence of many beings and things. Because of this, certain seasons are more appropriate for certain activities magically than are others. Activities to do with birth, growth, and renewal are best performed in springtime, while those of endings, death, and dissolution are best done at the beginning of winter. Similarly, certain activities are best conducted at sunrise, noon, sunset, or midnight.

22
The Winds

The Classical Winds

Early classical teachings tell of the four winds that correspond with the four directions: Boreas, Euros, Notos, and Zephyros. Ancient Greek mythology personified these winds as presiding genii in human form. Their origin-myth tells how at first the winds were under no will but their own, reckless and out of control. To curb their destructiveness, the gods decided to bring them under control and appointed the god Aiolos (Aeolus) to rule them from the island of Lipari in the Mediterranean.* Aiolos was under the supervision of the goddess Hera (Juno). Aiolos was empowered to keep them in a cave under the island, sending them out and bringing them back at his will. Aiolos commanded and controlled four winds called Boreas, Euros (Eurus), Notos (Notus), and Zephyros (Zephyrus), who were the sons of Astraios (Astraeus) and Eos (Aurora). Aiolos was depicted as an old man wearing a crown, clad in a cloak, and seated upon a mountain containing the cavern of the four winds.

---

*As will be seen, these earlier Greek gods and entities were often adopted into later Roman religion, with Latinized names (in parentheses here), although the Romans retained many of their own native deities as well.

The Tower of the Winds at Athens, built ca. 50 BCE
(photo by George E. Koronaios)

He and his winds were venerated widely at special temples. At seaports, seafarers made offerings at them to call for favorable winds and calm weather during their forthcoming voyages. Aiolos/Aeolus is the tutelary deity of sails, wind vanes, weathercocks, windmills, washing lines, kites, and the aeolian harp, whose strings produce the notes of the divine harmony when the winds blow through them.

Other ethnic traditions in Europe had their equivalent wind divinities. The Slavic god Stribog or Strzybóg (whose name has been interpreted as meaning "Wealth-spreader") was the ancestor of the winds and the eight directions. In the northern seas was, like Lipari, an Island of the Winds, a vague terrain that only appeared occasionally and then disappeared again. It was the Island of Buyan, which, according to the creation myth, was the first dry land created from sand brought up from the bed of the primal ocean by a dark diving bird (Pennick and Field 2003, 28, 30). Buyan was the residence of three winds: the north, east, and west. A traditional Russian description of the source of these winds is a small house that rotates on the feet of mice like the type of windmill called a buck- or post-mill. But it appears to be envisaged as a giant fan, a kind of reverse windmill that generated the winds. In Finland, a goddess called Tuuletar ruled the winds. Elsewhere, male deities are rulers of the winds. The Gauls ascribed the winds to a god called Vintios, who resided upon the holy mountain of the winds, Mont Ventoux in Provence, from which emanates the wind called Ventuoresco. Another Celtic wind-god was Borrum.

The original Greek four winds had a hierarchy. The north wind, Boreas, the "king of the winds," originated in Thrace. He is a harsh and wrathful character who travels through the upper air, enveloped in mists. In the lower air he creates eddies and whirlwinds in the dust that the Christians called "dust devils," ascribing them to the activities of evil spirits. His sons, Zetes and Calais, together known as the Boreades, were slain by Heracles (Hercules) and afterward appeared as the winds that blew for nine days preceding the Dog Days. The east wind, Eurus or Vulturnus, was depicted strewing flowers as he passed. The south wind, Notos (Notus), otherwise Auster, the "Father of Rain," was depicted pouring water from a vessel onto the earth, while the west wind, Zephyros, was shown garlanded with flowers. The Romans venerated Zephyrus as the consort of the goddess Flora. He is attended by the pleasant breezes called zephyrs, depicted as young boys with wings, forerunners of the *putti* or cherubs in later European art.

Although early perceptions described only four winds, the system was later refined into eight. A standard version emerged, which has continued until today. The names of the winds come from specific qualities of winds experienced in ancient Athens and later refined in southern Italy. The mainstream European tradition of the winds comes

Buyan, the island of the three winds

136   Cosmic Principles

from the Macedonian architect Andronicus of Cyrrhus, architect of the eight-sided Tower of the Winds at Athens, built around 50 BCE. It still stands. Andronicus's system describes eight basic winds: four cardinal winds—north, east, south, and west—and four others located equidistantly between them at the four corners of the heavens. On the eight sides of this building are sculptures representing the presiding genius of each corresponding wind depicted in winged human form. Originally, this octagonal tower was topped by a wind vane in the form of a triton holding a wand as a pointer. The Greek eight winds are (sunwise starting at the north): Boreas, Caecias, Apeliotes, Euros, Notos, Lips, Zephyros, and Skiron. On the eight-sided Tower of the Winds they are personified as carvings. The eight winds recognized by the Romans, which were ascribed the same qualities as those of the Greeks, are: Septentrio (north), Aquilo (northeast), Solanus (east), Eurus (southeast), Auster (south), Africus (southwest), Favonius (west), and Caurus (northwest).

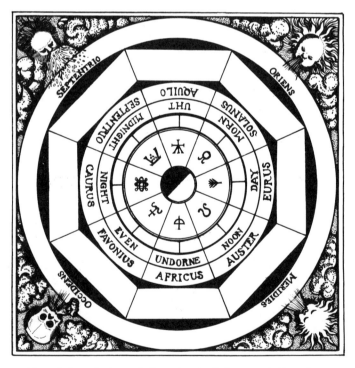

The eight winds and the wheel of time and directions

On each side of the eight winds is a subsidiary breeze that also has its own name.

The North Wind, called the "Sky-born Boreas" by the Greeks and Septentrio by the Romans, was perceived as king of the winds. Boreas is personified as a powerful bearded and winged figure, his cheeks puffed up with the act of blowing through a conch shell. The North Wind is a harsh and wrathful force that travels through the upper air, enveloped in mists, blowing the thistle heads of autumn across the plain. At ground level, Boreas generates whirlwinds of dust and raises waterspouts from the surface of the ocean.

The northeast wind, Caecias, is shown casting hailstones down from the sky; the East Wind, named variously Apeliotes, Vulturnos/Vulturnus, Euros/Eurus, and Solanus, is envisaged as an impetuous flying youth, his hair streaming behind him. He broadcasts seeds as he passes across the land, sowing the fertile land to bring forth flowers, fruits, and grain. The southeast, Euros/Eurus, is portrayed as an old man wearing a cloak; Lips, the southwest wind, steers a ship; and the northwest wind, Skiron, throws down fiery ashes from an urn. In the Roman tradition described by the architectural writer Marcus Vitruvius Pollio, from which comes the later European understanding of the winds, the northeast wind is called Aquilo; the southeast is Eurus; the southwest, Africus; and Caurus blows from the northwest.

The South Wind, called Notos/Notus and Auster in antiquity and Sirocco today in Italy, is described as the Father of Rain. Notos/Notus is personified as a tall man, his hair white with age, dripping wet with rain. In his hands, he holds a vessel from which he pours water on those below. His influence is believed to be harmful to human health. The West Wind, called by the Greeks Zephyros and in the Latin tradition Favonius, is depicted as a handsome youth garlanded with flowers, which he scatters across the Earth. He is supported by butterflies' wings and attends Flora, goddess of flowers. The pleasant, short-lived breezes called the zephyrs accompany him, personified as young boys with wings—an image that appears in Christian art as the cherub.

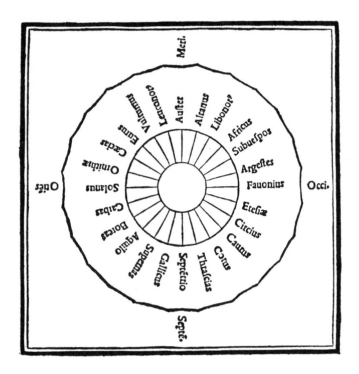

Winds and breezes according to Vitruvius, from the 1511 edition of *Ten Books of Architecture*

Vitruvius recounts that each of the eight winds had a subsidiary breeze on either side of it, creating a twenty-four-fold division of the horizon. To the west of Septentrio, the North Wind, is Thrascias, and to his east, Gallicus. Aquilo in the northeast has Supernas and Caecias to his north and south; Solanus, the East Wind, is flanked by Carbas on his north and the Ornithiae, which are intermittent breezes, on his south. The Southeast Wind, Eurus, is bracketed by Eurocircias and Volturnus. Auster, the South Wind, has Leuconotus to his east and Altanus to his west. Africus, the Southwest Wind, has Libonotus to his south and Subvesperus to his north. The West Wind, Favonius, has Argestes to his south and the intermittent Etesiae to his north. This wind-rose is completed by Caurus, whose flanking breezes are Circius to the south and Corus to the north.

These names and attributes of these eight winds are derived from a particular Mediterranean location and the prevailing climate of the era in which they were formalized. Each wind has its effect on humans, but although ancient writers ascribe certain physical or medical consequences to each of them, these were determined by observation at particular places, and the effects will be quite different at other places. However, they became standardized in the Western tradition and were linked by the Roman author Vitruvius to the bodily system of the four humors. Thus, the half from northwest to southeast, containing north and east, is wet. The other half, containing south and west, is dry. The half between northeast and southwest, containing east and south, is hot, while the other half containing west and north, is cold. This gives each quarter, and by association its winds, specific characters. The northern quarter is cold and dry; the eastern, hot and dry; the southern, hot and wet; and the western, cold and wet.

The eighteenth-century Temple of the Four Winds at Castle Howard, Yorkshire (photo by Gareth James)

Although the actual characteristics of the classical winds were not applicable outside Athens where they were first recognized—not even in Rome, despite the historical reality that they became adopted as fixed winds by Roman authors—they were nevertheless used to define the compass rose all over Europe, and even by the Spanish surveyors who laid out imperial towns in Central and South America. Old maps of many cities right across the Western world—including Saint Petersburg, Stockholm, Lisbon, Milan, Edinburgh, and Mexico City—have compass roses that show these eight Athenian winds. In Britain from the eighteenth century onward, temples of the winds were built near great country houses and at universities. The Temple of the Four Winds at Castle Howard (Yorkshire) by John Vanbrugh (1664–1726) still stands. It has four identical porticoes orientated toward the four cardinal directions. In 1819, the St Pancras New Church in London, designed by William Inwood (1771–1843), had a tower based on the Athenian Tower of the Winds. The architect Charles Holden (1875–1960) had connections with the church and in 1930 built the office building 55 Broadway, headquarters of the London Underground, which he called his "Tower of the Winds," with symbolic carvings of the winds at the seventh-story level. Later in the nineteenth century, a replica of the Athenian tower was built in Oxford as the octagonal tower of Green College. In 1992, the classical architect Quinlan Terry (born 1937) built a library at Downing College, Cambridge, with an octagonal tower bearing the Athenian wind names in Greek and a gilded wind vane in the form of a griffin, the emblem of the college.

Of course, the winds at Cambridge do not correspond in character with those of ancient Athens, and the winds that blow from these directions over all of these other cities have their own local characteristics. So, associating the Athenian meanings with these winds endows them with false symbolism. They are at best a very tenacious example of mythic continuity, for this is a conceptual system closer to magic than actual physical weather-lore. Nature does not conform to human-made systematization except in the most general cases. In practical

The Winds 141

Wind vanes of Cambridge, England: (*top*) griffin atop the octagonal tower of the winds, Downing College Library; (*bottom*) the wind vane of Emmanuel College Chapel

terms, the qualities of any named eight winds do not apply outside their proper area. When they spread out from their original place, the named winds became more a conceptual map of the directions than a system of any practical use. Those who depended upon the wind for their livelihoods—sailors and windmillers, for example—always had their own local names for the local winds, whose characteristics naturally vary from place to place, and because climate has never been a fixed system, but a changing one, they will have differed over time, too.

23

Specific Winds

All across the world, there are many names for specific winds. As we have noted, some European winds still bear the names of antiquity, but not necessarily describing the same directions. In alpine Europe, the warm dry wind leeward of mountains is called Föhn, a version of the Latin Favonius. In the Aegean, summer wind from the northeast or northwest is called Etesian (Meltemi in Turkey). In Provence, southern France, the Mistral (the "Master Wind") is the most famous wind. It is a northerly or northwesterly that blows along the valley of the Rhône River. In southern Spain, the south to southeast wind is called Solano. In eastern Spain, the wind called Llevantades blows from the north-northeast. Chicago is called the "Windy City" and its most notorious bitterly cold winter wind is called the Hawk. The song "When the Wind Blows (in Chicago)," written by Audie Murphy and Scott Turner, was a hit for pop singer George McCurn in 1963. Unlike the cold Chicago blast, the San Francisco Bay Area has the hot, dry offshore wind called Diablo (the Devil), while another strong offshore wind along the Californian coast is the Sundowner. Another powerful wind is the Chinook, a warm, dry westerly off the Rocky Mountains.

Many systems of the winds existed in Europe. Nuremberg

compasses of the seventeenth century have inscriptions that equate the winds with the weather: north, fair dry; northeast, bright cold; east, warm bright; southeast, fair middling; south, warm humid; southwest, rainy; west, cold humid; northwest, snowy. These are the weathers that were likely to be brought by the winds in that part of Germany at that time. Sailors on large lakes recognized the different winds predicated by the topography surrounding that particular lake. The Ammersee and Chiemsee in Bavaria each had their own local winds, recognized by sailors who plied their waters. Lake Garda in Italy also has named daily winds. From early morning until twelve noon, the wind called Peler blows from the north. Around midday, the wind turns and blows from the south, called Ora. In the winter, the wind Balin blows, and in summer, the westerly Ponale comes along the Ledro Valley, through which the Ponale River flows. On large lakes like Garda, the characteristics of the winds vary from shore to shore, depending on the topography.

Windmills with sails rotating in the horizontal plane originated in Normandy in the eleventh century. Originally, it was necessary to turn the mill into the wind, which required a subtle rapport with the direction and strength of the wind at any time. Only in the nineteenth century were windmills made that employed a geared fantail that turned the mill's sails automatically into the wind. Some windmills, especially in the Netherlands, had louvres or shutters that made a sound when the mill was not orientated properly into the wind. Windmillers also had their own wind-roses that varied depending in their location. Often they were displayed inside the mill. The standard "theoretical" winds named from the Athenian tower had no practical value—only the actual winds of the mill's location.

In Lancashire, northern England, the dialect word for a direction is *hæver*, defined as "a 'quarter' of the heavens, or compass, or directions"; a "lucky *hæver*" is a fortunate or desirable direction, as in the saying from Mellor and Ramsgreave, near Blackburn, where "the East is a lucky *haever*" (Harland and Wilkinson 1867, 149–50). The qualities of winds from a certain direction varies from place to place according to the local

Wind-powered sawmill *De Kat* at Zaanse Schans, the Netherlands

topography. The word *heaver* comes from the Lancashire dialect word *hive* (pronounced "heeve"), meaning "to blow," though *hæver* has the same meaning as the more widely used word *airt* that refers to one of the eight directions, implicit in the question "What *hæver* is the wind in this morning?" (Harland and Wilkinson 1867, 150).

The most celebrated named specific wind in England is in Cumbria in the northwest. There, the Helm is a destructive Föhn-type "lee-wave" wind that comes from the southwestern slopes of the mountain called Cross Fell into the Vale of Eden. But more generally there are specific northern English names for various winds. The Cat's Nose is a cool northwesterly; a Custard Wind is a cold easterly on the coast of northeastern England; Dryth is a dry northerly or easterly wind, and Fowan (the name, like Föhn, derives from Favonius) is a dry, scorching wind. A Piner is a strong north or northeasterly, while on the East Yorkshire coast, Robin Hood's Wind is a cold, raw northeasterly. In both England and the United States, a Plough or Plow Wind is a strong straight wind that precedes a thunderstorm.*

The winds are also significant in divination and magic. In the Northern Tradition, stormy winds were attributed to the fierce wind-giant Hrælsweg, who stood at the Eagle's Mount at the end of the Earth. Medieval authors noted that certain magical, divinatory, or alchemical procedures would not work when specific winds were blowing. It was known that windy weather in general disrupted operations of divinatory geomancy. Just as the Pagan Greeks had ascribed spiritual agency to the winds, so the early Christian Church deemed storm winds to be evil spirits determined to disrupt or destroy the human world order. In the eighth century, Archbishop Ecgbert of York (?–766 CE) called for bells to be rung against "the assault of whirlwinds, the stroke of lightnings, the harm of thunders, the injuries of tempests and every spirit of the storm winds" (Kittredge 1929, 158). A few years later, Archbishop Agobard of Lyons (ca. 769–840 CE). makes reference to magicians called *Tempestarii* who were reputed to call up storms. Although he wrote about them, he discounted the ability of magicians to control the weather, stating that only servants of God—not of the Devil—could do that.

Magic intended to call up or alter the strength of winds was conducted on land and at sea. In Britain, "Dobbie Stones"—small, flat boulders with a natural hollow—were used for raising the wind. Offerings of milk, brine, or ale were placed in the stones from the direction the required wind should blow. This was an instance of sympathetic magic based on the symbolism of the stone's structure. The cupped surface of the Dobbie Stone is a reflection of the dome of the heavens (the brainpan of the slain giant Ymir), a microcosm of the circle of the horizon and the rose of the winds.

---

*For further details about the winds, see my book *Creating Places of Power* (2022), 155–171.

Erik Väderhatt turns away an enemy ship by altering the direction of the wind (engraving from Olaus Magnus, 1555).

The celebrated Swedish king Erik Väderhatt (Eric Weatherhat, or "Erik of the windy hat"; 849–882 CE) was said to have power over the wind, with the ability to change the wind-direction merely by turning his cap into the appropriate direction. This was a signal for the demon with whom he was in league to alter the direction according to his instructions and that the king's hat "might have served the people for a weather-cock" (Spence 1920, 149). It was believed that he used his wind-control ability to drive away enemy ships from his land. This relates to the traditional Sámi "four winds hat," whose origin-legend ascribes its creation to a shaman who lived in a land where the winds blew from all directions at once. So, he bound the four winds magically in his hat and let them out only on condition that one would blow at a time. The traditional Sámi hat has four peaks that signify the four winds.

At seaports in the days of sail, women known as Sea Witches plied their trade, selling knotted strings or ropes to seamen who believed these would enable them to control the wind. The earliest reference to this practice is from the Isle of Man in chapter 44 of the *Polychronicon* (ca. 1250) by Ranulph Higden (1280–1364). Written in Latin, it was translated into English by John Trevisa (1342–1402), who wrote: "*For wommen þere selliþ schipmen wynde, as it were i-closed vnder þree knottes of þrede, so þat þe more wynd he wol haue, he will vnknette þe more knottes*" (Babington 1869, 43). In modern English this would be: "For women there sell shipmen wind, as it were, enclosed in three knots of thread, so that the more wind he [the sailor] would have, he will undo more knots." A form of binding-magic, the knots were said to contain or constrain the wind. Undoing a knot, purchasers were told, would increase the strength of the wind, and knotting the rope again would reduce it. Undoing one knot would produce a breeze; two, a strong wind; and three, a gale. Olaus Magnus (1490–1557) published an engraving of this practice in 1555.

Using magic knots to control the wind
(engraving from Olaus Magnus, 1555)

Traditional local knowledge of places makes reference to "wind-corners," often on the end of ridges, which amplify the power of the wind. These are sometimes dangerous places, where one can be blown over, and recreational flyers of kites or model aircraft see them crashing to the ground. (Drivers on highways sometimes feel this effect when traveling beneath overpasses.) The amplification of the wind is an effect of fluid mechanics, first described in mathematical terms by Giovanni Battista Venturi (1746–1822). In his architectural lectures from the early 1730s, Robert Morris (1701–1754) described places that amplify wind strength (1734, 87): "when the winds blow into them, they are keen and boisterous, because of the narrow passage through which they pass." Traditional buildings were orientated to mitigate the harmful effects of prevailing winds, and the Roman architect Vitruvius (85–20 BCE) recommended streets to be orientated with regard to the local winds. The city streets of Alexandria in Egypt took the prevailing wind into account (Nissen 1906, 95).

But the invention of the skyscraper in the late nineteenth century led to buildings which created harmful wind effects at street level. Modernity ignored traditions that had served people well for thousands of years. Built in 1902 in New York City, the Fuller ("Flatiron") Building at the intersection of Broadway and Fifth Avenue was the first to produce unwanted gusts of wind in the streets below, what are now called "pedestrian wind environments." Subsequently, these unwanted and sometimes dangerous or even lethal winds have been generated by many skyscrapers.

One of the more notorious recent buildings of this type was Bridgewater Place, a thirty-two-story tower built in Leeds, England, in 2007. It created a "wind microclimate" in Water Lane and the junction of Neville Street below, which produced gale-force gusts of wind measured to be between 67 and 79 miles per hour. People were blown over and in 2011 one person was killed when a truck was blown onto him. It took eleven years of incidents before a "wind scheme" was implemented for Bridgewater Place in 2018 that involved the construction of a canopy, five screens on the west side, and three "baffles" in Water Lane. This mitigated the worse effects of the building. Similarly, in London the thirty-seven-story "Walkie-Talkie" building at 20 Fenchurch Street produced "pedestrian wind environments" that required mitigating modifications. In 2019, building regulations were introduced in London to prevent such buildings being constructed, and the problem of artificially induced winds in "urban canyons" is now subject to worldwide study (e.g., Tominaga and Shirzadi 2021).

Wind Vanes and Weathercocks

Weather vanes have a considerable antiquity. As noted earlier, the Tower of the Winds at Athens was topped by a wind vane shaped like a triton with a wand as a pointer; it rotated on a fixed axis mounted on the apex of the octagonal roof. Brescia, Italy, had a weathercock on the Church of San Faustino Maggiore in the year 820 CE (Novati 1904, 497). In England in 862 CE Bishop Swithun (800–862 CE) put a weathercock on the cathedral at Winchester. (English folklore states that if it rains on Saint Swithun's Day, July 15, a rainy period lasting forty days will follow—however, this rarely happens.) In 925 CE the monastery of Saint Gallen (in present-day Switzerland) had its weathercock stolen by Magyar invaders. Westminster Abbey in London in 1065 is depicted in the Bayeux Tapestry, where a man on the roof is shown setting up a weathercock. In medieval Europe, vanes took many forms. A French adage tells us there are lions, eagles, and dragons on top of churches (Martin 1904, 10), and swan-shaped vanes were erected in parts of Germany, especially Oldenburg and East Frisia (Goethe 1971, 7–19). It is traditional to have letters for the four winds on short iron rods below the weathercock or vane. On traditionally orientated churches, this is not necessary, as the structure of the church expresses the directions, with the chancel and altar at the east end.

Wind vanes are important in traditional society because they indicate the likelihood of rain or snow when the wind blows from a certain direction. They are also valuable to sailors, who need certain winds in order to go to sea. Wind vanes and weathercocks are finely balanced artifacts that are driven by the prevailing currents of wind. The weathercock is designed so that its body is balanced on the staff on which it rotates, with its beak facing the direction of the wind. Weather vanes have an arrow that points toward the wind, the vane part facing downwind, as would a flag. Weathercocks and vanes move continuously according to the direction of the wind, yet they rotate around a fixed, stable vertical axis, thereby keeping in harmony with the wind no matter from what direction it emanates. A Latin motto associated with wind vanes reflects this function: *Officium meum stabile agitari*—"It is my function to remain stable while turning." This is the symbolic meaning of vanes and weathercocks, and the interpretation of this is that we must remain true to our core spirit while the conditions of the world change continually around us. The rune whose shape reflects the Viking Age wind vanes carried by ships

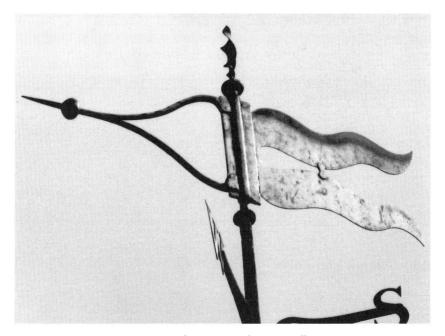

Ancient wind vane on Christ's College,
Cambridge, England

Weathercock emblem and motto—
"It is my function to remain stable while moving"

or set up on stave churches in Norway, is *Wunjo*, which means "joy," for joy is being. The traditional East Anglian sailing vessel called the Wherry had a similar *wane* on top of the mast. Set up on the highest point of the church, gilded vanes gleam in the sunlight just before dawn and just after sunset.

24

The Right Place at the Right Time

It is necessary to keep up the day.
—East Anglian Fenland saying

Traditional societies celebrate festivals thoughout the year, which commemorate important days that mark particular stages of the year. In the north, the physical fact of long days in the summer and short days in the winter is the common feature of traditional observances. The different ways of life—pastoral, agricultural, industrial, mercantile, and military—all have their contribution to make to days that mark the passing of the years. The solar year can be defined in ten different ways, depending on the cultural needs of the societies that used them. These are the ten possible year divisions. The year defined by the solstices can either be December–June–December or June–December–June. Equinoctial solar years can be September–March–September or March–September–March. These four divisions are physical, based on regular solar phenomena. The vegetation years are more flexible, based upon organic growth. Thus, there are two possible flower years: November–May–November and May–November–May. There are also

153

Pendant cross with sigils of the
four seasons from the foresters' tradition
in Alsace, France

two possible harvest years: August–February–August and February–August–February. The maritime years, based upon the favorability of the northern seas for sailing, are April–October–January–April and October–January–April–October, the months between April and October being the favorable ones.

Religious festivals are also linked with the seasons. In the north, winter darkness is more protracted than further south, and the midwinter solstice, celebrating the return of the light after the longest night of the year, is the major festival of the year. Celebrated with feasting and fires, disguises and games, it is related to the old Germanic Yuletide.* Most of these midwinter rites and ceremonies were absorbed into the

---

*Contrary to popular notions, recent research has shown that the winter solstice and the pagan Yuletide were not identical. The specific timing of the latter, which functioned as a "moveable feast," was based on a traditional lunar calendar and its relation to the solstice. See P. D. Brown, *Thirteen Moons: Reflections on the Heathen Lunar Year* (Gilded Books, 2022).

syncretic festival of Christmas, which is the most important festival in the present day. In medieval times, the agricultural year was regulated by the Church's "red letter days"—particular saints' days that either continued pre-Christian practice or coincided with it. Practically, these days were only an indication, as the fluctuations in the weather that might lead to an early or late harvest, for instance, were the real events that mattered. But the days were celebrated on the correct day in the calendar; this is the practice of "keeping up the day."

According to current Pagan folklore, the eightfold year in modern Paganism is reputed to have been devised in 1949 at a meeting in a London pub between the Druid Ross Nichols (1902–1975) and the Wiccan Gerald Gardner (1884–1964). The four "cross-quarter days" of Druidry, we are told, were added to the solstices and equinoxes celebrated by traditional witches. So, a year punctuated by eight festivals was born: Winter Solstice–Imbolc–Vernal Equinox–Beltane–Summer Solsice–Lughnassadh–Autumnal Equinox–Samhain. This legendary meeting of Nichols and Gardner has become a contemporary Pagan origin-myth. But even if it actually took place, it is is not the whole story. In 1906 Norman Lockyer (1836–1920) published *Stonehenge and Other British Stone Monuments Astronomically Considered*. In it, he described the "astronomical and vegetation divisions of the year," which produced a diagram showing eight divisions that included the solstices and equinoxes (Lockyer 1906, 23).

Twenty-six years later, in chapter 6 of his *Archaic Tracks Round Cambridge* (1932), the "ley hunter" Alfred Watkins (1855–1935) wrote of "Seasonal Alinements," where he credited Lockyer. Watkins detailed the "Celtic Vegetation Year," which has four quarter-days (1932, 27):

First Quarter-day (Brid—St. Bridget—Candlemas), Feb. 1–4.
Second Quarter-day (Beltaine—May Day), May 1–6.
Third Quarter-day (Lugh or Lug—Lammas), Aug. 1–8.
Fourth Quarter-day (Samhain—Martinmas—Mayor chosen), Nov. 1–8.

156 Cosmic Principles

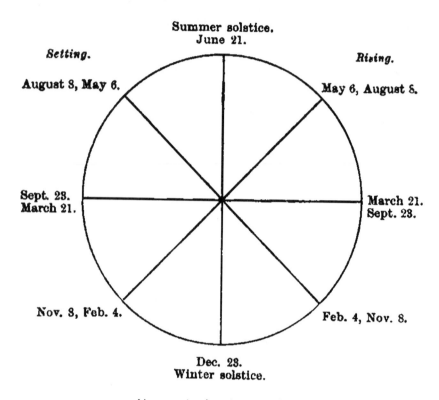

Norman Lockyer's year wheel

He also detailed the "Sun or June Year":

First Quarter-day (Shortest day—Mid-Winter—Christmas), Dec. 25–23.
Second Quarter-day (Equal day and night—Lady Day), Mar. 25–21.
Third Quarter-day (Longest day—Midsummer—St. John's), June 24–21.
Fourth Quarter-day (Equal day and night—Michaelmas), Sept. 24–23.

"These two tables together" Watkins concluded, "divide the sun-year (based on the solstices and equinoxes) into eight fairly accurate divisions." Suggestions of an eightfold year were also made seemingly independently by the Dutch prehistory researcher Herman Wirth (1885–1961), but the current system almost certainly was popularized in Pagan circles from the 1960s onward.

Ancient and contemporary events have one thing in common—they are "keeping up the day." A particular day in the year is recognized and celebrated by a public performance, whether it be a sacred day like Beltane or St. George's Day; a customary day like Boxing Day and Plough Monday; or a day that has been designated by a modern interest group, like Apple Day. Nation-states also designate days, such as Independence Day, or some particular date when a revolution occurred, or a war was won. This, too, is "keeping up the day."

Geomancy is all about *being in the right place at at the right time*, and the time when the first stone of a building is laid marks the vital moment when it begins to take on physical reality. Memorable rites and ceremonies are performed, and some kind of symbolic deposit is left buried beneath the foundation stone as a token of the act. Since early times, the horoscope of the instant of foundation was considered to denote the future success or otherwise of the building. The art of electional astrology seeks to find the most auspicious celestial configuration to lay the first stone of a building. An inceptional horoscope is drawn up in advance, and the foundation stone laid at the exact moment indicated by it. To the building, this is the instant of birth, equivalent to the natal time in human astrology.

In England, electional astrology was used in the foundation of colleges, institutions, and churches. For example, in Cambridge, the foundation stone of the west range of Gonville and Caius college was laid by the founder, John Caius (1510–1573), at 4:00 a.m. on May 5, 1565, at the rising of the planet Mercury. In London in 1675, John Flamsteed (1646–1719), Astronomer Royal to King Charles II (1630–1685; reigned 1660–1685), calculated the inceptional horoscopes for the Royal Exchange, the new St Paul's Cathedral and the Royal Observatory at Greenwich. The Royal Observatory election has the Sun in the ninth house, appropriate for the philosophical and scientific pursuit of astronomy. The rising sign is Sagittarius, which is the natural ruler of the ninth house, and the beneficent planet Jupiter, Sagittarius's ruler, is in that sign, almost exactly at the position of its rising. By electing the horoscope, buildings can be placed in a harmonious relationship with the celestial cycles, bringing the users into harmony with the Cosmos.*

---

*For further information on electional astrology in this context, see my book *Creating Places of Power* (2022), 257–81.

25

Nature and the Eldritch

The Anima Loci

The following text represents the key teaching of the Way of the Eight Winds. It deals with the themes that are expanded upon in various other sections of this book. *Anima Loci* was intended as an analytical description of the implication of the concept of the spirit of place (often called the genius loci), in terms of a reappraisal of the nature of place in the context of the religious and magical practices of consecration and exorcism or banishing. This teaching could be called a theory of practical geomancy according to well-understood ancient principles. Hence, it begins with a section on *önd*, then sanctification, followed by onlays, the state of *álfrek*, and the means of reanimating post-onlay places. It is given that the sacred nature of a place emanates directly from the Anima Loci and that any other usage of the place is an onlay derived externally, imposed by deliberate or accidental means over the original Anima Loci. Colors and patterns are metaphors for intangible natures.

In the original introduction to the text, I wrote:

Much but not all of what is called misleadingly "Earth Mysteries" can be described generally as "thing-oriented" work. Fundamentally,

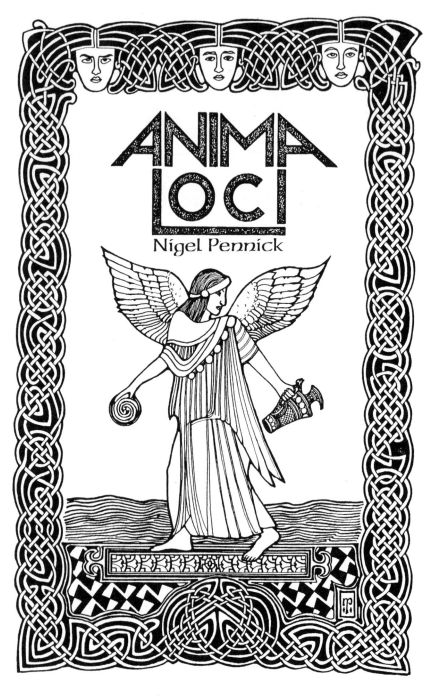

Cover of the Way of the Eight Winds'
Anima Loci publication

it is based upon the post-Renaissance spectacle of measurement and documentation of "objects." For this, data are gathered either with the assistance of technical instrumentation, or by means of residual magical techniques. Both are represented as claiming somehow to express the "true nature" or "hidden reality" of a given "ancient monument." Whether they are objectively "true" is debatable, but what both approaches do is to separate their users (and us) from a direct experience of presence at any place. . . . The Anima Loci view of landscape, presented here, is different. It is based on a traditional view of the world, that it is ensouled. The view is subjective, in that it treats the world as ensouled subject rather than inanimate matter.

Anima Loci: Principles

The principles of sanctification and desacralization view the world in terms of subtle elements that embody natural qualities but can also be affected by external actions. Naturally, everything that humans describe is explained in human terms. These descriptions are interpretations of reality according to the structure and function of human consciousness. We should always bear in mind that, while the descriptions fit very well into the perceived reality, we should never take them literally. Once they are taken literalistically, these perceptions degenerate into spectacle. Also, as Alfred Adler warned, what makes madness is literalism. The world's fundamentalisms—and their results—richly attest to the correctness of his assertion. "For hard are the gods on him who sees them manifestly"—Homer.

Places where the Anima Loci has manifested directly have always been marked and honored. Around the year 500 BCE princess Hagelochia of Sparta erected an image of Artemis with the following inscription: "This Artemis in the cross-ways did Hagelochia the daughter of Damaretus erect while still a virgin in her father's house; for the goddess herself appeared to her by the weft of her loom, like a flame of fire." This is a classical instance of a manifestation

An illustration from *Anima Loci*

of the Anima Loci. Many places have gained human recognition through epiphanies. Truth to the Anima Loci is truth to the nature of the place.

Önd

Throughout the world, traditional cultures have named the subtle "cosmic breath" that pervades all existence. It is best known in the West as the æther. In the Northern Tradition, where it is described well, it is called önd. According to this perception, önd is neutral in character. It is capable of picking up surrounding influences, behaving as a sort of medium for them. In a natural condition, önd is patterned in conformity with the natural colors and patterns of the place: it is in perfect alignment with the Anima Loci in its ever-altering fluxes of character. When human activity takes place, that, too, affects the patterns and colors of önd—is such cases the qualities of the Anima Loci are reinforced (sanctification), altered (onlay), or destroyed (*álfrek*).

Sanctification

Sanctity—the physical manifestation of the essential nature of a sacred place—comes into being when the Anima Loci is recognized. At such loci, the önd is patterned and colored with conformity the qualities of the Anima Loci. These patterns, never fixed, flow and change according to the qualitative changes of the Anima Loci. There is no dissonance. When the Anima Loci is recognized by human beings, then perfect harmony arises if human actions at the place reinforce, enhance, and develop the previously imperceptible potential. This enhancement comes about when the development takes the form of self-similarity, promoting the evolution of the hitherto-unmanifest qualities of the Anima Loci.

Enhancement is brought about by human activities that are in harmony with the Anima Loci. They are those things that repeat in a self-similar way the pattern-quality of the Anima Loci. They include pleasing artifacts, ceremonies, and activities that elicit a similar harmonious response in humans. Enhancing the Anima Loci is spiritual gardening, not trying to "command and control," but consciously participating in a self-ordering system. At places of sanctity, fully developed human beings can become outward expressions or embodiments of the Anima Loci. As time passes, through repetition and evolution, the place's *ørlög* is sanctified: the qualities of the Anima Loci are intensified.

By these means, the latent spirit of the Anima Loci can be brought forth into manifestation on the material level. Then, a truly sacred place has come into being. The invisible is made visible. This is the revelation of Paradise. Sanctity does not merely acknowledge or reproduce some specific perception of the Anima Loci: it creates a unique presentation of the Anima Loci that does not act as an intermediate filter, interpretation, or respresentation. Rather, nothing comes between: it is an enhancing gateway to the divine.

Onlays

An onlay comes into being when the önd of a site is altered by an act of will. This can either be a ritual act, such as exorcism or consecration, or an act of will that would not normally be considered magical, such as the unmindful construction of a secular building. Under an onlay, the qualities deriving from the Anima Loci are suppressed, yet still present. Because the patterns of the onlay are (by definition) different from those of the Anima Loci, there is a conflict between the önd patterns of the Anima Loci and those of the onlay. Thus, onlays must be renewed periodically, or the Anima Loci will remanifest, bringing the quality of the place back into line with the quality of the Anima Loci.

Álfrek

A place is rendered álfrek when the spiritual beings of the land are driven away. It is complete desacralization. The Anima Loci is destroyed. This can result from a too powerful onlay maintained over a long period. It is the ultimate result of an onlay that is in direct conflict with the Anima Loci. A place can also be rendered álfrek by physical destruction: if a holy hill is bulldozed away, or a hole for a metro station entrance is excavated where once was a sacred place, then the actual locus is no more, and it can have no *anima*. This type of álfrek is common in cities. If a place is rendered álfrek, this does not extirpate the önd, which remains present. It will be affected by whatever influences are brought there. For example, there can be on onlay upon an álfrek site. This gives us the means to do some sort of geomantic remedial work at álfrek places.

Post-Onlay Sites

Places where an onlay once existed, but where it is no longer operative, are *post-onlay sites*. If the place is not álfrek, then the Anima Loci is still present, even if weakened. She can re-manifest if the site is not overlain by a new onlay. A post-onlay site that is álfrek is open to any influence, conscious or unconscious, that might come into contact with it. The önd of the site will be patterned randomly, according to the influences. Álfrek post-onlay sites are particularly prone to destructive influences and new onlays that will be more powerful because they are not in conflict with the Anima Loci, which has been driven down.

Reanimating Post-Onlay Sites

If a place is not álfrek, then human actions can accelerate the return of the full influence of the Anima Loci. To do this, it is necessary to remove deteriorating onlay remnants, and to replace them with harmonious artifacts and activities. Remains that are neutral should stay as a witness to the *ørlög* of the place. The *ørlög* of the onlay will always be present, but the dwindling of its effects can be accelerated and obliterated. Then the character of the Anima Loci can shine through once more.

TABLE 1

CONDITION	TIME$_1$	TIME$_2$	TIME$_X$
PRIMAL	Although at any time, the Anima Loci and the önd are in harmony, their character is not constant (fixed), varying with time-cycles and other cyclic phenomena of Nature. The condition of ørlög of the locus is related to the time. There is no separation.		
SANCTIFIED	enhances Anima Loci ⟶ önd	enhanced and developed ørlög of enhancement ⟶	enhanced and developed ørlög of enhancement
ONLAY	alters önd ⟶ Anima Loci has some influence	diminishing Anima Loci influence progressive separation ørlög of onlay ⟶	onlay maintained ↓ loss of onlay T$_Y$ ⟶
ÁLFREK	produced where conditions destroy Anima Loci		
POST-ONLAY			Anima Loci remanifests

TABLE 2

PRIMAL	SANCTIFIED	ONLAY	ÁLFREK
ANIMA LOCI ↓ ÖND ↓ Human consciousness	ANIMA LOCI ↑↓ ÖND ↑↓ Human consciousness	ANIMA LOCI ↑↓ ÖND ↑ Human onlay	ANIMA LOCI DESTROYED ÖND ↑↓ Human actions
	Positive feedback	No feedback	Negative feedback

ÖND

PRIMAL

SANCTIFIED

ONLAY

ÁLFREK

Anima Loci
önd pattern
human pattern

TABLE 3

ANIMA LOCI

Patterns of önd through time under different conditions. Anima Loci pattern is shown as a bold straight line. Diminished Anima Loci as a straight line.

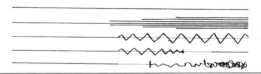

PRIMAL
SANCTIFIED
ONLAY
POST-ONLAY
ÁLFREK

Anima Loci processes

On Being Present

Without being present, we perceive the world as a secondhand experience—spectacle. Our personal and collective fictions and fantasies are projected onto outer reality, and we experience only a representation of Nature. When we are present, the externality of spectacle is rendered impossible.

The monetarist view of the world, currently being weighed in the balance and found wanting, states that nothing is sacred—the only significant factor about anything is its price. To these devotees of Mammon, holy shrines and sacred places have no intrinsic value. They are worth only what money they raise when they are put up for sale to the highest bidder. Heritage organizations, set up to guard these places for the commonweal, have betrayed the trust of those in whose name they act. Sacred places entrusted to them in perpetuity are put up for sale, perhaps to be destroyed by their new owners.

At the present time, the loss of ancient sacred sites through onlay and álfrek in all its forms is widespread. Contemporary times call for contemporary responses—being present and aware to the essential nature of sanctity, to what is meaningful, and to what is futile. This involves a letting go of attachment to ancient places that in many cases are likely to be álfrek. The continuity that these places represented is broken. It was broken when traditional society was disrupted by industrialization, world wars, and the development of mass culture. The common land was "enclosed," and taken forcibly into private ownership, away from the local people. The sacred places went with the land.

Far from being the solution to this disruption, the setting up of organizations and raising funds to purchase places when they are put up for sale is part of the problem. To participate in this system of ownership and management is to compound the issues. Such places, when in ownership of anybody other than mindful and reverent local people, suffer at best an onlay and at worst are reduced to spectacle. Sancity can be present ony when this local "ownership" is in the form of sacred guardianship. The Celtic concept of the *dewar*—the often hereditary, spiritual guardian—is of a totally different order. It is not ownership in the sense of title deeds to real estate, for that is itself an onlay stemming from feudalism. Dewarship is the mindful, sensitive communion with the Anima Loci that enables her to express herself however she will.

It is easier to assert the command-and-control syndrome over a locus than to be peaceful and listen. Command and control can be implemented at once, without regard for the Anima Loci. Being present, coming into harmony with the spirit of the Anima Loci, takes much more effort and sensibility. Furthermore, fewer people are capable of doing it. But unless dewarship is exercised, the fate of the Anima Loci at most places will be to suffer continued onlays and ultimately álfrek.

26

The Sacredness of Manifested Phenomena

Divine Immanence

The sacred is not separate from everyday life. Divinity is present in every physical object, containing and emanating divine realities. The understanding that all things are spiritually empowered is acknowledged and respected. Folk traditions and legends of the landscape throughout Europe assert that spiritual orderliness originates in the understanding that the land is ensouled. It has been taught since antiquity that a respectful, caring, spiritual awareness of the land brings peace and plenty, a society based upon goodwill, fecundity of animals, and abundant harvests. Variations in climate and landscape give each place its character; its hunting and farming; and its rites and ceremonies, festivals, and Gods. All who live close to Nature understand a oneness with the world. A state of heightened sanctity exists when the innate spiritual nature of any place is manifested there in visible, physical form.

Until the arrival of Christianity in Europe, there was no philosophical barrier between the lofty beings of heaven and lesser, earthly spiritual beings. The ensouled land was known to teem with spirits as a

170   Cosmic Principles

coral reef teems with fish. The spirits of the earth were viewed not as an evil "other," but as integral parts of a continuum in which the rocks and soil, plants and animals, wind and rain, and humans play their part as co-creators of life on earth. As in all traditional cultures worldwide, the ancient European understanding of the divine is the localized form of a general "organic religion."

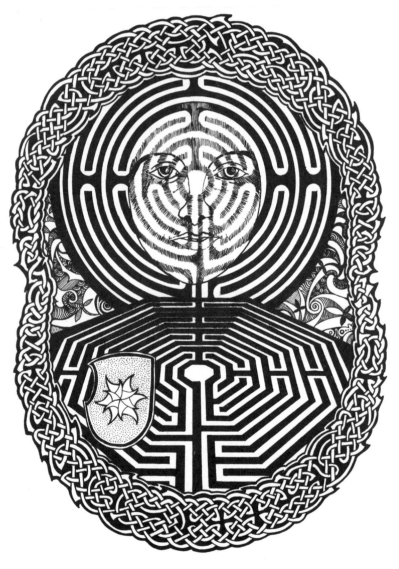

Divine manifestation—the Goddess in the Labyrinth

Ancient European ways acknowledge spirit guardians of fields and flocks; earth spirits; crop, water, and tree sprites; spiritual protectors of travelers and seafarers; supernatural beasts like trolls, water monsters, werewolves, and dragons; personifications of disease and death; and demons who bring bad luck. Ancestral holy places—homesteads, burial mounds, tombs, and battlefields—are held in veneration as places of the ancestral spirits. These are places where people can experience transcendent states of timeless consciousness, receive spiritual inspiration, and accept healing. All of these manifest as the innate spiritual qualities of places that the Romans conveniently characterized as the *genius loci*, the "spirit of the place."

The Way of the Eight Winds seeks to discover, express, and enhance the essence of the spirit present at any place. The location of buildings, especially those intended to honor the genius loci and the gods, was a matter of great importance in antiquity. Omens were observed to determine the spiritual suitability of a place for sacred rites, altars, temples, and burial places. Coming into harmonious confluence with the powers of a place was achieved through appropriate rites and ceremonies.

The Land Wights

Far truer is it to believe in fairies and in spirits than in nothing at all; for surely there is life all about us.
—H. FIELDING, *THE SOUL OF A PEOPLE* (1898)

As well as ancient Greek and Roman texts, certain ancient records from northern Europe—most notably, the Irish *Dindsenchas* and various Icelandic writings—preserve an understanding of the spiritual landscape that dates from pre-Christian times. During the ninth and tenth centuries, the uninhabited island of Iceland was colonized by settlers from Norway and the Western Isles of Scotland. Their religious response to the landscape is recorded in the *Landnámabók*, the book of land-taking. It is a unique record, for all other colonizations except the Seychelles and the Falkland Islands were of lands already inhabited by Indigenous peoples. Also, these settlers of a new land were not Christian, and therefore acutely aware of the spiritual nature of places. Certain areas were not settled at all, being reserved for the *landvættir*, the "land wights" or spirits of place. Ceremonies were performed in honor of these landvættir, and offerings left for them. For example, the *Landnámabók* records how Thorvald Holbarki recited a poem in honor of the giant that dwelt in Surt's Cavern. More generally, prayers were directed toward Helgafell, the Icelandic holy mountain. Before praying, devotees first washed their faces out of respect.

Spirits

To the ancients, the nymphs were located female deities, whom Hesiod (ca. 800 BCE) reckons numbered 3,000. Whether such numbers have any meaning more than the symbolic (like the celebrated 30,000 gods of Rome), Hesiod must have meant species of nymph, rather than individual beings. According to some ancient texts, the nymphs were believed to be immortal. But not all ancient Pagan commentators agreed, stating that although their lives were very long, nymphs finally died. According to Hesiod, their lifespan was several thousand years. But Plutarch (46–119 CE) disagreed and gave them only 920 years. There were two broad classes of nymph: terrestrial and aquatic. Three types of nymphs inhabited the water: those of the sea were the oceanids, or nereids; the naiads and potamides lived in springs, fountains, and rivers; while the limnads inhabited lakes and pools. The Lady of the Lake in Arthurian myth is clearly one of the limnads. In Provence, France, there is the Vallée des Nymphes (Valley of the Nymphs), where the numerous spouts of water that issue from rock faces are marked by sacred places of great antiquity.

Terrestrial nymphs include the napaeae, who inhabit hills and dales, and the oreads, who live in the mountains. The dryads and hamadryads are guardians of the trees and woodland. Dryads have the ability to wander at will beneath the shade of their holy trees and gather with other nymphs. But the hamadryads are restricted to individual trees in which they live and die. In pre-Christian times, sacred trees were universally respected for their indwelling spirits. Decaying trees were propped up, and had their exposed roots re-covered with earth so that their hamadryads would survive. No tree could be felled before ritual specialists had declared that the nymphs had departed from it. Though largely obliterated by utilitarian belief, the tradition still continues in certain places where *Gentle Trees* or *Fairy Trees* are held in great regard.

According to the *Ostentarium Arborarium* of Lucinius Tarquinius Priscus (king of Rome 616–579 BCE), an *Arbor Felix* was an auspicious tree under the protection of a god, thereby being even more sacred than those with indwelling hamadryads. Among these trees were poplars (*Populus* spp.), laurel (*Laurus nobilis*), and olive (*Olea europaea*). When King Charles III of the United Kingdom was crowned in 2023, he was anointed with consecrated oil from an *Arbor Felix*, an olive tree growing on the Mount of Olives in Jerusalem. In south Wales it was considered risky to build a cottage in or near the place where an elder tree (*Sambucus nigra*) grew. Elder trees have equivocal magical attributes, and are associated with the fairies (Trevelyan 1909, 316).

Taxonomy of the Indeterminate

In the first half of the nineteenth century, the folklore collector Michael Aislabie Denham (1801–1859) published numerous erudite articles on traditional lore and practices. His prolific works were anthologized after his death by the Folk-Lore Society and published in two volumes titled *The Denham Tracts* (1892 and 1895). In Volume II appears this remarkably comprehensive list of terrifying mythological, magical, phantom, supernatural, and otherworldly appearances and beings. It is an example of the sheer diversity of taxonomy of the indeterminate that we must deal with when attempting to define the unseen or half-glimpsed elements of our study.

Denham recalled a time "seventy or eighty years ago and upwards," when:

the whole world was so overrun with ghosts, boggles, bloody-bones, spirits, demons, ignis fatui, brownies, bug-bears, black dogs, spectres, shellycoats, scarecrows, witches, wizards, barguests, Robin-Goodfellows, hags, night-bats, scrags, breaknecks, fantasms, hobgoblins, hobhoulards, boggy-boes, dobbies, hob-thrusts, fetches, kelpies, warlocks, mock-beggars, mum-pokers, Jimmy-burties, urchins, satyrs, pans, fauns, sirens, tritons, centaurs, calcars, nymphs, imps, incubusses, spoorns, men-in-the-oak, hellwains, fire-drakes, kit-a-can-sticks, Tom-tumblers, melch-dicks, larrs, kitty-witches, hobby-lanterns, Dick-a-Tuesdays, Elf-fires, Gyl-burnt-tails, knockers, elves, raw-heads, Meg-with the-wads, old-shocks, ouphs, pad-foots, pixies, pictrees, giants, dwarfs, Tom-pokers, tutgots, snapdragons, sprets, spunks, conjurers, thurses, spurns, tantarrabobs, swaithes, tints, tod-lowries, Jack-in-the-wads, mormos, changelings, redcaps, yeth-hounds, colt-pixies, Tom-thumbs, black-bugs, boggarts, scar-bugs, shag-foals, hodge-pochers, hob-thrushes, bugs, bull-beggars, bygorns, bolls, caddies, bomen, brags, wraithes, waffs, flay-boggarts, fiends, gallytrots, imps, gyrtrashes, patches, hob-and-lanthorns, gringes, boguests, bonelesses, Peg-powlers, pucks, fays, kidnappers, gally-beggars, hudskins, knickers, madcaps, trolls, robinets, friars' lanthorns, silkies, could-lads, death-hearses, goblins, hob-headlesses, buggaboes, kows, or cowes, nickies, nacks (necks), wraiths, miffies, buckies, gholes, sylphs, guests, swarths, freiths, freits, gy-carlins (Gryre-carlings), pigmies, chittifaces, nixies, Jinny-burnt-tails, dud-men, hell-hounds, dopple-gangers, boggleboes, bogies, redmen, portunes, grants, hobbits, hobgoblins, brown-men, cowies, dun-nies, wirrikows, allholdes, mannikins, follets, korreds, lubberkins, cluricauns, kobolds, leprechauns, kors, mares, puckles, korigans, sylvans, succubuses, black-men, shadows, banshees, lianhanshees, clabbernappers, Gabriel-hounds, mawkins, doubles, corpse lights or candles, scrats, mahounds, trows, gnomes, sprites, fates, fiends, sybils, nick-nevins, whitewomen, fairies, thrummy-caps, cutties and nisses, and apparitions of every shape, make, form, fashion, kind and description, that there was not a village in England that had not its own particular ghost. Nay, every lone tenement, castle or mansion-house, which could boast of any antiquity, had its bogle, its spectre or its knocker. Every green lane had its boulder-stone on which an apparition kept watch at night. Every common had its circle of fairies belonging to it. (Denham 1895, 77–80)

Denham's catalog of supernatural and otherworldly powers, entities, and beings—just from England!—reminds us of the sheer abundance of forms that have been imagined, visualized, or sighted over a long period of time. Some are interpreted as the spirits of dead people; others as autonomous sprites that belong to an eldritch, otherworldly, realm that intersects with the everyday world at certain points and times. All of them have their conventional depictions, which may appear in vernacular art and as characters in fiction and performance.

27

Places of Spirit

European traditional spirituality is intimately tied up with landscape, climate, and the cycle of the seasons. The same features of landscape are held sacred in the Greek, Roman, Celtic, Germanic, Slavic, and Baltic traditions. They include mountains and hills, volcanoes, springs, rivers and lakes, ravines and caves, special rocks and trees. Each have their particular marks of veneration. Local people ritually ascend holy hills on the festival days of the sky gods. Offerings are cast into lakes and springs at certain times of year as offerings to the lake spirits in thanksgiving or propitiation. Holy trees are protected by fences, and decked with garlands and ribbons, and food is left for their indwelling dryads. Sacred signs and images of gods and animals can be seen carved on rocky outcrops or at stopping places along tracks and roads that were marked by shrines to local gods, places of devotion for travelers.

Other holy places with no particular natural features, but acknowledged as places of spirit, have been marked by posts, images, and temples. In Britain, Ireland, and Scandinavia cairns of stones were made where a sacrifice had taken place, or where a person had died. It is a sacred act for each wayfarer passing a cairn to place a stone upon it with a prayer for the spirits dwelling there. From at least the ninth century (but likely occurring much earlier), labyrinths made of turf or stones

Roman altar to the genius loci at
Bad Cannstatt, Germany

were used in spring rites, weather-magic, and ceremonies of the dead. There are tales in England of labyrinths being the dwelling-places of fairies. Early Christian churches were built on such sacred places when the old religion was destroyed. Places that could not be appropriated had their indwelling spirits redefined as legendary characters like Gogmagog or King Arthur, or hateful demons identified with the Christian Devil.

According to classical writers, the Druids, whose name meant "men of the oak tree," taught the doctrine of the transmigration of souls. In this belief, human souls at death are not extinguished, but enter into trees, rocks, or animals, or newborn humans. Thus, the individual is not a separate being, but part of the great continuum of all things. This is expressed in the traditional relationship of humans to their *Heimat*, where family, life, and place are indistinguishable. The ancestral dead were part of family and place, and the nonhuman spirits and deities of the place were acknowledged equally. It was a holistic life without the separation and alienation that all of us inevitably experience today. The ancestors played an important role in the everyday spiritual life of the common people.

An *idis* (Anglo-Saxon) or *dís* (Old Norse; pl. *dísir*) was the female ancestral spirit who was honored as a guardian of a clan, family, or individual that lived at her particular ancestral place. The dísir were worshipped collectively at special places in the ancestral landscape, often holy hills recalled today in Germany by names like Disenberg or Disibodenberg. Pagan Scandinavians celebrated a collective festival of the dísir called *Dísablót*, and temples were erected to their veneration where offerings were made for the good fortune of the family and the fecundity of flocks and fields. She also had her own shrine in the farmstead where prayers and offerings were made. The *ættardís* protected the family and the *barnadís* guarded over the children. Images of these ancestral spirits were set up in hofs and temples, and there were temples called *dísasalr* that were places specifically dedicated to particular dís. Such spiritual places were in the private ownership of the family who lived there. According to ancient custom, each holy place had its own living guardian, a member of the family which owned the land. In Scandinavia, public temples were the property of the hereditary keeper of the land; the same was the case in Britain with the Celtic holy sites known as *temenoi*. This was immutable ancestral property, which could not be sold, for there was an unbreakable personal relationship of the family members with the spirits of the place where they dwelt.

In Pagan Iceland, the office of *goði* (pl. *goðar*) originated in the priest of a tribe or clan who held a certain sacred place in common. Goðar were never full-time officials, rather hereditary landowners who had the duty to maintain ancestral holy places. In Iceland, the goði in charge of the temple at Kialarnes, the direct descendent of the first settler, Ingulf Arnarson, bore the title *Alsherjargoði*, "high priest." Iceland was divided geomantically into four quarters, each containing three jurisdictions, further subdivided into three *goðorð* (which designated the "authority of a goði"), each with its goði living at a particular holy place. In Iceland, the *höfuðhof* (main or public temples) were sometimes owned by women. In Scotland and Ireland, the office of the *dewar* (see chap. 25), the keeper of ancestral sacred things, continued in a Christian context until the last century, and remains as a Scottish surname.

The religious observance of pre-Christian northern Europe was centered not so much upon a chief deity, as upon the ancestors' spirits, located at an ancestral place. In early times, the king's ancestor was also the god of the tribe and the spiritual guardian of the tribal territory. This principle was maintained among the Angles and Saxons in England until well into Christian times, and the present King Charles III of the United Kingdom of Great Britain and Northern Ireland has a genealogy that is traced back to Woden. Seven out of the eight Anglo-Saxon royal genealogies began with Woden, and the eighth, Essex, with Seaxnet, tribal god of the East Saxons. The Swedish royal line also began with Odin.

In former times, the underlying theme of the spiritual in all of Europe followed the same ethos. The landscape of Europe was filled with sacred places where people acknowledged the indwelling spirits. These took many forms, but all were the focus of some human token to the spirits felt to be there. Christian missionaries made it a matter of course either to destroy these places completely, such as by cutting down the (ensouled) trees, or to construct Christian structures upon them and to banish the indwelling spirits by rites of exorcism. At that point, two different interpretations of the meaning of the same place came into being. Later, sectarianism and the decline of religion meant that even the holy places of Christianity were no longer considered sacred, and the appearance of the spirits of the land became classified as "the unexplained." We are still in this condition today. The elder faith and its truncated continuance in folk tradition have a vision of an ensouled landscape that is totally different from the modern worldview. But only through trying to recall the traditional understanding of the human relationship with the land can we recover something of the holistic life that once was the experience of everyone.

In parts of rural Britain, it is traditional to acknowledge the spirits of the land with offerings of food and drink. In Scotland and the north of England, Dobbie Stones by the gates of fields or by the back doors of farmhouses are sometimes encountered containing milk. Offerings of milk are poured into the depression for the local sprites in order to change the wind, though often it is said to be "for the cat." In East Anglia, the helpful guardian spirits of the land are known as *Hytersprites*. These are present within the parts of the landscape acknowledged as sacred by the elder faith.

There is a belief in East Anglia that each settlement has its own land-spirit guardians, which band together to form the *Ward*. These are beings who protect a village or town by night from both internal troubles and external dangers. At dusk each evening, the sprites who form the Ward assemble at a sacred place on the edge of the village, such as a Ward-hill, and then travel by way of certain spirit-paths to their watch-places. It is believed that the Ward-sprites are guardian spirits of individual people in the settlement, both living and dead. Their watch-places are the sacred stopping places of the geomantic landscape: the mounds, cairns, stones, shrines, crosses, and holy trees by the roads and paths that lead to and from the village. At night, if it has human acknowledgment and support, the Ward makes a protective spiritual ring around the place, giving protection against psychic attack from both the human and nonhuman realms.

But acknowledgment of each village's Ward is rare now. Bad places in the landscape, where humans intuitively feel psychically unwanted, are inhabited by *Yarthkins*. These are earth spirits that express positive hostility to human interference. Unlike Hytersprites, Yarthkins cannot be placated with offerings presented in pleasing and beautiful ways. In old Iceland, places with such spirits were just left alone, but when land began to be bought and sold as a valuable commodity, this way was not kept up, and techniques were devised to block or nullify their baleful influence. In East Anglia, traditional geomancy employs sprite traps, blocking stones, staves, egg-posts, and mirrors. As well as malevolent Yarthkins, certain places have "invisible presences" that are not pleasant to encounter. Each is described in local lore by a particular name, though its nature is imprecise.

Where helpful land spirits are no longer acknowledged, or have been driven away deliberately, the land is spiritually dead. In old Iceland this undesirable condition was called álfrek, and in East Anglia it is called *gast*. It is known that such sites, no longer tended by their spiritual guardians, will become barren and evil doings will happen there. This is the condition of many locations today. Miltary bases, car parks, airports, and landfills are prime examples of álfrek places.

Spiritual Enclosures and Enhazelled Fields

In medieval northern Europe and in later times there was a custom of setting aside pieces of land, which neither spade nor plough were allowed to touch. Typically, they were triangular corners of fields, dedicated by the peasant or yeoman who promised never to till the earth there. Inside the boundary, the pristine condition of the earth prior to its tilling by man is preserved. There, the land-wights still have a place to be, and the former "wilderness" is remembered. It is well known in Scotland, where pieces of fenced ground called the Halyman's Rig, the Gudeman's Croft, the Black Faulie, or Cloutie's Croft were places that traditionally neither spade nor plough were permitted to touch (McNeill 1957, I, 62). It also existed in southern England, as in the present author's grandmother's garden. In England, uncultivated triangular pieces of ground at a *trifinium*, the center of the junction of three country roads, were called No Man's Land, denoting their ownership by nonhuman entities.

This practice dated from pre-Christian times, when pieces of land such as these were actually sacred enclosures dedicated to religious rites and ceremonies. In Pagan Scandinavia, the *vé* was a triangular enclosure, set aside from the everyday world by a row of *bautasteinar* (uninscribed standing stones) or a fence called the *vébönd*. The Danish royal sanctuary at Jelling was such a vé (Dyggve 1954). After the Christian church became dominant, these were deemed heathen practices and were forbidden, hence the "Devil" names given to the Scottish Halyman's Rig. *The Devil's Plantation* was a name given to them in East Anglia, especially clumps of Scots pine trees that were markers for cattle drovers' tracks.

In Scandinavia, early Christian legislation forbade people specifically from worshipping at groves, stones, in sanctuaries, and at places designated *stafgarðr* ("fenced enclosures") (Olsen 1966, 280). Elder trees often grow in such places, and veneration of this kind of tree was banned as a "heathendom" in England by King Edgar (ca. 944–975; reigned 959–975). Also, in his laws known as the *Dooms*, Knut (Canute), king of Denmark and England from 1020 to 1023 CE, asserted: "Heathendom is . . . the worship of heathen gods, and the sun or moon, fire or flood, fountains or rocks or forest trees of any sort" (Larson 1912, 276). Pagan worship continued much longer in eastern Europe. According to *Helmold's Chronicle* (1156), the grove at Stargard in Pomerania (modern-day Poland), sacred to the Slavonic god Prove, was enclosed by a fence (Váňa 1992, 178, fig. 44). In Britain, medieval stone crosses, where they remain, and twentieth-century war memorials were erected on such pieces of ground, continuing their spiritual status. In the countryside of Poland to this day, one can see crosses by the roadside and at "no man's land" triangles, with fences around them.

In Anglo-Saxon England, temporary enclosures for judicial single combat and even full-scale battles were cut off from the everyday world by a fence made of hazel (*Corylus avellana*). All round the place of combat, hazel-poles were set up, marking the perimeter of the enhazelled ground where the battle was to be fought. The area was chosen, and the poles were set up by the heralds in charge of the proceedings. Once a battlefield had been enhazelled, it was dishonorable for an army to scour (pillage) the country around it until after the battle was won. The decisive Battle of Brunanburh, fought in the year 937 CE, in which English forces under King Æthelstan defeated the much larger confederation army composed of Scottish, Welsh, Irish, Danish, and Norwegian units, was a formal challenge held upon an enhazelled field.

28

Trees, *Temenoi*, and Places of the Ancestral Spirits

If you do nothing else, whenever you can, plant a tree.
It will be there when you are gone.
—HARRY W. SMITH (1867–1944),
DESIGNER OF PEASHOLM PARK,
SCARBOROUGH

The tree is the most apparent symbol of the Cosmic Axis: a living being linking the underworldly soil through the middleworld suface to the upperworld of the air. As a living being, it exists within a specific time, having been born from the seed, growing through to maturity, reproducing, living to old age, and then dying. The lifespan of many trees are several times as long as those of human beings. Also, unlike a human, who is a unique individual, trees can be sustained and regenerated by cuttings, and even in some species, by suckers arising from the roots when the trunk has been cut down. The tree is a world in itself, providing shelter for many animals and birds, also algae, fungi, lichens, and epiphytic and parasitic plants. When the tree dies or is killed, it is transformed into fuel and material for practitioners of woodcraft, carpenters, joiners, cabinet makers, and instrument-makers. These skilled craftspeople who make things from wood know that each kind of tree has its own unique characteristics.

Trees have also been sacred in their own right and as an integral part of sacred places. Classical writers tell how in ancient Greece some shrines evolved from sacred trees. The oracle at Dodona was a tree

Sunbeams through the forest in Schwarzwald, Germany

whose leaves were used in divination. The Celtic Druids of Gaul and the British Isles held *nemetona* or holy groves of trees in awe. They were sacred places entered only by members of the priesthood. In his *Pharsalia*, the Roman author Lucan (39–65 CE), writes of the Druids of Gaul who lived in deep groves and remote woodlands: "They worship the gods in the woods without using temples," noted his scholiast (Jones and Pennick 1995, 81). The modern place-name element *nemet-* (or Nympton in western England) denotes the site where a Celtic holy grove once existed. The goddesses Nemetona and Rigonemetis are named as the indwelling protectors of sacred groves.

Individual sacred trees were a feature of holy places throughout pre-Christian Europe. Like the nemetona they were protected from the outer world by consecrated fences, and their indwelling spirits were honored with rites and ceremonies. But if trees are held sacred by one religion, another may decide to destroy them, so incoming conquerors or missionaries cut down the holy trees of the peoples they subdue. In Ireland, Saint Patrick and his followers felled the trees venerated by the elder faith. The name of the city of Derry recalls the sacred oak grove that grew there in the days of the Druids (*dair* being the Irish word for "oak"). In Gaul, Saint Martin of Tours destroyed sacred trees, and the holy oak tree of the Old Prussians at Romowe, on the southern shore of the Baltic, was felled in person by the Grand Master of the Deutsche Ritterorden (Teutonic Knights) during their crusade against the Indigenous religion there in the thirteenth century. But in other places, changes to religion or regime were not so harsh to ancient sacred trees. In Britain, ancient yew trees exist in the enclosures around many ancient churches. Some are very old indeed, and it is likely that they are even older than the Christian religion at those places. Perhaps they are the trees of the elder faith, or descendents of them.

The Celtic *temenos* was the central place of collective worship that appears to have been derived from the sacred grove. It was an enclosure, generally square or rectangular, defined by ditches, in which ceremonial gatherings took place. In central Europe, these enclosures are known

Sacred tree with image of Our Lady, Fraueninsel, Chiemsee, Bavaria, Germany

as *Viereckschanzen* ("four-corner ramparts"). They contained sacred stones, ceremonial fireplaces, a tree or pole, and wells and shafts for ritual offerings. Compressed earth at such places attests to ceremonial perambulation or dances around the spirit tree or post that was central point. The May tree or Maypole is clearly part of the same tradition.

The Wildwood

The wildwood was the primal woodland that grew after the ice retreated at the end of the last Ice Age. Civilization in central and northern Europe was originally represented by villages that were founded in clearings in the forest made for the cultivation of crops. The greenwood was felled and the soil was plowed. The wood of the trees was fashioned into buildings, utensils, tools, and vehicles. The edge of the woodland became a boundary, a frontier, which acquired many

The charcoal burners Cook and Bowtle at their lodge in the forest of Essex, England, ca. 1900

symbolic meanings. This frontier was the transition point where human control began and ended. Symbolically, the wildwood is the untamed opposite of the civilized, settled world of organized humanity. The careful control of cultivated land contrasts with the uncontrolled realm of the wildwood; civilization is cut from the woodland but is always confronted by uncontrolled Nature. There is a tension between cultivated land and the uncultivated wildwood; any settlement abandoned by humans will soon revert to woodland within a few years.

Cultivated land and the wildwood represent a duality: between domesticated animals and wild animals, and between sown crops or plants—which are literally "planted" in tilled soil by human hands—and vegetation, which grows unplanted according to its own biological nature. The wildwood served as a place of escape for fugitives and criminals, for the rule of law of cultivated land contrasts with the lawless woods. Brigands, outlaws, and those on the run found refuge in the wildwood. The famous legend of Robin Hood and his Merry Men tells how they lived hidden in the forests of Barnsdale and Sherwood in northern England, and in his *The Wind in the Willows* (1908) the pagan author Kenneth Grahame (1859–1932) located the destructive opponents of his riverbank animals in the Wild Wood.

The spirits of the wildwood were recognized in ancient times: Abnoba, goddess of the Schwarzwald (the Black Forest, south Germany), was equated by the Romans with Diana. Vosegus was god of the forests of the Vosges mountains in Alsace. Medieval carvings of foliated human heads, known today as the "Green Man," are believed to be personifications of the vegetation-spirits of the greenwood. Phytomorphic foliated masks that are known from Roman metalwork and architecture appear to be representations of Sylvanus, tutelary god of forests, fields, and farming. In Oxford, the medieval shrine of the patron saint, Frideswide, has heads of the saint surrounded by forest leaves. Legend tells how, in Anglo-Saxon times, she was a Christian princess who fled forced marriage to a Pagan lord and sought refuge in the trackless wildwood.

The medieval European wildwood was haunted by the Woodwose (Anglo-Saxon *wuduwāsa*), a wild man of the woods covered in leaves and with long hair. In myth, the Wild Man may be a child abandoned in the wildwood but found and nurtured by bears or other animals. The Wild Man may be a cursed man put under a magic spell or otherwise driven to madness, as in the Arthurian story of Sir Tristram. In eastern Europe, the wildwood holds the *leshy* (Polish *leszy* or Czech *leši*), a forest-living trickster portrayed either as a man with goat's legs and hoofs, or as a gray-bearded man wearing a cone-bearing green cloak. It leads travelers astray, sweeping snow over their footprints so that they cannot retrace their steps (Anglickienė 2013, 137). Traditional camouflage worn by huntsmen and outlaws is also part of this current, the Lincoln green clothing of Robin Hood being a classic example.

Occasionally, the inchoate denizens of the wildwood may cross the borderline and impinge upon civilized society. Incursions by wild animals, brigands, and outlaws are always a threat. Beings from the wildwood may be captured and exhibited as examples of the "Other." *Valentine and Orson* was a mummers' play performed widely in northern Europe. The story tells how twin brothers were abandoned in the wildwood and left to die. However, Valentine was rescued, being found by nobles and brought up as a chivalrous knight, while Orson, referred to as Sansnom ("No-name"), was raised by bears and grew up to be a Wild Man of the Woods. The story is based around their encounter when Orson is captured and their later adventures. The contrast between nature (the barbarism of Orson) and civilization (the order of Valentine) reflects the dangerous, lawless, untamed wildwood as contrasted with the chivalric refinement of courtly life.

To lose oneself in the wildwood is to lose one's mind. In the wildwood, one becomes nameless, *Sansnom*—that is, without identity. It is a reversion to the state one had before one recognized one's identity. The story of Sir Tristram likewise sees him flee into the wildwood where he loses his mind and wanders naked as a Wild Man. Rescued from his plight, he is brought back unrecognized and takes some time before he resumes his identity. Similarly, in the year 573 CE, the Celtic bard Myrddin Wyllt (Merlin the Wild) was a witness on the losing side of the carnage at the Battle of Arfderydd in what is now southern Scotland. He lost his mind with grief and fled into the great Caledonian Forest where he lived among the wild animals and acquired the gift of prophecy.

There is a legend in northern Europe of a vast hall in a clearing somewhere deep in the trackless woods. Called *Le Pavillon des Chasseurs* in France and the *Jägerhalle* in Germany, this "Foresters' Hall" or "Woodmen's Hall" is a kind of Valhalla for the shades of departed foresters. The wildwood surrounding this eldritch hall teems with wildlife that includes now-extinct European animals such as the aurochs and others such as the wild boar, wisent (bison), and elk, whose range is now restricted to small areas of the continent. The hall contains the spirits of those who once were great hunters—but only those who hunted for necessity, not for sport or the pleasure of killing.

The Hunters' Hall recalls the great woodlands that once existed right across central and northern Europe, and the abundant species of animals and birds that dwelt there, now destroyed. The wildwood was destroyed because its animals were hunted to extinction and its timber similarly was exploited for use and profit. In North America, railroads were built through the primal forest. The trees were felled to prepare the trackbed; they served as railroad ties, fuel for the steam locomotives, and as building material for the log cabins of the settlers. Trees also became telegraph poles set up alongside the track to carry wires for communication. As modernity marched onward, the wildwood declined.

29

Numinous Places in the Land

All places are meaningful, but places where something human happened—or is believed to have happened—are uniquely specific. They are landmarks associated with particular stories or mythological and historical events. As the Irish writer James Joyce (1882–1941) noted, "Places remember events." Whatever the event and whoever the personage, the place is made notable and special by the interweaving of topography, history, religion, myth, and the institutions that carry on and commemorate the event in observances, rituals, and performances.

Examples and Manifestations of Interpretation

Human language describes, but it is essentially metaphorical. Whenever we read or hear what people say about things, we must always be aware of the vast diversity of opinion and theory upon the meaning and description of them. In order to delve into the principles that underlie them, we must distinguish the exoteric from the esoteric. The name *rhinoceros* may appear impressive, but it is only made up from Greek words meaning "nose" and "horn"—thus, a "nose-horn," which does not sound so grand. Indeed, in German the animal is called a *Nashorn*. The nature of a rhinoceros is something other than the names humans use to describe it. The subtle exoteric perception of things varies even between closely related cultures. The following example is relevant in the approach of the Way of the Eight Winds to aspects of its geomantic subject matter, which are bewilderingly confused by disparate terminology, theories, and belief systems. Things that appear straightforward, such as the typical English "landscape garden" surrounding a stately mansion, can have a complex history that remains almost unrecognized (see the discussion of feng shui below).

Metaphors of Earth Energies

> *We live in the midst of invisible forces whose effects alone we perceive.*
> —DION FORTUNE (1890–1946)

Enthusiasts for "earth energies" frequently claim that their personal speculations are the definitive definition of these subtle powers. The Way of the Eight Winds recognizes that there is a multiplicity of traditional understandings, some from antiquity or traditional cultures, and others framed in scientific terminology. Each different descriptor has subtle differences from every other one. It is only through a recognition of their symbolic nature that they can be reconciled as various human responses to the unseen.

The "influence of surroundings" that Charles Leadbeater described in 1909 has been viewed in recent years as coming from what were described as "telluric currents" or the "earth spirit" and are now called "earth energies." But "earth energy" is yet another modern metaphor based upon scientific descriptions of various electromagnetic emanations or states of matter, including magnetism, microwaves, X-rays, radiation, and plasma, though not specifically any of them. But earlier metaphors also exist, based upon prescientific and poetic worldviews.

These currents that streamed across the earth or just below the surface through the "veins of the countryside" are part of many visions of the landscape, traditional, speculative, and fanciful. They point to some truth, but in themselves are *metaphors* for the ineffable.

All of these are, in one way or another, metaphors for flow—that which cannot be grasped. Some are connected with the breath, such as the Greek *pneuma*, breath/spirit/soul, the "wind of the spirit." The equivalent of this in East Anglian tradition is *spirament* or *sprowl*. Another metaphor is the "universal plastic medium" or *æther*. The Indian word *prana* (Sanskrit for "breath" or "life force") has been used to describe this power, as has the Northern Tradition word *önd*. It is related to the "animal magnetism" of the discoverer of hypnosis, Franz Anton Mesmer (1734–1815); the *odyle* or "Odic force" of Karl Ludwig von Reichenbach (1788–1869), which he described as "an imponderable force allied to magnetism"; the *Archée* (universal cosmic force) of Joseph Saint-Yves d'Alveydre (1848–1909); and also the *orgone* of Wilhelm Reich (1897–1957). A book published in 1871, titled *The Coming Race*, introduced a fictional force called *vril* to the public. Written by Edward Bulwer-Lytton (1803–1873), it was an early science-fiction novel and a bestseller. "Vril" was soon taken literally, and the concept was absorbed into speculations to the point where Bulwer-Lytton was later hailed as an adept of the occult sciences. For example, in 1880 *The Mahatma Letters* to the Theosophist A. P. Sinnett (1840–1921) from his Indian correspondents referred to vril as "the common property of races now extinct" (Barker 2021, 2). From the late nineteenth century, Western anthropologists wrote of the power called *mana*, from the Polynesian and Micronesian tradition, where it was described as "the force that permeates everything." References to mana became popular in the wake of *The Coming Race*. The word was long in use by anthropologists and occultists alike. The Native American *manitou* of the Algonquians and *orenda* of the Iroquois were also considered parallels of mana.

Chinese *feng shui*, meaning "wind and water," refers to both metaphors and has its own "energy" *ch'i* or *qi* (or the Taoist *wu wei*, which has been described as "sparkly life energy"). In 1905 Helena von Poseck (1859–1953) wrote of the "evil breath" blocked by Chinese geomants. This was not human breath, she remarked, but "the dreaded breath is of a more mysterious and spiritual nature" (von Poseck 1905, 368). The Theosophists called this energy "etheric current," and Leadbeater explained (1900, 112): "There are great etheric currents constantly sweeping over the surface of the earth from pole to pole in volume which makes their power as irresistable as the rising tide." In *The Fairy-Faith in Celtic Countries*, W. Y. Evans-Wentz (1878–1965) recounted that (1911, 33): "an Irish mystic, and seer of great power, with whom I have often discussed the Fairy-Faith in its details, regards 'fairy paths' or 'fairy passes' as actual magnetic arteries, so to speak, through which circulates the earth's magnetism."

In his 1966 work on the Chartres Cathedral, Louis Charpentier (1905–1979) described the *woivre* as a poetic image of telluric "currents that 'snake' through the ground" (Charpentier 1972, 20). This is in turn linked with the "serpent power" that was called "a flow of current" and "terrestrial magnetism" by John Michell (1933–2009) when describing the Chinese *qi* of feng shui that powered the "dragon paths" or *lung-mei* (Michell 1969, 73), which the twentieth-century British town planner Patrick Abercrombie (1879–1957) had called the "local currents of the cosmic breath" (Abercrombie 1933, 230). Another poetic metaphor came from the Spanish poet Federico García Lorca (1898–1936). He wrote of *duende*, originally the name of a terrestrial dwarf but also a word that also describes an exceptional quality of passion or inspiration. According to García Lorca, it is a mysterious force that everyone feels, but no philosopher has explained. *Duende* is another word that has come to be associated with specific powerful places.

Early twentieth-century water diviners (dowsers), seeking scientific terminology, named their art *dynamic activity* and then *radiesthesia*. The celebrated French dowser the Abbé Alexis Mermet (1866–1937), who patented a special dowsing pendulum, claimed that the human sympathetic nervous system picked up "rays" emanating from a radiesthetic field (1959, 39): "everything takes place as if all bodies emitted undulations and radiations." In the early 1960s, Watkinsian ley-line enthusiasts merged with UFO investigators who claimed that these lights in the sky had been observed to travel in straight lines across the country. Believing them to be alien spacecraft, they postulated that the leys emanated a subtle energy that the aliens could use to power their interplanetary craft. What power they used for flying in interplanetary space was not stated.

Dowsers then began to discover ley lines and some suggested that they could be used to "heal the earth" or be manipulated to quell social disorder. These ideas originated in Germany, where Ernst Hartmann (1915–1992) and Manfred Curry (1899–1953) had dowsed *Erdstrahlen* (Earth radiation or Earth rays) that they claimed formed net- or grid-patterns across the Earth's surface (Hartmann's grid was a different size from Curry's, of course). Erdstrahlen, it was believed, caused "geopathic stress," which led to harmful effects on people living in such places. Piezoelectric effects of geological fault lines in the rocks below were suggested as generators of "earth lights" that were not visiting alien spacecraft but natural phenomena (Devereux 1982). In the twenty-first century the theory became current that these "earth lights" are composed of "self-illuminated intelligent plasma," which causes "consciousness interaction fields" that produce the effects once attributed to fairies on their ride along their trackways (Little and Collins 2022, 200). As common beliefs change over the years, new parables and metaphors emerge that are framed in the language of the era, just as "the Force" from the 1976 movie *Star Wars* and its many spinoffs has fed into the mix. Those looking for scientific explanations follow Elbert Hubbard (1856–1915) in the belief that "the supernatural is the natural not yet understood."

The concept of lines of energy exists in the established churches, too. In 1906 the Roman Catholic prelate Monseigneur Robert Hugh Benson (1871–1914) wrote a piece titled "In the Convent Chapel" in his devotional work, *The Light Invisible*. This story tells of the interaction between a praying nun and the Tabernacle of the Reserved Sacrament (consecrated host) in the chapel. Benson likened the link to a drive band between wheels in a factory or the electric wire between telegraphists. He presented this transmissible force as lines that carried emanations for good across the world. Benson wrote (1906, 120): "There ran out from this peaceful chapel lines of spiritual power that lost themselves in the distance, bewildering in their profusion and in the intensity of their hidden fire."

A religious investigation into "earth energies" appeared from the Church of England in 1972, which approached them from a Bensonian direction. The findings were in a report titled *Exorcism*, commissioned by Dr. Robert Mortimer (1902–1976), then bishop of Exeter (Devon, England). The commission was chaired and the report edited by Dom Robert Petitpierre (1903–1982), the leading Anglican Benedictine exorcist at the time. Ecumenically, the commission included a leading Jesuit exorcist from the Roman Catholic Church. Though it was hardly noticed outside churchly circles at the time of publication, it is a remarkable document with a bearing on practical geomancy.

The report is a manual of exorcism of people and places, with analysis and recommendations for the Anglican clergy. Of most interest to geomants is its opinion on place. The bishop's commission distinguished three kinds of forces, which it suggested may be operating at any given place: those that are wholly human; those that are impersonal; and those that are demonic. They claimed that there were certain places where psychic disturbances occurred. They called places exhibiting this phenomenon "strained" by the effects. These are places where apparitions of the departed, poltergeists, aspirations, levitations, and other psychic phenomena are perceived to occur. The commission concluded that these phenomena can be "place memories," manifested at places that bear the psychic trace of some earlier personal action, thereby repeating the event in some way. It claimed that these are rarely more than 400 years old.

The commission asserted that some happenings it has investigated were "haunts" deliberately instigated by magicians, and they said that houses or sites used for "sexual misbehavior" also generate these energies. It is an identical process that Benson ascribed to his nun, but with other results. They also determined that an office of an organization dedicated to greed or domination can act as a "dipersal center" for such psychic disturbances. Finally, what the commission described as "demonic interference" was said to be common on desecrated sites such as ruined sanctuaries. This report remains the major thinking on what we call geomancy in the Church of England, though it is rarely mentioned in public. It is yet another metaphor that has attempted to explain "earth energies."

30

Feng Shui

Chinese feng shui became popular in the West from the 1970s onward, and it had an especial vogue in the late 1990s. But it has a much longer history in the West, having been instrumental in altering the British landscape in the eighteenth century. There are many schools of feng shui, which have different approaches. Some use a specialized geomantic compass called a *lo pan*, while others are based upon the analysis of landforms or the astrological influences. Within these schools are many lineages and currents, handed on from generation to generation.

Feng Shui in the West

The history of Chinese geomancy, feng shui, is also often misunderstood. Feng shui has been known in the West since at least the sixteenth century, when Jesuit missionaries to China began to bring back accounts and artifacts to the West. A feng-shui compass was exhibited in London in 1600. The Danish antiquarian Ole Worm (1588–1654) owned one and it was put on show in his "Cabinet of Curiosities" at Copenhagen. In 1655, after his death, an engraving of it was published by his son at Leiden in Holland in *Museum Wormianum* (Golvers 1994, 331–50). The Latin commentary about the compass included a description of the

Chinese *ba gua* geomantic mirror with the
eight trigrams and corresponding constellations

eight trigrams, the first to be published in Europe. Later books such as *Feng-Shui* (1873) by the reverend Ernst Johann Eitel (1838–1908) also had relatively detailed descriptions of the compass, so its meaning and function were not unknown in Europe from then onward, though it is clear that the Compass School was not the main inspiration of European landscape design influenced by feng shui.

In 1685 William Temple (1628–1699) wrote an essay, "Upon the Gardens of Epicurus: or, Of Gardening," in which he referred to irregular planting:

> for there may be other forms wholly irregular that may, for aught I know, have more beauty than any of the others; but they must owe it to some extraordinary dispositions of nature in the seat. . . . Something of this I have seen in some places, but heard more of

it from others who have lived much among the Chinese; a people, whose way of thinking seems to lie as wide of ours in Europe, as their country does. (Faber 1983, 142)

Temple noted, however, that although the Chinese landscape laid out was "without any order or disposition of parts that shall be commonly or easily observed . . . and, though we have hardly any notion of this sort of beauty[,] yet they have a particular word to express it, and, where they find it hit their eye at first sight, they say the *Sharawadgi* is fine or is admirable" (Faber 1983, 142). In other words, it was not random: there were principles, but these were not easy for the noninitiate to see.

Temple's essay was the beginning of the reaction against straight-line planning that led to what was called the "English Garden," which was actually the result of feng-shui principles being applied in a European context. Writing in 1712 in the London magazine *The Spectator*, Joseph Addison (1672–1719) explained:

> Writers, who have given us an account of *China*, tell us, the Inhabitants of that Country laugh at the Plantations of our *Europeans*, which are laid by the Rule and Line; because, they say, any one may place Trees in equal Rows and uniform Figures. They choose rather to show a Genius in Works of this Nature, and therefore always conceal the art by which they direct themselves. (issue of June 25, pp. 101–2)

Feng shui also influenced the eighteenth-century British landscape gardener and architect William Chambers (1722–1796). Chambers traveled extensively in China and absorbed the principles of feng shui, which he applied to his gardens and buildings in England. His book *A Dissertation on Oriental Gardening* (1772) contained the principles of feng shui, which British writers since William Temple had called *sharawadgi*, a word probably derived from Japanese, meaning "not being symmetrical" (Faber 1983, 142). Following Temple, Chambers bewailed the fact that there were no skilled practitioners of the art in Britain (1773, 3): "Is it not singular then, that an Art with which a considerable part of our enjoyments is so universally connected, should have no skilled professors in our quarter of the world?"

The "English Garden" landscape design became so well established by the nineteenth century that its feng-shui origin was almost forgotten. In the nineteenth century, writings on feng shui ignored the fact that it had been incorporated into the British landscape for more than a century. So, the English writer Charles Dickens (1812–1870) is said to have followed feng shui. When on his travels he always moved his bed into a proper north–south orientation, wherever he slept (Ackroyd 1990, 222). In 1873, the reverend Eitel, a Protestant Christian cleric who had been sent by the London Missionary Society to China, published *Feng-Shui, or the Rudiments of Natural Science in China*. Chapter 4 of his book is titled "The Breath of Nature," and in chapter 3 he describes the meanings of the rings on the geomantic compass (Eitel 1873, 33–44). The earlier uses of feng shui in Europe seem to have been unknown to Eitel and other writers of the period. At the end of the nineteenth century, the doyen of the Spiritual Arts and Crafts, the architect and designer William Richard Lethaby, made reference to aspects of feng shui in his highly influential book *Architecture, Mysticism and Myth* (1891).

In the early twentieth century, articles were published in English on feng shui in China in *The East of Asia Magazine* by Western authors such as Helena von Poseck and James Hutson. Around the same time, leading architects of the Arts and Crafts movement—including Hugh Mackay Baillie Scott (1865–1945) and the Cambridge University professor of architecture, Edward Schroeder Prior (1852–1932)—were very aware of the location of their buildings, constructed so as to harmonize with their sites and possess a soul (Baillie Scott 1906, 73–75). The aforementioned town planner Patrick Abercrombie incorporated some feng-shui principles into his work. In his 1933 book *Town and Country Planning*, he quoted a Chinese text (uncredited) that described the planner as a person who was able to reconcile various different elements according to the "local currents of the cosmic breath," and added that while such esoteric principles were not appropriate in their entirety in modern practice, "it should be possible to evolve a system of landscape design which will be authoritative enough to prevent brutal outrage on one hand, and a misguided attempt at bogus naturalism on the other" (Abercrombie 1933, 230–32).

When Plymouth's city center was rebuilt to his collaborative designs with James Paton Watson (1898–1979) following its wartime devastation in 1940–1941, they made a completely new street plan based on an axial avenue, a north–south "via sacra" toward the sea. Called Armada Way (recalling the Spanish invasion fleet defeated in 1588), the main council offices on it were located at a place determined by feng-shui principles. The ancient quarter called the Barbican, which was relatively undamaged, retained its sixteenth-century street plan. According to the commentator David Matless (1993, 168), Abercrombie presented feng shui as a doctrine of intervention, seeking an evolving functional aesthetic harmony between humanity and the environment. Of course, when built, the architecture was 1950s concrete modernism, neither traditional vernacular Western English nor Chinese in materials or style.

Fusui (feng-shui) temple in Peasholm Park, Scarborough, Yorkshire, England, designed by Harry W. Smith, 1911

Many of the British landscape architects from the eighteenth to the twentieth centuries had fully integrated feng shui into their practice. Apart from the occasional pagoda, pavilion, or "Chinese Temple," their work did not look Chinese because the essential principles rather than the outward form were followed. Subsequently, as at Stowe in Buckinghamshire, the Chinese-style buildings have been demolished while the European Classical ones remain. The largest remaining antique pseudo-Chinese building in Britain is Sir William Chambers's 1761 Pagoda at Kew Gardens in southwest London, a monument to an earlier recognition of feng shui. In 1911 in his design of Peasholm Park at the seaside town of Scarborough in northern England, Harry W. Smith (1867–1944) applied *fusui* (feng-shui) principles to the design of "Japanese" public gardens that also survive with oriental buildings on an artificial island in a serpentine lake. Similarly, more recent Chinese geomantc buildings exist in a park at Mannheim in Germany.

Japanese geomantic compass

31

Crossing the Borderlines

There are seven kinds of boundaries: physical, cultural, legal, conceptual, sacred, magical, and eldritch.

All living things exist because they are separated from everything else by physical-biological bodily boundaries that defend them against destruction. The membranes that enclose the smallest unicellular organisms are boundaries that ensure their existence. To humans, borders create real psychological and psychic effects. Conceptual boundaries are often couched in binary opposites: Us and Them; the sacred and the profane; the sheep and the goats; citizens and foreigners; native and exotic species. These boundaries, imaginary and real, are a language perceived through codes. We construct identity by examining differences and embodying them in boundaries.

The boundary itself has physicality—it is the contact point between two different things contiguous with one another. The nature of the two different things may be defined in many ways, according to the seven categories listed above. The contact between two different things at the boundary does not preclude interaction. In the case of enclosures, whatever their size may be, the edge between them creates an interaction of the inside and the outside. The inside and the outside exist within the same space; it is only the boundary that divides them.

Boundary marker of Saint Vedast Parish,
city of London, 1725

British National Borders, the Debatable Lands, and the Landsker

Great Britain has a number of ancient borders between the three countries that exist on the island—England, Scotland, and Wales. The 160-mile-long border between England and Wales dates from around the eighth century CE; some of it is Offa's Dyke, a linear earthwork built on the orders of the King of Mercia, Offa the Great (740–796; reigned 757–796). Part of this dyke is earlier, having been radiocarbon dated to between 430 and 652 CE. The border was fixed in 1536 and finalized in the Local Government Act of 1972, when the disputed county of Monmouthshire was included in Wales.

The border between Scotland and England, 96 miles long, was defined in 1237 by the Treaty of York when King Henry III of England (1207–1272; reigned 1216–1272) and Alexander II of Scotland (1241–1286; reigned 1249–1286) agreed it. But one section, called the Debatable Lands, remained unresolved until 1552 when a Commission of Scots and English adjudicators divided this territory between the two countries. From Esk to Sark, English and Scottish workmen built the Scots' Dyke, two ditches in parallel with the earth from each making a bank in the middle. On either side of this double ditch and bank, thorn hedges were planted. Paths in the fields on either side were made crooked, with unexpected bends to prevent a practical line of fire along them toward the other side.

Two different human-made landscapes run up against one another in Pembrokeshire, west Wales. Once called "Little England within Wales," part of the county was settled by English and Flemish people around the year 1100 as a result of the Norman conquest of England in 1066. The area of settlement was laid out according to Anglo-Norman principles of land ownership and use, while the remaining Welsh part continued the traditional Celtic principles. The imprecise boundary between the two different systems, which was not a wall or fence or even marked on the ground, nevertheless remains. It is called the Landsker Line.

Industrial Boundaries: Barbwire and Barbarism

In the nineteenth century, metal production and manufacture on an industrial scale enabled the construction of a new kind of boundary. One of the most useful inventions that came out of industrial Norwich, the capital city of East Anglia, England, was chicken wire. From the textile weaving industry came an application of weaving iron wire, devised in 1844 by Charles Barnard (1804–1871), and chicken wire was born. This enabled boundaries to be erected to keep small livestock, such as poultry or rabbits, in enclosures, and give some protection against predators such as foxes. This was a useful product, later expanded into more sturdy chain-link fencing, that eventually created the longest fences in the world. Rabbits were introduced to Australia in the early nineteenth century, and after only a few years had multiplied to the extent where they were considered a pest. The wire mesh that originated in Norwich

Behind the chicken wire,
Dry Drayton (Cambridgeshire, England)

was used on a monumental scale in Australia to prevent various species, introduced and indigenous, from living in sheep-farming areas. Rabbits, dingoes (wild dogs), and emus were exterminated in the areas inside the fences.

The Wild Dog Barrier Fence, or Dingo Fence, intended to keep wild dogs out of southeastern Australia, was constructed in the 1880s and eventually ran from the Eyre Peninsula to Jimbour, 3,488 miles away with only a few breaks at transport crossings. State organizations were set up to survey, construct, and maintain these monumental borderlines. The fence built by the Darling Downs–Moreton Rabbit Board on the Queensland–New South Wales border, included both wire mesh and barbwire. The State Barrier Fence of Western Australia, otherwise called the Vermin Fence, was the result of a Royal Commission convened to discuss the problem of rabbits. This fence was constructed between

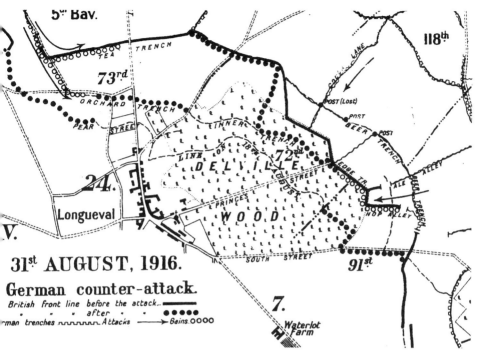

Boundaries in World War I trench warfare, Delville Wood (Loungueval, France), on August 31, 1916. The author's great uncle, Sidney Dale, was killed in that wood at the age of twenty-two. His body was never found.

1901 and 1907. Others were built later in Western Australia, including a north–south section built in 1950 that at 1,139 miles long was the longest unbroken fence in the world (Crawford 1969; Broomhall 1991).

The invention of barbwire (aka barbed wire) was instrumental in enclosing the land of the United States that was formerly unbounded territory traversed by Native Americans and indigenous wild animals, most notably the buffalo. Devised just after the end of the Civil War by several inventors including Louis Francis Janin (1837–1914) and Lucien B. Smith (1839–1891), it was perfected and patented by Joseph Farwell Glidden (1813–1906) of DeKalb, Illinois. Barbwire was the industrial version of thorn hedges and bramble thickets that controlled livestock in the traditional landscape of Europe. Originally

Barbwire on the Western Front, World War I—artist's impression of combat in the trenches of the Battle of the Somme, 1916

intended to keep cattle within defined tracts of land, it soon proved useful as a defender of borders, being rolled out on the southern border with Mexico to keep out people as well as livestock. In 1895, at the Battle of Magul in Mozambique, southern Africa, the Portuguese Army first used barbwire as a defense during a war against the Indigenous inhabitants of the colony. Later it was used in trench warfare in the hostilities between Russia and Japan in southern China in 1905. But its greatest use was in the fortified front lines in France and Belgium in World War I (1914–1918), where vast entanglements of barbwire defended the trenches, redoubts, and bunkers from attack by the enemy. Huge numbers of men on both sides of the conflict died entangled in barbwire amid the machine-gun fire and artillery bombardments. An ironic British soldiers' song of the time, "Hanging on the Old Barbed Wire," has as its final verse:

> *If you want to find the old battalion,*
> *I know where they are.*
> *If you want to find the old battalion,*
> *I know where they are.*
> *They're hanging on the old barbed wire.*
> *I've seen them, I've seen them,*
> *Hanging on the old barbed wire.*
> *I've seen them, I've seen them,*
> *Hanging on the old barbed wire.*

And of course barbwire is notorious as the means for millions to be held prisoner behind it in the concentration camps and gulags of twentieth-century and later tyrannies.

Walls

The Great Wall of China; the Devil's Dyke, the Wansdyke, and Hadrian's Wall in England; Offa's Dyke delimiting England and Wales; the Roman *Limes* in western Germany; and the Danevirke (Dane-Work) in Schleswig-Holstein, northern Germany, are all ancient linear earthworks and walls constructed to define borders and defend territory against outsiders. Hand-built by slaves and conscripted peasants, many such walls still define territory long after their use has passed. At the time it was constructed, part of the Great Wall of China was deemed to have had a geomantically detrimental effect, having destroyed the veins of the earth.

A defensive boundary: the ruins of the medieval town wall of Conwy, Wales

The Iron Curtain that emerged after World War II was a notional barrier between Eastern Europe, under communist control, and democratic Western Europe. In 1945, Germany, which had been destroyed in the war, lost part of its territory to Poland and the Soviet Union, and the remaining land was occupied by the victorious allies. Germany did not exist as a state at all until 1948, when it was divided along the line between the Soviet occupation in the east and the French, British, and American-occupied territory in the west. Two states came into being, the eastern one with a communist government under Soviet control: the Deutsche Demokratische Republik (German Democratic Republic aka East Germany). In 1952 the East German government constructed a fence with barbwire and observation towers along its entire border with the Bundesrepublik Deutschland (the German Federal Republic aka West Germany). This was not intended to keep people out, but to keep them in. There was a 500-meter-wide zone inside the fence from which all inhabitants were forcibly removed, and all buildings demolished. Further in, there was an exclusion zone in which only those deemed loyal to the regime were permitted to live. It was the physical manifestation of the "Iron Curtain" that divided the European continent. It all went down in 1989.

Similarly, individual cities have been divided by walls and barbwire. At the time of writing, there are walls through the cities of Belfast in Northern Ireland and Nicosia in Cyprus, intended to keep mutually hostile communities apart. But the Berlin Wall was the most notorious of these intracity walls. In 1945 the city of Berlin was occupied by the Allies and divided into four zones: the Soviet zone in the east and the Western Allies' three zones in the west. By 1961, the East German authorities were so worried about their citizens "defecting" to the west that a wall was constructed to prevent the citizens of East Germany from escaping into West Berlin. Finally, in 1989, along with the fence that divided the two Germanies, it was torn down. But not before hundreds of people had been killed attempting to cross it. During the "Cold War," Checkpoint Charlie was from 1945 a notorious crossing point for the border between West and East Berlin; later, from 1961, it became a small gap in the notorious Berlin Wall. It was a perilous place where any mistake in one's behavior could lead to dire consequences, for border guards are trained to exercise paranoid suspicion of even the most innocuous travelers. Now it is a curiosity of history, and the former border is indistinguishable in most places. It is as if it was never there. It is an example of the transitoriness of human-made borders.

Streets, Boulevards, and Railways as Boundaries

In London, the fashionable Regent Street was designed by John Nash (1752–1835) and built in 1811 as an upmarket shopping street. But it also had a less obvious barrier function as the boundary between the poor eastern side, which included the sordid slum district of St Giles, known as the Rookery, and the rich West End where the grand houses of the upper class were situated. Later in the nineteenth century, the Parisian boulevards designed in 1854 by Baron Georges-Eugène Haussmann (1809–1891) served similarly to cut off and enclose areas where different classes lived. Railways driven through cities in the nineteenth century also had the effect of cutting off poor areas from richer ones, and "living on the wrong side of the tracks" became a euphemism for ghettos—areas of poverty and deprivation generically named after the Ghetto, the quarter in medieval Venice where Jews were compelled to live.

Boundaries are not eternal. In the long run, they change. One needs only to look at old maps to see that the boundaries of nation-states have been defined at a certain point in history and then defended as if they had always existed. Over the centuries, territories have expanded and contracted, or even ceased to have national importance. In Europe, former states such as Frisia, Brabant, Savoy, Burgundy, and Catalonia are now subsumed into larger entities. Brabant is split between Belgium and the Netherlands; Frisia between the Netherlands and Germany; and Burgundy between France and Switzerland. Many national boundaries run across and divide formerly unified territories. Lands that were part of subsequently disintegrated empires are now nation-states that generally preserve the boundaries once imposed by their former colonial masters. Most African nations have such borders, as do the states that broke away when the Soviet Union collapsed. Many wars continue to be fought because these borders are disputed by people both inside those more recent nation-states and others outside of them.

Even totally invisible human boundaries nevertheless are real. The house I lived in as a boy was in the London Borough of Holborn, but the pavement and road in front of it was in the Borough of St Pancras. This meant that the refuse collectors from Holborn had to have special dispensation to operate in St Pancras in order to pick up our garbage. The boroughs were a modern version of the parishes, where a particular church had jurisdiction over its own area. The parish marker illustrated here is from the parish of St Vedast in the City of London. It dates from the rebuilding of the city after the Great Fire of 1666, when all boundaries had to be resurveyed.

These are the "borderline cases"—liminal areas that are spiritually on the edge. The Last Chance Saloon in Summer County, Kansas, built in 1869, was the last place cowboys on the trail could drink alcohol before crossing the border into "Indian Territory," where alcohol was prohibited. It has become a metaphor now: "drinking in the Last Chance Saloon." Some state lines are places where bikers riding legally without helmets are forced to don them immediately as they cross the line. And speed limits on roads may change when one crosses into another jurisdiction. In Europe, mobile phone (cellphone) signals immediately display the next country's server immediately as the border is crossed, even though the Schengen Agreement means that people can cross it at will without border guards intervening. Another boundary-derived saying is "You must toe the line." Some sports insist that the ball or bat or foot must be completely over the line—that is, beyond it—while for others being on the line itself is sufficient. Where *do* we draw the line?

Sacred Boundaries

Each temple had its sacred *temenos* around it, an enclosure in which certain profane activities were not permitted because such acts would desecrate the holy space. The warning *"Procul, O procul este, profani"* from the sixth book of Virgil's *Aeneid* told those who were unsanctified

Access points across boundaries are marked by pillars, either holding gates or symbolic, such as Boaz and Jachin in the biblical Temple of Solomon, depicted in an eighteenth-century engraving by John Sturt, and the pillars that echo them at the entrance to the Naval Hospital at Greenwich, London.

to stand aside and not enter the sacred space. Only those who had been purified were fit to enter the temenos.

Seven Stages of Sanctity

The town of Beverley (Yorkshire, England) was a place of sanctuary. Once a fugitive criminal had crossed the town boundary and entered Beverley, then they could claim sanctuary from prosecution and be absolved of their offenses. The shrine at Beverley was accorded its privileges in 937 CE by King Æthelstan (894–939; reigned 924–939) in honor of Saint John of Beverley, who had been buried there two centuries earlier. The town was a Holy City plan, entered through four gates. There were seven zones of increasing sanctity in the Beverley sanctuary. On the four approach roads, a mile and a half from the center, were stone crosses that marked the line of the Outer Bounds, the transition point from the secular world into the sanctuary. Inside the town itself was another boundary, the Second Bounds, also marked by stone crosses. Inside this was the churchyard, in which stood the minster church. This was the third level of sanctity. Once inside the church nave, there were further boundaries to cross: into the chancel, and then into the Sanctuary containing the High Altar. By the High Altar

A sacred enclosure: the shrine of the Black Madonna at Ludwigshafen, Germany

was the Frithstool, a stone seat on which the fugitive had to sit to be freed from prosecution. This was the most sacred of the seven zones of sanctity. Law officers pursuing criminals could still arrest them within the boundaries, but had to pay an ascending toll of fines, depending in which zone of sanctity the arrest took place. The fines doubled up from the first through the succeeding ones until the sixth. If the fugitive had reached the Frithstool, however, and was dragged from it to be arrested, this was not permitted. The person carrying out the arrest at the Frithstool was rendered *bōtlēas* ("irredeemable") for profaning the sanctuary, which meant they were declared outlaw and hunted down without any possibility of sanctuary for themselves. Those who claimed sanctuary by sitting on the Beverley Frithstool had to either live for the rest of their lives within the town boundary or they could swear to abjure the realm (go into exile), when they were given safe passage to the nearest port or the Scottish border.

32

The *Locus Terribilis* and the *Locus Amoenus*

Bad Places—the *Locus Terribilis*

Tradition teaches a spiritual awareness of places humans can and cannot enter. People living a traditional, self-reliant life—without powered machines and the backup of rescue services—have a subtle recognition of all conditions around them. The acknowledgment of debilitating places in the landscape was a feature of traditional life in Scotland and Ireland until the twentieth century. Local traditions always asserted that there are places where human beings were not welcome and ought not to enter. These places are not intrinsically bad, but it is certain that human presence there is inappropriate. The name for such a place is *locus terribilis*. There are many kinds of natural places whose physical characteristics are hostile to prolonged human existence. Some are just physically dangerous. More subtle than these are the spiritually bad places whose character—seen traditionally as an indwelling spirit, the genius loci—is inimical to human presence. In more "New Age" terms, these are seen as harmful energies. Among human-made "bad places" are locations used for the burial of the dead and sites of human violence, murders, atrocities, and battles. They have the potential to make human life there difficult or impossible. For other beings, both spiritual and physical, these places may be good.

Just as it is not very wise to camp in an enclosure around an electricity substation, so equally to enter a locus terribilis is to court fatal peril. To build a house and live on such a spot is even more risky. However, it is only human to wish to explore and transgress, so unknowing, foolhardy, or self-centered people have built upon a locus terribilis. People often build against their better judgment and try to live in places that are not conducive to human life on a sustainable basis. The inevitable catastrophic consequences of their recklessness are recounted in folktale and legend. Dearth and disease, derangement, destruction, and death have fallen upon those who dared to dwell upon those places where we must not be. This is not necessarily because the genii loci have actively punished the transgressors, but because it is a natural consequence of such an action.

In former times, places occupied by hostile spirits or menacing presences were just left alone, but when the land began to be bought and sold as a valuable commodity, the old ways of reverencing places were not kept up. In Ireland and Scotland such hostile places were recognized as the Scots *fainty grund* ("fainting ground") and the Irish *féar gortach* ("hungry grass" or "hunger-stricken earth")—signifying ground where one walking there would suddenly feel faint from no apparent reason. Writing in her *Ancient Legends, Mystic Charms, and Superstitions of Ireland* (1887), Lady Jane Wilde (1821–1896) told of the *Fair-Gortha* (*féar gortach*) or the "hunger-stricken sod," as a locus terribilis where, "if the hapless traveller accidently treads on this grass by the road-side, while passing on a journey, either by night or day, he becomes at once seized with the most extraordinary cravings of hunger and weakness, and unless timely relief is afforded he must certainly die" (1887, II, 69). In Scotland it was deemed necessary to carry a piece of bread in one's pocket when going to such a place, and from Ireland is a record of a woman who always kept some "stir-about" porridge in a pot, ready to feed wayfarers who succumbed to the harmful place close to her cottage (Warrack 1911, 162).

Lady Wilde also wrote of another herb, or fairy grass, called the *Faud Shaughran*, or "stray sod" (1887, II, 68–69):

> [W]hoever treads the path it grows on is compelled by an irresistible impulse to travel on without stopping, all through the night, delirious and restless, over bog and mountain, through hedges and ditches, till wearied and bruised and cut, his garments torn, his hands bleeding, he finds himself in the morning twenty or thirty miles, perhaps, from his own home. And those who fall under this strange influence have all the time the sensation of flying and are utterly unable to pause or turn back or change their career. There is, however, another herb that can neutralize the effects of the *Faud Shaughran*, but only the initiated can utilize its mystic properties.

Getting lost or rather led astray by spectral beings was a hazard of travel in former days. In Wales, the Gwyllion, who appeared as old women, would entice wayfarers away from their mountain roads to their doom (Sykes 1890, 49). In the Fens of East Anglia and Lincolnshire in eastern England, spectral lights—said to be the sprite Will O' the Wisp—enticed travelers from their causeways into creeks and sinkholes, where they drowned. Those who strayed from their path were said to be "Will-led." The reverend R. M. Heanley wrote (1902, 6, 7): "the older labourers still speak with bated breath of the 'Gabblerout' of the Wild Huntsman, and the wandering souls of children who have died without baptism whom he chases, and whom you may see for yourselves as 'willywisps' flitting across the low grounds most nights of the year."

Whenever we find ourselves in Perilous Spaces, we must always be aware and retain our concentration. We must follow the old adage: "Keep within the compass, then you will be sure to avoid the problems that others must endure." Keeping within the compass means not overreaching our bodily space in dangerous situations, thereby losing our balance. This is a teaching that many ignore to their own destruction.

No Man's Land

The term is of English origin. It comes originally from a triangular piece of ground at a trifinium, a place where three roads meet. It was neither part of the road, nor of the land beside the roads, and consequently belonged to no one. These pieces of land share the eldritch quality of the corners of fields and gardens called by names like the Devil's Plantation and the Clootie's Croft. Occasionally, a house was built upon one, which took the name "No Nation Place" or "Republic Cottage," for it was an extraterritorial place in no parish or county. Modernization of the road network has largely destroyed these eldritch triangles. During World War I the name "No Man's Land" was applied to the terrain between the opposing trenches in trench warfare—territory occupied by neither side in the conflict, a life-threatening locus terribilis.

The *Locus Amoenus* and Other Places

Seek Paradise.
—CHALDAEAN ORACLES OF ZOROASTER

The antithesis of the locus terribilis is the *locus amoenus*. European medieval romances tell of a place in this world that is not an otherworldly realm of faërie or the eldritch world, but an earthly paradise. This is the locus amoenus, the "lovely place," which medieval art depicts as an enclosed orchard or garden that grows green all year round, with flowers and fruits, birds and bees. It is otherworldly because the cares of everyday life do not exist there, and its climate is ever temperate. A more ancient version of it is the Garden of Alcinous in *The Odyssey*. Medieval Europe's luxuriant herb gardens belonging to Jewish physicians and

Christian monasteries were a real version of the locus amoenus, where curative plants were grown to heal the sick. The layout of these herb gardens was geomantic, and the patterns of planting recalled the divine order of the Cosmos, as with the legendary locus amoenus.

Legend tells of another non-eldritch "otherworld" that goes by the name of the Earthly Paradise. This is a larger version of the locus amoenus: an entire land of peace, tranquility, and spiritual perfection. The Earthly Paradise is somewhere to be found in this world, but in imprecisely remote locations such as Avalon, Magonia, the Well at the World's End, or the Wood Beyond the World. Some earthly paradises, such as the Irish *Tír na nÓg*, were said to contain a Fountain of Youth, in which aged people could enter the waters to be miraculously transformed, emerging rejuvenated in the full vigor of someone less than half their age. Those living in such places became immune to the passage of time. These were mythic places that never existed beyond the human imagination and longing, though certain locations were said to be portals into these realms. In Ireland, the deep lakes of Lough Corrib, Lough Gur, and Lough Neagh were believed to provide entry to Tír na nÓg. Giraldus Cambrensis (Gerald of Wales; 1146–1223) told of the *Insula Viventum*, an island where the inhabitants knew no death. It was identified as *Inish na mBeo* (Island of the Living) in Lough Cre, east of Roscrea (County Tipperary). For centuries, Western explorers searched the world in vain hunting for these European lands the mythic land in Asia of Shambhala and in South America of El Dorado, while the Christian Socialists sought—equally in vain—to build an Earthly Paradise here and now.

Another form of the Earthly Paradise is the mythical Land of Cockaigne, illustrated most notably by Pieter Breugel the Elder (ca. 1525–1569) in his painting of 1567. Here, in a land of plenty that contrasted with the periodic shortages and famines of the real world, the houses are roofed with pies, cooked birds fly into one's open mouth, roast pig runs up to be eaten, and the fountains run with an unceasing flow of ale and wine. The Land of Cockaigne is a celebratory excess of a never-ending carnival of food, drink, music, dance, song, and lovemaking, where work is unknown and everything is free.

In Holland, the legend of Cockaigne was transformed later into *Luilekkerland*, which is a children's paradise of glittering candy and sugary drinks. In Germany it became *Schlaraffenland* "Lazy-monkey Land," and in the United States it was specifically the hoboes' paradise, the Big Rock Candy Mountains, where no one had to work and cigarettes grew on trees amid the "birds and the bees" common to the locus amoenus. After World War II, theme parks became pale material manifestations of the Land of Cockaigne, though nothing in them was free. Filled with tumultuous drunken crowds and the continuous uproar of the carnival feast, Cockaigne has a quite different character than the regimented expensive conformity of the theme park with people standing in line to take their turn on mechanical rides. But Cockaigne, Luilekkerland, Schlaraffenland, and the Big Rock Candy Mountains are also far distant from the eldritch world. For those who enter faërie do so as lone individuals, and their feasting—remember never to eat otherworldly food!—is among nonhuman eldritch beings.

Political idealism also postulated mythic lands, of which in 1516 Thomas More (1477–1535) gave the generic name *Utopia* (lit. "No-place"). Another such utopia is *Erewhon* (an anagram of "Nowhere") as depicted in the satirical 1872 novel of that name by Samuel Butler (1835–1902). In the twentieth century, attempts by political activists to impose by force their own sectarian versions of Utopia led to the oppression and death of millions who could not or would not conform to the imperatives of their theoretical systems. During the nineteenth and twentieth centuries, fantastic fiction juvenilized these wondrous worlds of the medieval imagination. In 1865, Charles Lutwidge Dodgson (1832–1898), writing as Lewis Carroll, created Wonderland; in 1904, J. M. Barrie (1860–1937), Neverland; and in 1950 C. S. Lewis (1898–1963) wrote of Narnia. Subsequently, myriad fantastic lands, benign and malevolent, have come from the pens and word processors of authors worldwide and continue to do so in increasing numbers.

33

The Sacred and the Profane
Archaeology

Procul, O procul este, profani!
(Away! O be gone, ye who are unsanctified!)
—Virgil, *Aeneid*

It is commonplace today that archaeologists enter and violate places of ancient sanctity in their quest for knowledge. Seeking ancient foundations and artifacts, they have dug beneath the Church of Saint Dionys in Esslingen, Germany; the Urnes stave church in Norway; Saint Peter's Church, Barton-upon-Humber in England; and innumerable less-well-known churches in many other lands. But the significant shrines of the Christian religion also have been excavated, including the Church of the Holy Sepulchre in Jerusalem, which was the burial place of Jesus; the holy of holies of Roman Catholicism, Saint Peter's Basilica in Rome; and York Minster, an ancient archepiscopal seat of the Church of England. Also in Jerusalem, Israeli archaeologists have conducted excavations beneath the Al-Aqsa Mosque, the third holiest shrine in Islam. All of these, and many other sacred sites dug into, are currently consecrated places of worship, where the dead of generations are buried.

The sacred rites of passage of the community are celebrated within these places, as they have been for upward of one thousand years. Generations of devotees have sought solace and strength in their faith upon this holy ground. Generations of priests have conducted the proper sacred rites for them at the correct times. They are sanctuaries, places of true spiritual power. But the implications of this seem to matter not at all. In their search for information, unknown artifacts, and the furtherance of their careers, archaeologists have obtained dispensation to dig within sacred grounds—and they do.

Perhaps this violation of the sacred originated centuries ago with the excavation of the abandoned holy places of Egyptian religion. The guardians of those holy sites were long dead when archaeology was invented, and the places were shunned by the dominant religion, Islam, and the Ottoman Empire's colonial rulers of the land who profited from excavations. Mummies were a lucrative trade, being exported for use as medicine. There is a thin line between archaeology and grave-robbing. Later, imperial agents and settlers in colonial lands dug into the holy places of the local people whom they had subjugated or exterminated so they could remove any interesting and valuable artifacts they found. The locals were in no position to object, and the results of this plundering still echo through the law courts today. Following the precedent set by the excavation of shrines of extinct religions and Indigenous sacred places, it was only a matter of time before the archaeologists turned their attention to the sacred places of their own culture, within their own lands.

Any idea that to disturb the earth beneath these and other venerable buildings might have an effect upon sacredness, seems to have been dismissed. For the disturbers have been given permission by the very priests who are guardians of these sacred places. It is not really the fault of the archaeologists, whose task it is to dig the earth for meaningful remains. It is the priesthood—which is supposed to be the repository of traditional understanding—that permits these grounds to be violated. If they would only refuse, then not an ounce of sacred earth would be moved. More than anything else, the acquiescence of the priesthood to the archaeologists' demands demonstrates a failure of faith in their traditional upholding of sanctuary. The guardians of these sacred sites have abrogated their sacred duty.

Because archaeology is a scientific discipline, it views all places and artifacts neutrally. The value placed upon a sacred place by a devotee cannot be taken into account, except as an area of sociogeographical study. Even the bones of the dead—who were once living beings like you and me—are no more than "material remains" to be hauled out from their resting places and taken to a laboratory for scientific analysis. But on a human level, the removal of one's ancestors' bones to a museum (or a labeled cardboard box in the museum basement) is at best an indignity and at worst, sacrilege. Who would not feel outraged if an archaeologist dug up one's grandmother just to put her skull on show in a museum cabinet? To those few religious people who still have a sensibility for the holy, to dig in holy ground is equally outrageous.

The fact that archaeologists can dig beneath churches and take away foundation deposits, the bones of saints and laity alike, demonstrates that, in general, the clergy is not aware that any difference can be made by doing so. This seems to be the case, because in many churches, the priests have removed the relics from view so that tourists can see the building more easily. A sad example is the Florence Cathedral in Italy, where the reliquaries and their contents are now in a museum, rather than serving as foci for a form of religious devotion within a tradition that goes back 1,600 years. Now they are there merely as a spectacle, to be viewed only as curios, high art, or examples of superstition superseded by modern materialism. Whatever spiritual virtue they might contain is discounted. When the little things are no longer held to be sacred, then also are the greatest.

Geomantically, digging away beneath churches profoundly alters the ground upon which the building stands. Whether or not the original church was an onlay, built on the site of a Pagan temple, whose site was divined by an augur or sybil, it was certainly founded with rites and ceremonies that served to empower the building with spirit. Geomancy teaches that there are subtle forces in every place, and that at those with particular qualities, sacred places have come into being. It is clear from the wealth of traditional lore across the whole of Europe, that churches are such places. If the sacred is not just a human construct, but actually emanates from the power within the earth at certain places, then to dig there without the traditional geomantic precautions runs the risk of destroying that power. Those who dig—and those who give them permission to dig—do not know this or do not think it is a worthwhile tradition to maintain. Either way, the special nature of the earth at that place is forever altered.

The inviolable nature of sacred places was formerly enshrined in law. It was recognized that shrines, churches, and graveyards could not be interfered with for any reason. In former times, the Free Miners of the Forest of Dean, on the borders of England and Wales, were allowed to dig on any land except the King's Highway, orchards, and churchyards. To violate a churchyard in order to mine coal was unthinkable. But today, archaeologists can and do mine the bones of the dead in churchyards. Once tradition, founded on a spiritual as well as a practical understanding of being, is lost, then all is profaned, and the holy disappears.

The rediscovery of the remains of the English king Richard III (1452–1485; reigned 1483–1485) was in a car park that stood on a long-abandoned monastic site. This empty space in the city of Leicester had once been the site of a monastery where the king's body had been taken after his death in battle at Bosworth Field in 1485. The monastery, perhaps an onlay on an earlier Pagan sacred place, was destroyed in the Protestant reformation, and for several hundred years, various buildings existed on the site until they were finally demolished, and a car park was built there. Remarkably, the remains of King Richard rested there undisturbed until 2016, when they were discovered and reburied in Leicester Cathedral.

PART III
Geomancy

*There is no person alive or who has lived that was not born at a specific place and time; every one of us comes from a place, and we remain located somewhere for the whole of our lives. Certain places are ensouled—*numen inest*—and allow us to come into contact with the powers and entities of the eldritch world, while others are desacralized, where whatever ensoulment there once was, has been destroyed by human activity.*

34
Physical Elements of Geomancy

Geomancy represents a traditional understanding of the defining elements of any landscape, both natural and human. Natural features are mountains, rocks, and caves; springs and rivers; and trees. Human-made features are standing stones, posts, roads, crossroads, doors and entrances, buildings, labyrinths. We will focus on a few of these features below.

Mountains

Mountains in various parts of the world are considered the "world mountain," the central pivot of the world that related to the omphalos and the Cosmic Axis. William Lethaby notes (1891, 74):

> This world-mountain was Nizir to the Chaldaeans, Olympus to the Greeks, Hara Berezaiti to the Persians of the Avesta, and later Alborz and Elburz.... At its apex springs the heaven tree on which the solar bird is perched. From its roots spring the waters of life—the celestial sea, which, rushing down the firmament, supplies the ocean that circumscribes the earth or falls directly in rain.

Devil's Arrow megalith, Boroughbridge
(Yorkshire, England)

In Europe, particular mountains, revered by the elder faith, are recognized as holy to this day. In France, the "White Mountain," Mont Blanc, is the holy mountain of western Europe; Ventoux in Provence was the Gaulish holy mountain of the winds, dedicated to the wind-god Vintios. Other sacred mountains are Helgafell in Iceland; Říp in Bohemia, the place of the Czech ancestors; the Disenberg, Hörselberg,

Wurmberg, and the Brocken in Germany, associated with the ancestral dísir and the goddess Venus; and the Polish holy mountains of Łysa Góra (Bald Mountain) and Ślęża. The Pennines in England and the Apennines in Italy are named for a Celtic god of high places, Poeninus, who was assimilated with Jupiter by the Romans. The shrine of Jupiter Poeninus at the Great St. Bernard Pass on the Swiss-Italian border, called Mons Jovis (the Mountain of Jupiter) in Roman times, was converted into a Christian monastery dedicated to Saint Bernard.

Most notable mountains had their particular tutelary deities. In Arcadia, Greece, Mount Kylline (Cyllene) was sacred to the god Hermes, for it was deemed to be his birthplace. He was worshipped there as Hermes Kyllenios. Elsewhere in Greece, Saint Elias took over sacred mountains from the sun-god Helios. Around the year 50 BCE in Gaul (modern France) the Romans built a temple of Mercury (their version of Hermes) upon the Puy de Dôme. It was dedicated to Mercurius Dumiatis. Hermes/Mercury can be seen as a forerunner of the Christian Saint Michael, an archangel that originated in Jewish tradition. Both Hermes/Mercury and Michael have the attribute of the psychopomp, who conducts departed souls into the next world. Like the Egyptian god Anubis, Michael is depicted holding a pair of scales in which the departed soul is weighed and judged.

In several places in Europe are hills and mountains dedicated to Saint Michael. Near Abergavenny in Wales is the Skirrid, called the "Holy Mountain." Formerly, its summit bore a chapel dedicated to Saint Michael, used until 1680 by Roman Catholics long after Catholicism was banned in Britain. Its sacred nature is apparent in local folklore, as for many centuries, soil from it was taken and scattered on farmers' fields to enhance fertility. It was also used to consecrate the foundations of new churches and was thrown on coffins during burials to protect the dead. Another holy mountain of Saint Michael is the Heiligenberg near Heidelberg in Germany. The Sankt Michaelskloster at its apex occupies the site of a Roman temple of Mercury and a surviving votive stone bears the name Mercurius Cimbrianus.

In western England there are several holy mountains dedicated to Saint Michael. The most notable are Glastonbury Tor and Saint Michael's Mount in Cornwall. But two smaller ones, Burrow Mump at Burrowbridge in Somerset, and Brent Tor on the edge of Dartmoor (Devon), are also geomantically significant. Saint Michael's Borough or Burrow Mump, recorded in 1480 as Myghell-borough, stands near the confluence of the River Cary and Parrett. Brent Tor has the Church of Saint Michael de Rupe (St Michael of the Rock), which, unlike the ruined Churches on the Skirrid, Burrow Mump, and Glastonbury Tor, still holds religious services. In France, across the sea from Cornwall, is Mont Saint-Michel, a coastal holy mountain that bears some resemblance with its Cornish counterpart, Saint Michael's Mount: they are liminal spaces, reachable from the mainland only at low tide. Both mountains have the legend that Saint Michael appeared upon them, as does Monte Gargano in northern Apulia, Italy. The Santuario di San Michele Arcangelo there is feted as the oldest shrine in western Europe where the archangel manifested himself. Other more localized Christian saints also have their own holy mountains. Saint Bernard, who took over from Jupiter, has already been mentioned. The holy mountain of Ireland, Croagh Patrick, is sacred to Saint Patrick, founder of Christianity in that land, while the holy mountain of Alsace, France, is dedicated to Saint Odile, whose monastery stands at its high point.

In western Europe, as a result of the Counter-Reformation, Catholic Christians created Calvary Mountains, where a steep pathway to the top reproduced the Stations of the Cross, along which pilgrims could reenact the journey of Jesus to his crucifixion on top of the hill of Golgotha. In 1981 in Yugoslavia (now in Croatia), Mount Podbrdo near Medjugorje was the site of an apparition of the Virgin Mary. Subsequently, it became a pilgrimage shrine, an example of a modern holy mountain coming into being as a result of an ostentum. The Brabant mystic Hadewijch (1220–1260) had several visions, which she recorded as poems. One was a vision of a holy mountain upon whose summit was the highest being whose countenance expressed God's power.

Rocks

Rocks, boulders, and caves are striking elements in the landscape, which can strike fear or awe into the beholder. Often shaped into fascinating or ominous forms by millennia of weathering, they remain as outstanding landmarks, visible from far off. Weathered rocks such as the Externsteine in Germany and the granite Tors of Dartmoor in western England have been visited by wayfarers and pilgrims who left enigmatic carvings and excavated caves in them in which ascetics sometimes lived and meditated. They are places of heightened vision that inspire mystics and poets. A famous hymn, "Rock of Ages," was written in 1776 by the Reverend Augustus Toplady (1740–1788), having been inspired by his refuge in such a fissured rock in the neighborhood of Cheddar, western England. Smaller unworked rocks and boulders, ranging from ten-

The Externsteine (Westphalia, Germany), center of ancient and contemporary mystic rituals

foot megaliths to boulders a few feet across, also are places of eldritch vision. Arthur Machen recalled being captivated by such numinous stones (1922, 25): "Before an oddly shaped stone I was ready to fall into a sort of reverie or meditation, as if it had been a fragment of paradise or fairy land."

Hills and Burial Mounds

In northern Europe, folk-moots, the forerunner of parliaments, were held on *moot hills*, the burial mounds of ancestors, the aid of whose spirits was invoked in decision-making. To this day, the ancient moot hill at Tynwald on the Isle of Man is used for the ceremonies of the official opening of the House of Keys, the Manx Parliament. As the geomantic center of the island, the hill was constructed from earth

The octagonal Red Mount Chapel at King's Lynn
(Norfolk, England)

brought from the seventeen parishes of the Isle of Man, and the annual ceremony of the House of Keys is held on the summer solstice. Thus, Tynwald is not only at a special place and composed of special materials, but is activated at a special time of year (Michell 2009, 77–103).

Rivers

Philosophically, one can never step into the same river twice. A metaphor for life is the "river of no return," flowing form its source to the sea, just as one's life begins with birth, flowing thence inexorably to the end in death. Spiritually, the flowing of the river into the sea symbolizes the reunion of the individual soul with the All.

Eddies and Currents: *Manred*

The word *manred* comes from Welsh Bardo-Druidic teachings.* It refers to the underlying matrix of matter, the "swirling patterns" or atoms, molecules, and geometrical relationships that compose matter. Celtic art can be viewed symbolically as displaying the interpenetrating strands of manred, which also parallel the Northern Tradition concept of the Web of Wyrd. The ancient Irish seeresses called *banfáithi* stared into the swirling waters of rivers in order to see visions or tell fortunes. In Wales, the medieval writer Giraldus Cambrensis related how Llangorse Lake (Llyn Syfadden) possessed red and green oracular streaming patterns flowing there (perhaps they were algal blooms or the result of a vision). Streaming patterns of the tides can be observed in the estuarine parts of great rivers, such as the Tyne at Newcastle-upon-Tyne in northern England.

Each river also has its spirit, and many rivers are still called by versions of their divine names. The Seine and Saône in France recall the

---

*For more background, see chapter 35 below.

Physical Elements of Geomancy 237

Holy well of Saint Odile at Mont Sainte-Odile (Alsace, France)—
a well whose water is used to heal eye problems

goddesses Sequana and Souconna, respectively; the Severn in England, Sabrina. River deities were honored with festivals and sacrifices. Local legends tell of some rivers how the indwelling spirit demands at least one human life a year. One such is the river Trent in England, whose powerful tidal bore is personified as the Eagre or Aegir, which may reflect the name of the Norse sea-god, Ægir. In the Baroque era, sculptured personifications of the local river became popular adornments for aristocrats' parkland. At Schwetzingen in southern Germany is a sculpture personifying of the river Donau (Danube), whose source is close by; while in a park at Richmond, to the west of London, is a statue of Father Thames modeled by John Bacon the Elder (1740–1799) and cast in Coade stone. Images personifying Father Thames also adorn several public buildings in central London. These are part of a larger renaissance in the acknowledgment of spirits of place at that time, for the naiads and potamides lived in springs, fountains, and rivers, while the limnads inhabited lakes and pools. Holy wells are by their nature indwelling-places of spirits. A holy well is not a deep well in the ground, but a flowing spring of water. They are places of healing and seership.

35

The Cosmic Axis

The Cosmic Axis has been mentioned above in its mythological and symbolic aspects. There are two distinct but related themes associated with the Cosmic Axis. The first is a spiritual model: a metaphor envisaging or explaining phenomena encountered by the journeys of the spirit, inside and outside the physical body. The second signifies a group of phenomena connected with the physical geolocation of an object as a wordly image and reflection of a cosmic reality. But the symbol of the tree as sustainer of life works on all levels.

The Cosmic Axis itself is a conceptual pillar, sometimes a tube, that has its lowest point beneath the surface of the earth on which we walk, just as a tree has its roots invisible in the soil. The axis passes from the realm beneath the earth, passes through the earth's surface, and ascends straight toward the heavens. It is a pillar that stands as a stable axis at the center of the world, linking those things that are below with those that are above. This threefold structure appears to reflect a cosmology that can be fitted readily to the worlds of Norse cosmology and Welsh Bardo-Druidic tradition, though neither expressly refer to the tree in this way.

This spiritual cosmology, part of modern Druidry, is said to come from some allegedly ancient manuscripts discovered in Raglan Castle, Wales, which, according to the founder of modern Druidry, the Welsh

As above, so below. Lichfield Cathedral
(Staffordshire, England)

Bard Iolo Morganwg (Edward Williams; 1747–1826), had been collected by the Glamorgan Bard Llewellyn Sion (ca. 1560–1616) (Williams Ab Ithel 1862–1874).* Highly contested at the time, it was published in the nineteenth century as part of the Celtic Revival and tells of cer-

---

*This history is discussed in greater detail in my book *Celtic Tree Alphabets: Mystic Signs and Symbols of Ogham and Coelbren* (Destiny Books, 2024), 115–38.

tain "circles" of being (*cylchau*, sg. *cylch*), which are envisioned to be arranged vertically on the Cosmic Axis. This Bardic cosmology teaches the transmigration of souls between various cylchau. The lowest cylch is an underworld called Annwn, paralleling the Christian Hell, but unlike that place of eternal torture, it is a place of lower insensate matter and organisms that have not progressed sufficiently to enter Abred, the middle world in which we live. Humans who suffer *obryn*, transmigration of the soul into a lower organic form, are also present in Annwn.

Above Annwn is the middle world, Abred (equivalent to the Northern Midgard), also called Adfant, the "place with the turned-back rim," a mythic way of dealing with the contentious edge of the flat Earth present in this cosmology. In Abred, humans undergo a series of reincarnations, the nature of their return depending upon the spiritual worth of their previous life. The next cylch is Gwynvyd, a heavenly upperworld "in which are all animated and immortal beings" (Williams Ab Ithel 1862–1874, I: 222–23), a realm containing "cessation of evil; cessation of want; and cessation of perishing" (Williams Ab Ithel 1862–1874, I: 176–77). The uppermost or innermost is the Circle of Ceugant, where there is only God. The authenticity of the Iolo manuscripts is rightly suspect and heavily disputed, yet within them is a spiritual tradition that has been highly influential on modern Druidry.

The Cosmic Axis is also portrayed as a World (or Cosmic) Mill, with a rotating millstone (the sky) on a static millstone (the Earth). This mill is an image of fate or destiny, grinding out well-being or catastrophe, and inexorable outcome, the mill of God, grinding slowly. It is an ancient pre-Christian adage, cited by Sextus Empiricus in the second century CE: "The millstones of the gods grind late, but they grind fine." The kenning *Amlóða kvern* (Hamlet's Mill) appears in this cosmic context in the Old Norse text *Skáldskaparmál*.

Physical Manifestations of the Cosmic Axis

In eighth-century Saxony there stood a holy column in a sacred enclave called the Eresburg. It is not known how ancient this pillar was, but

Classical image of the sacred pillar called the Irminsul

there is evidence for tall posts set up in the Iron Age sacred enclosures in Germany now known as *Keltenschanzen* ("Celtic fortifications"). Today, the site of Irminsul, as it was called, is the church of Obermarsberg in Westphalia. The medieval text *Translatio S. Alexandri* by Rudolf of Fulda (ca. 800–865 CE) tells that the Irminsul was a large wooden post set up in the open: "In their language it is called 'Irminsul,' which in Latin is the 'universal column.'" Because the Irminsul was the prime religious structure of the Saxons, it was destroyed in the year 772 CE on the orders of the Emperor Charlemagne (747–814 CE; reigned 768–814) to signify the subjection of the conquered Pagan Saxons to the Christian power of the Holy Roman Empire. However, the tradition of erecting tall posts was not stamped out, for it continues to this day in customs such as that of the Maypole.

Pagan Trackways, Spirit Paths, and Royal Roads

Walking along ancient paths and tracks is a means of experiencing the influence of surroundings, coming into rapport with the physical landscape and perhaps experiencing eldritch presences. The Way of the Eight Winds has conducted numerous geomantic walks in numinous places and encouraged participants to do so elsewhere whenever possible, cultivating their awareness of the subtle qualities they might encounter.

The Cosmic Axis 243

Maypole at Ickwell, Bedfordshire, England, on May Day 1997

Pathways in the Landscape

In certain landscapes local people recognized invisible otherworldly paths that ran across the country between notable features associated with the spirits of the land. These may have been tracks on which religious processions took place in Pagan times. The *Capitularia Regum Francorum*, dating from the days when Frankish kings attempted to destroy non-Christian beliefs and practices, tells of the "Pagan trackway" called *yrias*—sacred paths marked by rags and shoes, along which processions were made. These tracks were among "the irregular places which they cherish for their ceremonies." A "Pagan trackway" of the Viking Age still exists in Sweden. Known as the "cult road" at Rösaring, it meets at its southern end with a stone labyrinth and a burial-ground. It is about 10 feet (3 m) wide, has a north–south orientation, and runs along the top of a ridge for 600 yards (540 m). Ancient royal roads also have a spiritual dimension, being under the protection of the king—legendary, historical, or present-day. In Britain, the Royal Mail still reflects this regal connection by transporting postal traffic along the roads.

Spirit Paths and Fairy Tracks

In Ireland, some people who suffered misfortunes and ill health, understood that the cause was living in a house built at a "contrary place." The worst contrary place of all was on a fairy track, along which the "good people" processed at certain times. In Scotland, these spirit paths were used by the Fairy Rade, the fairies' expedition on May Day to attend their great annual feast (Warrack 1911, 163). W. Y. Evans-Wentz noted (1911, 38): "When the house happens to be built in a fairy track, the doors on the front and back, or the windows if they are in the line of the track, cannot be kept closed at night, for the fairies must march through." But elsewhere the fairies were believed to pass straight through stone walls (Evans-Wentz 1911, 68).

Building on a fairy path is not recommended, for the fairies who process along it at certain times of the year will punish anyone who has blocked their way. Those who knew would avoid the problem by granting a right of way. Fairy paths were allowed to pass beneath buildings constructed across the way leaving the right of way unobstructed. In Scotland, this feature is called a *closs*. On Dartmoor in the west of England, an ancient track called the Mariners' Way runs through the central passage of an ancient traditional longhouse at West Combe. John Michell tells how Paddy Baine built his house with its corner blocking a fairy path. The house was psychically disturbed, so he consulted a woman who knew how to remedy such problems. She advised him to remove the corner, which he did, and after that all was well (Michell 1975, 88). The mid-twentieth-century theory of *Erdstrahlen* (Earth rays) and "geopathic stress" is an interpretation of fairy paths in modern "scientific" terminology.

In Wales, the fairy folk known as the *Tylwyth Teg* ("Fair Family") have paths like the Irish little people, on which it is death to a mortal who meets the Tylwyth Teg when walking (Michell 1975, 150). In Brittany, the *Ankou*, the King of the Dead, the shade of the last man in the parish to die, travels with his entourage along certain special paths. To meet with them is to die (Michell 1975, 218). Evans-Wentz notes that fairies were in some places believed to be the spirits of the departed (Evans-Wentz 1911, 33). Related to this is the Wild Hunt such as the Norwegian *Oskorei*, which was said to ride through the air on dark, wild horses. The word *oskorei* derives from the Old Norse words *öskrligr*, meaning "fearful, terrible," and *rei*, a "procession on horseback," hence the "fearful procession" or "terror-ride." This ride, like the Fairy Rade, was believed to be an assemblage of the spirits of the dead who in their lives were not evil enough to be doomed to go to Hell, but who remained unsettled spirits after death. After dark, people feared to travel in case the Oskorei should abduct them. The sign of the cross on a house door was considered an appropriate apotropaic sigil to ward off the riders of the Oskorei.

There are geomantic techniques for mitigating the harmful effects to humans of spirit paths, and they are part of traditional systems of knowledge. Light travels in straight lines, and it is a widespread folk belief that mirrors reflect not only visible light but also intangible spirits. All over Europe are traditions of straight spirit-paths along which, at certain times, travel dangerous inhabitants of the otherworld. Like light, spirits travel in straight lines and unless something is done to stop them, they will enter dwellings whose entrances (windows and doors) are approached by lines of sight. To prevent this happening, mirrors, often in the form of silvered glass balls (called "witch balls" in England), are placed at strategic points to reflect the perceived intrusion. A parallel tradition exists in feng shui, where the octagonal *ba gua* geomantic mirror performs the same function. Perseus, when slaying of the Gorgon Medusa, viewed the monster in his mirrorlike polished shield, for to view her directly meant turning to stone. In eastern England, in addition to mirrors, the traditional Nameless Art of East Anglia employs sprite traps, blocking stones, staves, and egg-posts. The downside of the art of blocking and entrapment of spirits is that the precautions must be reinforced periodically or the harmful effects will appear once more before long.

36

The Road Leads Us On

Royal Roads

The personification of natural phenomena and landscape features is a tradition that figures significantly in the lore of ancient roads. In northern Europe, the origins of many ancient roads are credited to great kings of legendary history. The semi-mythical *History of the Kings of Britain* (ca. 1136) by Geoffrey of Monmouth (ca. 1095–ca. 1155) recounts how the roads of Britain were built by order of Belinus, one of the kings of the ancient Britons. According to Geoffrey, Belinus ordered four roads to be built across Britain, which led in straight lines between cities (Geoffrey of Monmouth 1966, 93). These were called the Four Royal Roads of Britain and were protected by a law that punished anyone who committed an act of violence upon them. The "king's highway" was sacred ground. Historically, these four roads were surveyed and built by Roman engineers in the days when Britannia was a province of the Roman Empire. It is possible that earlier roads existed along parts of their courses. But those who lived in later times where such major projects were no longer possible often ascribed the great straight roads and colossal earthworks of the past to the labor of giants or the Devil. Myths emerge from mysterious places and unaccounted relics.

There were similar royal roads in Ireland, too. Tara of the Kings (*Teamhair na Rí*) was the ancient royal capital of Ireland, and the Five Royal Roads of Ireland radiated from its center. They were: *Slige Midluachra*, which ran to Emain Macha near Armagh in the north; to the northwest ran *Slige Asal*; to the midwest, *Slige Mor* connected Tara with Uisnech, the *Navel of Ireland,* where stood the omphalos, and on to Galway on the west coast; *Slige Dala* linked Tara to Tipperary in the southwest; and to the south *Slige Cualann* ran to Bohernabreena, south of Dublin. Like their counterparts in Great Britain, these Royal Roads had a spiritual dimension that guaranteed royal protection of those traveling along them.

In Sweden, the legendary King Onund the Land-Clearer was credited with creating the country's roads. In *Ynglingasaga* Snorri Sturluson (1179–1241) tells that Onund's roads ran through forests, across bogs, and over the mountains. So, the king was called Onund Road-Maker. The time of his reign was notable for fruitful seasons, caused clearing the forests for cultivation. A historic road-making northern monarch was Haraldr Blátönn Gormsson (910–987) known as Harald Bluetooth, king of Denmark and Norway, who around the year 980 CE ordered the survey and construction of a highway along the Jutland Ridge. The road, which is called *Hærvejen* (the Army Road) or *Oksevejen* (the Oxen Way), was laid out so that it avoided the necessity to cross most of the rivers on the route. Narrower roads ran from the Jutland Highway to the main towns.

Difficult places on roads and trackways—places of passage—have accordingly been places of spiritual assistance. In the days before bridges, fording a river was a hazardous, possibly life-threatening, necessity. A shrine before a ford allowed the wayfarer to call upon the spirits to allow him or her to cross the river, then, once crossed successfully, to give thanks for safe passage. Passes through mountains are similar.

A major shrine dedicated to the Gallo-Roman deity Jupiter Poeninus stood above the alpine pass between France and Italy now called the Little Saint Bernard. Corresponding mountain passes were sacred to the goddess Brigida, who under various similar names was venerated widely as a goddess of fire, poetry, and transition.

37

Stonehenge

Stonehenge is the most notable stone circle in Great Britain, unique because of the lintels that still cap some of the stones. Unlike the seemingly rough stones of some megalithic circles contemporary with Stonehenge, the uprights are carefully hewn and the capstones fitted upon tenons that reflect the craft of carpentry. It has always been known that Stonehenge was built so that during the Summer Solstice the sun could be seen to rise above a particular stone called the Friar's Heel or Heelstone when viewed from the center of the circle. In recorded times, local people went to the circle at sunrise at midsummer to view this event. It is clearly an alignment toward a significant sunrise.

Various antiquarians, surveyors, and visionaries have written of the alignments that emanate from or pass through the stone circle and their meaning, both practical and symbolic. This tradition goes far back. The mystical dimension appears in eighteenth-century Druidic speculation. John Wood the Elder (1704–1754), architect of the most famous streets of the city of Bath, incorporated symbolic forms in his work. The Royal Crescent and the King's Circus are his most notable buildings, symbolizing the Moon and the Sun. The circular Circus was laid out after Wood's death by his son, but to the Elder's design. According to

Stonehenge trilithons and Heelstone

John Wood the Elder, the ancient Druids embodied their arcane knowledge in emblematic form in the symbolic designs of their temples and their relationship with one another across the landscape. His 1747 book *Choir Gaure* detailed Stonehenge and the stone circles at Stanton Drew. Wood saw Stonehenge as the model for his King's Circus, laid out as thirty houses upscaled from the dimensions of Stonehenge as he had measured it. In 1981 Alvin Holm determined that the center of the Circus lies on a line between the stone circles at Avebury in the east and Stanton Drew in the west, the line itself being oriented on the equinoctial sunrises.

In 1846 the reverend Edward Duke (1779–1852) published his *The Druid Temples of the County of Wilts*, in which he described a straight line linking what he saw as "druidical sanctuaries" (ancient earthworks and megalithic stones) at Winterbourne Bassett, Avebury, Silbury Hill, Walker's Hill, Marsden, Casterley Camp, and Stonehenge. Duke equated these places with the geocentric planetary orbits he called the "Mundane System": Venus with the stone circle at Winterbourne Bassett, the Sun and Moon with Avebury, and the Earth by the enormous ancient mound called Silbury Hill. Almost a century and a half later, Michael Dames suggested that Silbury Hill symbolizes the Earth Mother goddess. Continuing Duke's alignment, Mars is signified by Marsden, Jupiter by Casterly Camp, and Saturn by Stonehenge.

In the 1890s Colonel Duncan Alexander Johnston (1847–1931), director of the British state mapmaking organization called the Ordnance Survey, noted during his survey of Wiltshire a straight north-south line linking Avebury, Silbury Hill, Stonehenge, Ogbury Camp, Old Sarum, and New Sarum. In 1904 this discovery, and the work of the reverend Duke, was taken up by Francis J. Bennett, who published a paper in *The South-Eastern Naturalist* titled "On the Meridional Position of Megaliths in Kent Compared with those of Wilts, and Also with Those of Earth-Works and Churches." Bennett found similar alignments farther east, in Kent, with "a general north and south trend." He surmised that these sites may have been linked by a *via sacra*, a sacred pathway. Bennett's longest alignment was in Wiltshire, which ran from Binknoll Camp through four churches, Avebury stone circle and earthwork, Silbury Hill, Easterly Camp, Stonehenge, Ogbury Camp, Old Sarum, Salisbury, and Clearbury Camp.

In 1906 Norman Lockyer published the results of his work since 1901 on the astronomical alignments of Stonehenge. In *Stonehenge and Other British Stone Monuments Astronomically Considered* he related the orientation and alignments of Stonehenge to the ancient uses of the circle, attested to by existing local folk traditions. The 1909 edition of the book demonstrated that some of the sight lines from Stonehenge exhibited "the inter-relation of monuments" by passing through other ancient landscape structures. The original line promoted by Duke was seen by Lockyer to be part of a triangle of alignments.

Stonehenge 253

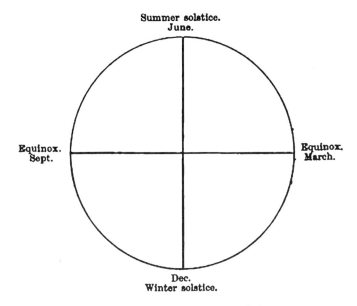

The four Astronomical Divisions of the year

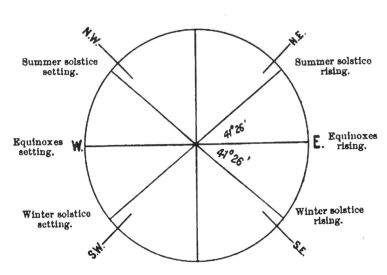

The various bearings of the sun risings and settings in a place with a N. latitude of 51°

Stonehenge astronomical divisions of the year according to Norman Lockyer

Alfred Watkins, still the most famous exponent of landscape lines, explained how he "discovered" them (1922, 9):

> A visit to Blackwardine [on June 30, 1921] led me to note on a map a straight line starting from Croft Ambury . . . over hill points, through Blackwardine, over Risbury Camp . . . the straight lines to my amazement passing over and over again through the same class of objects.

He called these lines *leys*, a word that originally meant "clearings," not straight lines. Later exponents renamed them *ley lines*. These lines, he claimed, were ancient British trackways. However, Watkins as a fifteen-year-old in September 1870 had attended an antiquarian meeting at the Green Dragon Hotel in Hereford, where William Henry Black (1808–1872) gave a lecture about straight alignments of ancient sites across the British landscape and beyond. Either Watkins had forgotten this, or perhaps he devised a good story. Later commentators expanded the Watkins story further to reposition him riding on horseback (he went to Blackwardine by motor car), from which he received a vision of lines of light shining as a "fairy chain" across the Herefordshire hills. Myths emerge in every age, and John Michell (1933–2009) called Watkins's revelation an "extraordinary moment of clairvoyance" (Michell 1969, 70). In his *The Old Straight Track* (1925) Watkins naturally wrote about the "alinements" (alignments) at and around Stonehenge.

In 1948 K. H. Koop (dates unknown) expanded Norman Lockyer's triangle to a system that extended across Salisbury Plain on which Stonehenge is located. In the early 1960s, Ross Nichols, founder of the Order of Bards, Ovates & Druids and member of the earlier group the British Circle of the Universal Bond, published the mimeographed booklets *The Timestones of the Druids: Archaeology, Observation and Tradition at Stonehenge* and *The Mysteries of Avebury: the Avebury-Stonehenge Axis of the Powers*. The latter work explained Edward Duke's

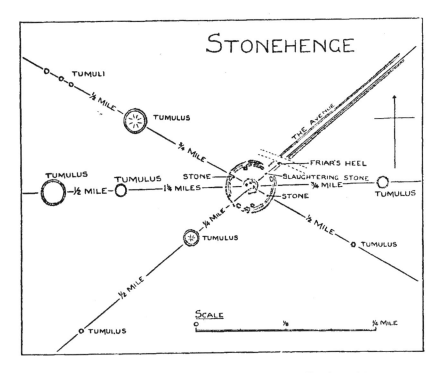

Stonehenge's "alinements" according to Alfred Watkins
(from *The Old Straight Track*, 1925)

planetary system in the alignment of sacred places; Nichols wrote of Stonehenge being a center of a "social-religious faith" and a place of mantic power: "What we can tell is that sensitives feel as a physical thing the power of these circles and the 'mana' of certain great stones" (*Mysteries of Avebury*, p. 7).

The Stonehenge line has yet another mythic dimension. There was a town built in the prehistoric defensive earthwork called Old Sarum whose inhabitants by the thirteenth century were in daily conflict with the military garrison also stationed there. The town authorities decided to construct a new town and move out. Local legend tells how the site of the new town, which became Salisbury, was divined by shooting an arrow from the ramparts of Old Sarum. The new city was laid out in the year 1220. Where the legendary arrow was shot is along the alignment noted by Bennett in 1904. Divination by arrow appears in several English legends, most notably the site of Robin Hood's grave by his last shot as he was dying.

Mythology and symbolism, ancient and modern, meet at geomantically significant places.

Stonehenge plays an important role in British mythology, earth mysteries, and Pagan religion. Participants in my geomantic tours aways wanted to visit Stonehenge, though the intrusive elements of modernity in the shape of parking lots, a tunnel under the road, tarmac paths, and barbwire fences somewhat shocked them as such necessary adjuncts of tourism are never shown in the stock photographs of this megalithic masterpiece.

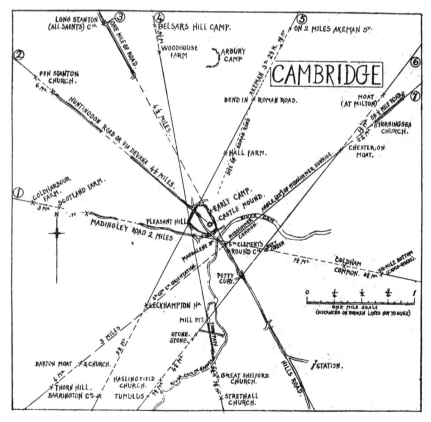

Ley lines—Alfred Watkins's "alinements" around Cambridge (from *Archaic Tracks Round Cambridge*, 1932)

38

The Crossroads

Where two roads or tracks cross, there is a place of transition where the wayfarer has the opportunity to choose which direction to take. Because four pathways meet at the crossroads, there is an awareness of the other two directions present there—above and below. Symbolically, at the crossroads the axis linking the underworld with the upperworld intersects this world on which we walk. Here the distinction between the physical and nonmaterial worlds appears less certain, and the chance of encountering something supernatural seems more likely.

Crossroads possess the power of transformation. Stories and legends from Europe, Africa, and America tell of people exhibiting exceptional abilities after visiting the crossroads. For there dwell otherworldly beings who may transmit their inspired knowledge to humans. In west Africa, the horned god Eshu sits at the crossroads to assail or assist the traveler. He is the lord of beginnings and tranformations who gives gifts to those who stop at the crossroads, ask him for help, and give him something in return. Eshu gives his devotees the ability to make the best of desperately unfavorable situations, the manifestation of pure potency that empowers a seemingly miraculous transformation whose outcome is nevertheless ambivalent. In North America, Eshu was assimilated by the clergy with the Judeo-Christian Devil, seemingly because of the element of tricksterism and misrule ascribed to him and his depiction as horned.

Folktales from the state of Mississippi recount how average banjo or guitar players would go to a crossroads at midnight and encounter a being who would tune their instrument after which they performed as inspired virtuosi. By the twentieth century, this figure was called the Devil, as in Mississippi bluesman Robert Johnson's (1911–1938) seminal 1937 song "Me and the Devil Blues," which is in the context of African American crossroads spirituality referred to in another of his songs, "Cross Road Blues." Similar otherworldly Bardic inspiration is also told in different contexts of Scottish and Irish pipers and Manx fiddle players. The musician returned from the encounter at the crossroads a changed person, now with the power of virtuosity. The present author's song, "Have You Ever Seen the Devil?" written in 2015, has the chorus:

> *Wait at the midnight crossroads,*
> *The Devil will come soon.*
> *You'll always hit the target,*
> *Play your instrument in tune.*

This refers to the person who impersonates the Devil who oversees intiation ceremonies of rural fraternities in eastern England, as well as the central European practice of gaining marksmanship at crossroads and the American one of obtaining musical prowess there.

There is no presence without time, and it is within time that all physical things exist. In his seminal book *Architecture, Mysticism and Myth*, William Richard Lethaby explained this pattern in a sacred context (1891, 53): "The perfect temple should stand at the centre of the world, a microcosm of the universe fabric, its walls built four square with the walls of heaven." The geomancy of traditional towns, among them Oxford, Chichester, and Llanidloes, reflects this cosmological principle. A crossroads or church at the central crossroads, the carfax, marks the omphalos, the local "center of the world." Everything else there, the town and the landscape around it, relates to this central point. While the Roman *Cardo* tended to be north–south, the *Decumanus* was often aligned on significant sunrises such as midwinter solstice. A quarter of a mile from where this was written is a major multilane highway, now called the A14, whose alignment was laid out in the mid first century CE by Roman engineers as part of an imperial road called Via Devana. It is orientated upon midwinter sunrise and midwinter sunset, the same orientation as the axis of Stonehenge and the street grid of Beijing (Nissen 1906, 90).

Places where tracks intersect are considered dangerous and are believed occupied by special spirit-guardians because they are places of transition where the middleworld and the underworld intersect. Gateways are also transition points, but they differ from crossroads in that we must turn back if we are not to enter them. Crossroads are liminal *loci* of transition, and the crossing of roads is a place of physical and spiritual dangers. Here the distinction between the physical and nonmaterial worlds appears uncertain, and the chance of encountering something otherworldly is more likely than at other places. In the Roman Empire, crossroads were acknowledged with a *herm*, an image of the god of traffic and trade, Mercury (Hermes). This god, who indicates the right road and guides the traveler's footsteps, was the generalization of the particular spirit of each individual crossroads. In Celtic mythology, the god Lugh indicated the right road at such places and was a guide to the traveler's footsteps. Like Lugh, Mercury and Odin are gods of the dead, divinities of the crossroads, and later Christians, having destroyed the earlier religions, set up stone crosses where the Roman *herms* or posts sacred to Mercury, Lugh, or Odin had once stood.

As *Hangatýr*, Odin was also the "god of the hanged," and often gallows and gibbets were set up at crossroads for the execution of criminals. An example of an ancient crossroad execution-ground in England was the famous Tyburn, London, which stood at the crossing point of the Roman road running northward toward Edgware and the Roman road heading toward the west, now Oxford Street. The author's forebear,

John Austin, a highwayman, was the last man to be hanged at Tyburn, in 1783. In England until 1823, the bodies of people hanged there were often buried at the crossroads, as were those who were deemed to have committed suicide. The lore of crossroads, and tales of transformation at them, is universal.

Physically, crossroads are urgent places, where the wayfarer must make a decision about which direction she or he will take. Deciding to go straight ahead is equally a decision not to take one of the other paths. So, symbolically, the crossroads is a metaphor for any place or time where we must choose between alternative courses of action. As central points, whose ways radiate in all directions, they provide access to the world above and the world below, so crossroads are good places to make magical changes. Using a ceremony, we can give away our harmful feelings at a crossroads and make a new start. Objects bearing harmful forces may be smashed there to dissipate their energies. Like casting metal or dice, there is a stark irrevocability of the moment of definition. The random possibilities become determinate immediately after the casting takes place. The crossroads thereby marks symbolically and in reality a place and time from which there is no turning back. Crossroads divination was conducted in Britain and other parts of Europe and is associated with the belief that the Devil (the Christian interpretation of the ancient crossroads gods) could be made to manifest at such intersections. Crossroads lore also included the idea that spirits of the dead could be "bound" (immobilized or rendered powerless) at crossroads—specifically, suicides and hanged criminals, but also marginalized people including witches, outlaws, and gypsies. The belief was that since straight routes could facilitate the movement of spirits, contrary features like crossroads and stone or turf labyrinths could hinder it.

39

Labyrinths

The Unicursal Labyrinth

The labyrinth is a unique human artifact. It is a pathway that leads without branches from the outside inexorably toward the center. It can be any size, from a small coin to a labyrinth a hundred feet across cut in turf. To the uninitiated, the pattern is inscrutable and must be traced with a finger on small ones or walked in the large ones. Because of this confusing pattern, labyrinths have been used the world over as apotropaic devices, warding off bad luck and trapping evil spirits. Labyrinths are pathways marked by walls, either of turf, ditches, or stones. The solid pattern of the labyrinth contains a space through which people can enter, leading them inevitably from outside to the middle. Thus, the important part of the maze is the pathway, not the walls. The void in the solid is what we travel through. In Christian tradition, the labyrinth symbolizes is the path of life and spiritual development. Our transient existence moved in the void within the constraints of matter.

The related myths of the metalworkers Daedalus (Crete) and Wayland the Smith (Scandinavia), both of whom created labyrinths, tell of this interaction of solid and void. In metal casting, the metalworker first makes a matrix, a model carved from wood or fired in pottery.

Then this matrix is impressed into a material that makes a mold. The original solid shape of the model now becomes a void, into which the molten metal is poured. It cools to make a copy of the original matrix. The mold is then broken, and the metal object released. The solid of the matrix becomes void in the mold and then solid again when the metal fills it. Casting metal makes manifest materially the mysterious interconnection between presence and absence, here and not-here, solid and void, positive and negative. For "original and cast show the same image and are equally beautiful," as the Dutch Theosophical architect J. L. M. Lauweriks (1864–1932) observed. Depressions in the mold become raised areas, and the raised areas of the mold become depressions. What was hollow is now solid and what was solid is now hollow. Casting metal is a metaphor of human life—we are created in a vessel called the womb, we are released into the world when this mold is broken open, we are here—and then we are gone.

In northern Europe, labyrinths made of turf or stones were used in spring rites, weather-magic, and ceremonies of the dead. There are tales in England of labyrinths being the dwelling places of fairies. Local lore also identifies labyrinths as dwelling places of fairies, earth spirits, or land-wights. The turf labyrinth at Asenby in Yorkshire, England, was in a hollow on top of a small hill called the Fairies' Hill, where those who ran the maze would kneel when they reached the center "to hear the fairies singing" (Allcroft 1908, 602).

Another important function of labyrinths is to trap evil spirits in their confusing patterns. When laying their nets, fishermen in Sweden would walk a labyrinth to trap harmful entities that sought to hinder their work. The *smågubbar* ("little people") were malicious land-wights who would always follow fishermen around until they went on board. So, the fishermen would go into the center of a labyrinth, and the smågubbar would follow them in, getting confused in the process. Then the fishermen would run out of the labyrinth to their ship and cast off before the smågubbar could reach it. Walking a labyrinth prevented the wights from coming on board ship and thwarting the haul.

The rite of activating a labyrinth magically was by walking to the center and out again without stumbling. One foot wrong, and bad luck would mar the voyage.

The harmful northwest wind was a particular concern of Scandinavian labyrinth magic. It was believed that the wind spirit would get trapped in the labyrinth, thereby reducing its strength. Inland, in northern Sweden and Finland, labyrinths were made by Sámi reindeer herders as magical protection against predatory wolverines.

There are more than five hundred ancient stone labyrinths documented in Scandinavia and Iceland, though only one in the British Isles. They are made of rounded stones that range in size from pebbles to boulders, laid on the earth or on rock surfaces. Some are close to prehistoric burials or grave-fields, and it is likely that some may date from the Bronze Age, though most are thought to be less than 900 years old. In Great Britain, the most ancient labyrinths are cut into the greensward, and given the alternative name "turf mazes."

In the days of sailing ships, fishermen in the Baltic Sea also built labyrinths on rocky islands and walked through them to improve the weather. In Sweden in 1973, Eva Eskilsson from Härnösand recounted that a former ship's pilot had told her that when mariners were delayed by bad weather and could not sail, they would build labyrinths of stone so that the wind would get caught up in them and so reduce in strength (Kraft 1986, 15). In 2013, in "Weatherwatch: How to Catch the Wind in a Trap of Stone," an article about Scandinavian labyrinth magic, the British *Guardian* newspaper reported that weather magic was still employed by New Age practitioners who constructed temporary labyrinths with biodegradable paint to keep the weather clear at outdoor events (Hambling 2013). In the 1990s, the present author made sawdust labyrinths in the Green Area at the Strawberry Fair on Midsummer Common in Cambridge for the same purpose.

The labyrinth is not a puzzle maze in which one can get lost. There are two basic principles—the *path to the center* and *there-and-back-again* (the path through the center and out again without turning back). The

264 Geomancy

Out-and-back labyrinth pattern of Baltic design

Original labyrinth design by the author, 1990

classical labyrinth embodies seven steps that reflect the sevenfold transformation present in the seven stages of initiation. When we traverse the labyrinth, we encounter its turning points, which have progressive symbolic and psychic effects, paralleling the progressive purifications of initiation.

A Physical Example: The Saffron Walden Town Maze

Another element of labyrinths is sexual in nature. An eighteenth-century manuscript tells that the "Town Maze" at Saffron Walden in Essex, England, was a gathering place for young townsmen who had a system of rules connected with walking the maze. Wagers in gallons of beer were made. A young woman stood at the center, called "home," while a boy tried to get to her in record time without stumbling. Presumably, the most agile youth then consummated his victory. Similar games or rituals are recorded from Sweden. The Scandinavian labyrinth name *Jungfrudans*, "young woman's dance," recalls places where these rites were performed. The Town Maze at Saffron Walden is the largest surviving ancient turf

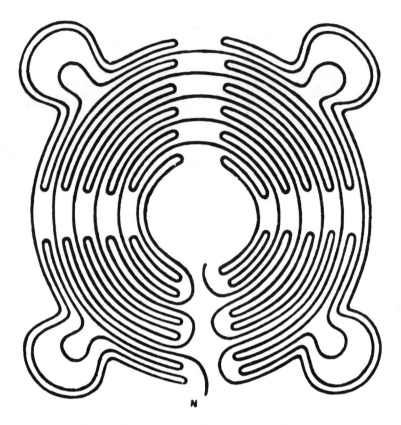

Plan of the ancient turf maze on the Common at Saffron Walden (Essex, England)

maze in England. Writing at the turn of the last century, the reverend George S. Tyack noted (1899, 196):

> There are local records which prove the great antiquity of a maze at this place. The design is peculiar, being properly a circle, save that at four equal distances along the circumference the pathway sweeps out into a horseshoe projection . . . the four corners, variously called bastions, bellows, ears, or horseshoes, are named after the towns which they face: north-west, Cambridge; north-east, Newmarket; south-east, Chelmsford; and south-west, Stortford. These names infer that the labyrinth is a conceptual microcosm of the district.

40

Geomantic Protection

Windows and doors are places where harmful people and evil spirits can enter a dwelling, so it is traditional to protect the frames by amulets and talismans. The Jewish *mezuzah* is a protective talisman fixed to the frame of an entry door. Made of parchment, the mezuzah has the word *Shaddai* written in Hebrew on one side, and on the other, two passages from the biblical book of Deuteronomy.

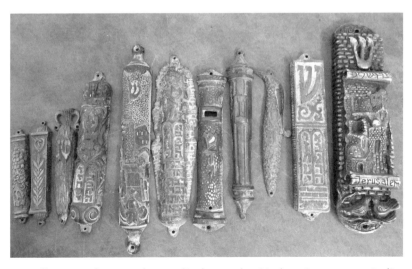

A collection of mezuzahs on display at the Madras Synagogue, India (photo by Chennaidl)

Vernacular buildings in northern and central Europe traditionally have signs on doorframes and gables. In timber-frame buildings, they are carved and painted. Doorposts are protected by a double triangle known as the "*Dag*-sign" and in northern England it appears on the speer-posts beside the hearths of Yorkshire cottages. These are called *witch-posts*, although this designation only dates from the 1930s after one was donated to a museum. As with the textual mezuzah, spells were also written to protect non-Jewish buildings. The Scots expression "*Arsé-Versé*" (English "Arsy-Farcy") denotes a spell on the side or back of the house to ward off fire (Warrack 1911, 9). The dialect word *arsy* means "backward" so the spell refers to something written backward or on the back side of the house.

In the United States, Pennsylvania Dutch barns are noted for their ornate painted roundels called *hex signs*, though this designation is—like the "witch-posts"—a modern term devised by folklorists. Many of these are geometric, but there are also stars, "sunbursts," birds, hearts, tulips, and tree-of-life motifs painted in bright colors. The four emblems of British and American playing cards—diamonds, hearts, spades, and clubs—are also used as protective signs. They signify the four elements: diamonds representing the element of earth; hearts, water; spades, air; and clubs, fire. Traditional knot patterns of various kinds are used as protection, as well as the related pentagram ("the symbol at your door," see below) and labyrinth. The latter includes a notable sixteenth-century labyrinth carved in stone on the building called *Zum Irrgarten* ("At the Labyrinth"), in Augustinergasse, Zurich, Switzerland. The function of these deliberately intricate patterns is to ward off, confuse, or entangle evil spirits that attempt to enter the house, intending harm. A horseshoe nailed above the door serves the same purpose.

The pentagram was used in medieval magic as an apotropaic sign. It appears in the verse romance *Sir Gawain and the Green Knight* (late fourteenth century), which tells how the English call it the "endless knot." This is a sigil with many names; pentacle, pantacle, pentangle, pentagramma, Solomon's seal, the flaming star, the rempham, and the

Geomantic Protection 269

Nineteenth-century house with protective runes in brickwork in St Ives (Huntingdonshire, England)

270 Geomancy

Protective labyrinth on the house *Zum Irrgarten*,
Augustinergasse, Zurich, Switzerland
(photo copyright Tauav / Adobe Stock)

Druid's foot (German *Drudenfuss*). Although in modern times it has been traduced in popular literature as an evil sign (and appears on the flag of Morocco), the five-pointed star drawn by a single line is important in sacred geometry because the fivefold division of the circle is the starting point for the geometric proposition known as the golden section (see below). Medieval and later folk magic ascribed the pentagram a protective power. In English folk tradition it appears as a threshhold glyph in the counting song "The Twelve Apostles":

> *... Four for the Gospel makers.*
> *Five for the symbol at your door.*
> *Six for the six proud walkers. ...*

In 1893, the pioneer folksong collectors Lucy Broadwood (1858–1929) and J. A. Fuller Maitland (1856–1936) explained that this "five for the symbol" signifies the pentagram (Broadwood and Maitland 1893, 154–59).

There is a protective tradition in religious buildings, too. Because stone chuches have survived for much longer than secular timber buildings, we know more about them. Guardians and attendant figures, images of devotion, holy symbols, and sacred forms provide protection

Pentagram amulet of copper, England, 1970s

against negative forces and destructive elements. Carved dragons' heads on the upper part of buildings were common in northern architecture including the timber stave churches of Norway and Romanesque stone gateways in Normandy and England. Gargoyles, grotesque figures that serve as water spouts, are named for the French *gargouille*, meaning a "gullet" or "throat." Gargoyles are mainly in the form of dragons' heads, lions, and demonic or humanoid forms, sometimes obscene. They are amuletic, protecting their churches against demonic attack. There is a tradition that malevolent spirits can be enchanted into an imprisoned state within these stone carvings where they serve as active repellents of the free-roaming destructive spirits of the air. The origin-myth of gargoyles tells how in Rouen, Gaul (modern France), in the year 635 CE, Bishop Romanus slew a fire-breathing monster named Gargouille. The dead monster was put on a pyre to be burnt, but its neck and head remained unburnt, for they were fireproof. So, the head and neck were

Gargoyle on the Church of Our Lady and the English Martyrs, Cambridge, England, 1880

set up on the outside of the church to frighten away other demonic entities. Gargoyle lore tells how evil spirits were sometimes bound into the stone images, their power being used to frighten away other evil entities. In Scotland, a harmful spirit called Quhaip served to protect cottages, for it was supposed to haunt the eaves of houses on the lookout for evildoers (Warrack 1911, 436).

PART IV
Makings

Those who pursue mindful arts and crafts create artifacts that are of practical use, aesthetically pleasing, and empowered with spiritual virtue. Their forms and functions express the materials from which they are made and the place from which they come.

41

The Spiritual Arts and Crafts

Know what you have to do, and do it.
—JOHN RUSKIN (1819–1900)

We who follow the precepts of European Traditional Spirituality attempt to encapsulate this deeper reality in everything that we do, thereby acting in harmony with the seen and unseen worlds. Naturally, the artifacts that we make, both transient and permanent, ideally will partake of this harmony, because they are personal, located in place and time yet embodying aspects of the eternal. There is no place for destructive competition in the achievement of the work. For through peace and concord, small things increase; through discord, great things diminish. We must always take the time necessary to accomplish the task, not to hurry or skimp the work so as to reach a rapid conclusion. For patience is the ornament, guardian, and protector of life. "Almost right" is wrong. When we recognize these principles and strive to apply them in our lives and work, then we are in harmony with the deepest roots of being. Spiritually, there is a unity between the maker and the made. The act of making is primal when it expresses the fullness of being. The ensouled artifact is eternal in that no further degree of wholeness or presence can be reached beyond it.

Ancient Skills and Wisdom

Trust only in Nature and respect her laws.
—WENZEL HABLIK (1881–1934)

The skills to make things oneself are essential in traditional society. When, from the mid-eighteenth century, the Industrial Revolution rolled across the world, the rural poor retained personal craft skills that were downgraded in mechanized towns and cities. Those whose work was free, individual, or in some way not allied to the urban collective or tied to the military-industrial complex, continued their traditional lives until they were overwhelmed by modernity. Their home-knitted garments and self-made tools and utensils were dismissed by urban dwellers as rustic, rural, or primitive, obviously inferior to manufactured merchandise. This idea, of course, was wrong, but it was promoted by those whose business it was to manufacture the necessities of life for the urban proletariat. But embedded in these country and coastal crafts were traditions that stretched back for thousands of years. They embodied meaningful symbolism and the magic of making, affirming the positive values of continuity and self-reliance. In a real sense, these artifacts were empowered by the "living signs" they bore, ornament in the original Roman sense of *ornare*, the process of making something fit for the entry of the gods, that is, ensouled. The emblems of "folk art"—as academe categorized traditional utensils, tools, furniture, trappings, vehicles, and buildings—constituted a symbolic system in its own right, with roots in ancient skills and wisdom emanating from archaic prehistory.

The Arts and Crafts movement of the late nineteenth and early twentieth century fought back against this materialistic tide of manufacture. The guiding ethos of the movement, founded in London in 1888, was to express innovative creativity within tradition. One of the key tenets at the beginning of the movement was to encourage mindfulness in place of the careless way of working that had accelerated the decline of crafts in the nineteenth century. The designers of the Arts and Crafts movement learned from continuing local tradition, both through studying extant buildings and artifacts and from tuition by local craftsmen and members of surviving guilds. Symbolic and religious traditions, too, were significant elements.

In addition to the materialistic and commercial view of making things, there is another sort of relationship that exists between people and artifacts. Whatever is created by the craftsperson in the spiritual arts and crafts is primarily for use, instruction, or delight. It is made with a loving and respectful spirit for the service of the divine power and the common good of the community. The moral philosophy inherent in the spiritual arts and crafts means that the craftsperson is always aware that the work has a wider dimension than the pursuit of profit or fame. It is for the good of all. As the pioneering architect Edgar Wood (1860–1935) wrote:

> Who works not for his fellows starves his soul.
> His thoughts grow poor and dwindle and his heart grudges each beat, as misers do the dole.*

Of course, all of the materials we must use originate in the world in which we live. In his *Summa Theologica*, Thomas Aquinas (ca. 1225–1274), explained: "Man is not the founder of nature; by art and virtue he makes use of natural things for his own benefit" (Gilby 1951, 283). Art is the operative link between the imagination and the final result, the process which J. R. R. Tolkien called *sub-creation*, that

---

*This is the text of the carved stone inscription at the monumental stairs leading to his 1889 Place of Contemplation in Jubilee Park, Middleton, Lancashire (now Greater Manchester), England.

is, using the given materials of Creation in a new way that nevertheless operates according to true principles. In an analogous way, the Theosophical master of symbolic geometry, architect Claude Bragdon (1866–1946), asserted that the function of true art is to express the "world order" through the transient things that people may make with their hands, so that the great can be sensed in the little, and the permanent in the transitory. Art involves nature, tradition, and innovation. "Art is a blending of nature and will" wrote Ralph Waldo Emerson (1803–1882), and sculptor Auguste Rodin (1840–1917) noted that "An art that has life does not restore the works of the past: it continues them." In the mid-twentieth century André Malraux asserted that art is a revolt against fate.

The Spiritual Arts and Crafts master William Richard Lethaby wrote (1911, 14): "In becoming fit, every work attains some form and enshrines some mystery." Mind and hand are inseparable. Artifacts gain an inner consistency when the act of making is indistinguishable from the spiritual path of the maker. To the artist, there is a spiritual connection with the world, a oneness of the maker and the made that is analogous to the union of the lover with the beloved, or to the devotee with the gods. The Spiritual Arts and Crafts seek to realize spiritual ideals materially through a process that itself is the craftsperson's spiritual journey. They are based on the principles of traditional craftsmanship, in which, as the medieval German mystic Meister Eckhart (ca. 1266–ca. 1338) taught, "working and becoming are the same." Traditional spirituality is not just an inward thing: it must manifest materially. But there is a difference to be understood in the way things are made. In 1818 Samuel Taylor Coleridge made a very significant observation when he drew a distinction between mechanic and organic form. Form is mechanic when on any given material we impress a predetermined form, one that does not arise necessarily out of the natural properties of the material. On the other hand, organic form is innate, it develops from within so that the fullness of its development is one and the same with the perfection of its outward form. On the spiritual level, this is analogous with the relationship of *önd* with the Anima Loci. Sanctification is organic, while an onlay is mechanic.*

"Those who lead the contemplative life and do no outward works are most mistaken, and on the wrong tack," said the medieval mystic Meister Eckhart, for "no person can live the contemplative life without a break": "afterwards his duty lies in doing outward works" (Backhouse 1992, 137). This is a spirituality independent of religious denominations and belief systems; it is the world of the worker, the artisan whose function is to deal with physical reality firsthand. The realities of doing necessitate a practical approach in which the unquestionable presence of the materials always overrides abstract human theories and dogmas. This is not the dialectical materialism preached by modernity: the vision is that of the poet, not of the cleric or the accountant. Things made with this perennial recognition are vessels of the spirit. Makers who follow the Spiritual Arts and Crafts tradition recognize that these metaphors of human existence are present within making and the artifacts produced. It maintains and develops by self-critical renewal these spiritual and traditional currents whose values are not the same as those implicit in the mainstream of industrial design and the mass media. This symbolism of aesthetic embodiment has not gone away just because the discourses of modernism and postmodernism have discounted the meaningfulness of symbols, except as a means to hegemonic power.

Masters of the traditional guilds taught their apprentices the fundamental Five Precepts, which must be followed in making things. They are the most basic expression of true principles:

1. Suitability for purpose
2. Convenience in use
3. Proper use of materials
4. Soundness of construction
5. Subordination of decoration to the four preceding rules

---

*For a deeper exploration of sanctification and onlay, see chapter 25, "Nature and the Eldritch."

On a materialist level, the catchphrase "form follows function" is an exoteric reflection of this holistic understanding. It was quoted in the late nineteenth century by the Chicago architect Louis Sullivan (1856–1924), and his disciple Frank Lloyd Wright (1867–1959) reworked it as "form and function are one." But an imagination that is not free to partake of Nature in all her plurality and multiplicity, but instead is subject to the censorship of theory, doctrine, and dogma will be channeled ever more narrowly into a dead end, and instead of liberating and promoting abundant life, it will inevitably serve as the engine of monomania and oppression.

Existence is a process of continual creation, destruction, and re-creation; formation, transformation, and re-formation—states of being that mutate and flow from one to another and yet more, ceaselessly. Matter acquires actual being by taking on a form, as Thomas Aquinas noted. Creativity involves recognizing the potential within anything material and using intuition and skill to bring it into visible, tactile, usable form. Making anything is a function of human consciousness—the making of meaning—but even ultimate perfection is transitory. The fleeting arrow of life is the individual's small part of a much greater whole in which boundaries and definitions are the provisional condition of the present moment.

All visible and invisible manifestations of existence emanate from true principles. Through the Spiritual Arts and Crafts, the process of living becomes a spiritual journey in which we act by choice that originates in considered principles, not through obedience to external forces. It is a form of caring—caring to do things well. The Amsterdam architect Karel Petrus Cornelis de Bazel (1869–1923) saw this as the striving of artists to reach their own deeper essence. In succeeding, the artist produces a reflection of the universal, which nevertheless respects the mundane purpose of the work. To do this is to participate in the replenishing of the world. The opposite of this is carelessness. The Arts and Crafts architect Charles Francis Annesley Voysey (1857–1941) noted that mechanical work can be produced without the worker's consciousness being engaged in it, and, worse, in most cases can only be produced by the elimination of all human thought and feeling. Mechanically performed work is thus the antithesis of ensoulment of the artifact.

By Hammer and Hand All Arts Do Stand

The hammer is the essential tool of the smith and the carpenter, and figures from European mythology such as Hephaistos, Daedalus and Wayland, Vulcan, and Thor all relate to the magic powers of the hammer. The West African god Shango is also part of this current.

The hammer of the god Thor, Mjöllnir (the "Crusher"), is a symbol of power that was used in Norse religion as an instrument of

By hammer and hand all arts do stand

consecration. The sign of the hammer was sacred in Norse religion, and talismans of Mjöllnir were (and are) worn by devotees. In Viking times, fathers made the sign of the hammer over the family meal, plowmen made the sign over the fields, and *goðar* made it over couples in marriage ceremonies.

Nails and chains are artifacts made originally by hand as the essential crafts of the blacksmiths. Both nails and chains possess magical lore beyond the innate structural and magical virtue of the metal itself. In the late Roman Empire, iron nails marked with images and inscriptions were used in magical rites. "God-nails" (*reginnaglar*) were elements of the sacred array of Viking Age halls and temples, and the old English expletive "God's Nails!"—whether or not it refers to the nails with which Jesus was nailed to the cross—is an expression of the magical power of nails. Nails driven into doorposts for good luck can be seen at many old inns in Great Britain. The motto, "By Hammer and Hand All Arts Do Stand," is used by craft guilds in many cases, including the various local Scottish incorporations of Hammermen.

42

Sacred Geometry

The principles of sacred geometry transcend all sectarian religious doctrines. Sacred geometry is a technology that aims to reintegrate humans with the cosmic whole. It works, as electricity or mechanics do, for anyone who fulfills the criteria, no matter what their principles or aims. Sacred geometry has been applied to Pagan temples of the Sun, shrines of Isis and Osiris, tabernacles of Jehovah, sanctuaries of Marduk, prayer halls of Confucius, Islamic mosques, Christian churches and cathedrals, tombs of saints of all stripes, mausolea of monarchs, memorials to those slain in war, university libraries, and even two London Underground stations. Geometry is usually included in the discipline of mathematics. However, historically, geometry predates mathematics, being a much more fundamental order of things than mathematics, which is a creation of the human intellect.

The Art of Line

The Art of Line involves developing the ability to think and visualize in three dimensions—or four, if we include the necessity to perform the procedures sequentially in time. It is the meeting of hand and mind. The Art is applied geometry practiced without the abstract formulæ of theoretical geometry. Those who have mastered the Art have become spatial visionaries. We are able to envision the creation of structures in space without measurement. Yet they are by no means abstract, for by means of the Art this tower was erected. The stones that compose it were cut precisely to size and shape by the techniques of stereotomy, arrived at without calculations, by drawing alone. This is the practical result of mastering the Art of Line, known to the French journeymen as the *trait*. Through the Art, we bring into physical being those autonomous imaginative forms that are not immanent in the material substance of the world. The essentials of successful work are to know yourself, use the tools properly to structure experience, organize your thoughts, and make the basis of all things spiritual.

Ratio and Proportion

It is proportion that beautifies everything. The whole Universe consists of it, and musicke is measured by it.
—ORLANDO GIBBONS,
FIRST SET OF MADRIGALS (1612)

We are so used to counting in tens, using decimal coinage and metric measurements, that it is difficult sometimes to think in other ways. The decimal system is not the natural way of measuring. Traditional measure is totally practical. It is based upon the requirements of cooking, handicrafts, agriculture, and trade. It emerges directly from the characteristics of the materials being measured, and not from mathematical theory. These weights and measures are physical; they relate to the human body and natural objects, and they are interconnected in subtle ways. Traditionally, length, weight, and capacity are divided by halving. A unit of anything is divided into two halves, then halved again to produce four quarters, then halved again to produce eight eighths, and so on. This can be done by eye, or by folding anything foldable. Three such divisions cut the item into eight equal parts, and in natural measure

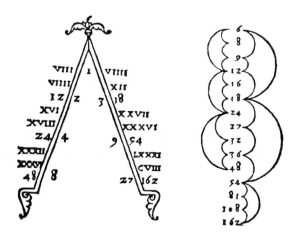

Renaissance harmonics diagrams

3, 4, and 8 are significant numbers. Traditional weights and measures as well as time were based on an eightfold system (see below). Eight is significant also because it also occurs in the eightfold division of space into the eight airts, the octave of the musical scale, and the thirty-two divisions of the compass rose (8 x 4). But precise units, while necessary for activities such as cooking, trade transactions, and construction, are ruled by proportion: they are not necessary to proportion. Proportion is the mathematical relationship between different parts of things, and the dimensions of them are irrelevant.

Jacopo de' Barbari (ca. 1470–ca. 1516) stated that "there is no proportion without number, and no form without geometry," and Gerrit Rietveld (1888–1964), Dutch founder of the movement *De Stijl*, observed in 1930 that "we cannot conceive of existence without space." When humans make things on a human scale according to true principles, then they may produce ensouled artifacts. In the sixteenth century, Guilio Delminio Camillo (ca. 1480–1540) noted that in ancient Egypt "there were such excellent makers of statues that when they had brought some statue to the perfect proportions it was found to be animated with an angelic spirit: for such perfection could not be without a soul" (Yeats 1966, 159).

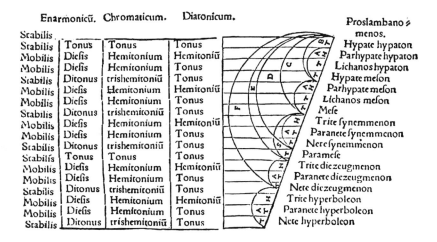

Harmonic ratios according to Vitruvius

The relationship of music to proportion was discovered by Pythagoras, who observed that the octave of every note played by a string of any length is produced exactly halfway up that string. In turn, the octave of that note is halfway up at a quarter of the string length, and so on. The actual measured length of the string does not matter. It is the ratio that is significant, not the measure.

The mathematician and philosopher Theon of Smyrna (70–135 CE) tells how the four main harmonies of the diatonic scale combine the numbers 1, 2, 3, and 4 as the *Musical Tetractys*. These four harmonies are the fourth, which is the ratio 4:3; the fifth, 3:2; the octave, 2:1; and the double octave, 4:1. By combining these in proper ways, all forms of music and architecture can be made, for there are limitless possibilities of combination. The Music of the Spheres, in all its complexity of endless realignments, changing relationships, and new harmonies, thereby reflects the limitless combinations of the elements that allow the multiplicities of the existent world to have their being. These musical numbers also produce harmony when applied to architectural proportion, symbolically relating the structure to the inner workings of the Cosmos.

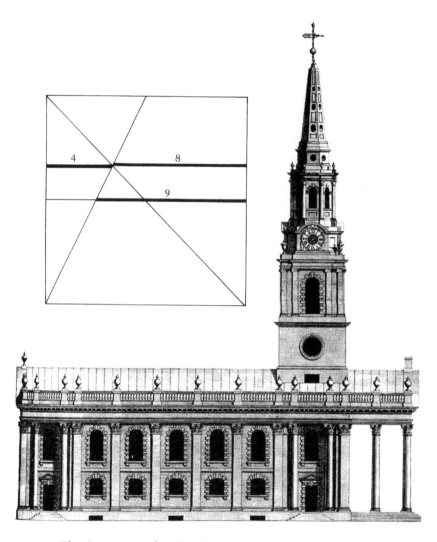

The Symmetry of Order: St Martin-in-the-Fields Church, London (1722), designed by James Gibbs with dimensions determined by the Helikon diagram, with the ratios 4:8:9.

Timeless spiritual principles are brought into physical presence through sacred geometry. Justness of Proportion on the physical level reflects the Divine Harmony on the cosmic one, the gateway to a knowledge of higher realities. This is the "symmetry of order" as James Gibbs called it.

The Helikon and the Golden Section

The Helikon (or Ptolemy's Helikon) is a geometric system noted by Claudius Ptolemy (ca. 100–170 CE) and most associated with the renaissance architect Sebastiano Serlio (1475–1554). It is a particular division of the square whose ingenious geometric division produces

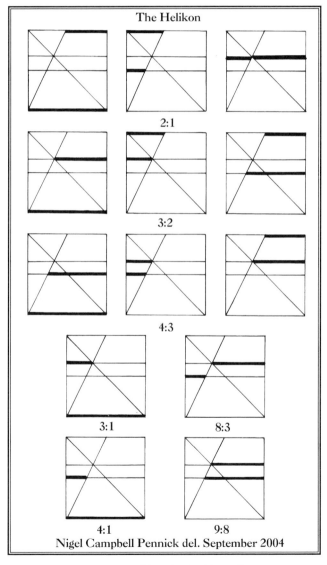

Ratios generated by the Helikon diagram

whole-number ratios. The golden section or golden cut is a proportion that exists between two measurable quantities of any sort when the ratio between the larger and smaller one is equal to the ratio between the sum of the two and the larger one. Geometrically, it is the ratio in the pentagram between the side of the inner pentagon and its extension into the pentagram, a ratio of 1:1.618, mathematically symbolized by the Greek letter Φ (*phi*). In any increasing progression or series of terms with Φ as the ratio between two successive terms, each term is equal to the sum of the two preceding ones. Because of its unique properties, displaying the geometric principle underlying the growth of living things, visible in such things as the Nautilus shell and the Sunflower, it is a sigil of life and the power of unlimited extension (Pennick 1980, 25–28; Pennick 2005c, 64–65).

Paramateric Diagrams

A *paramateric* diagram is a parameter for a design in graphic form, containing within itself the necessary proportions and sometimes keys to the geometry of a structure. There is a collection of 596 drawings that once belonged to an eighteenth-century British secret society of Jacobite or Rosicrucian tendency. The collection is linked with John Byrom (1692–1763) but contains earlier material from the seventeenth century (Hancox 1992). Byrom's diagrams each consist of a series of concentric circles at seemingly irregular intervals, with associated dots and straight lines. Some are clearly geometric diagrams in the medieval *ad triangulum* and *ad quadratum* systems, which determined the layout of medieval churches and cathedrals, or are related to the Thibault diagram. From the main body of concentric circles emerges a linear component, with divisions related to the main body, but extending beyond it. They denote the relative dimensions and proportions of components of classical buildings. Paramateric diagrams such as these, used by a classical architect, would provide the means to produce a classical building embedded with that particular form. However, the same parameters

Sacred Geometry 291

An example of paramateric sacred geometry

used by a modernist architect would create a modernist building that nevertheless would have the same particular form and proportions. In the Rhineland of Germany is a tradition that the steeple-top spheres on which weathercocks are mounted contain all the information needed to rebuild the church if it were destroyed. This information is not a manuscript with a plan, which would be destroyed by fire, but lines engraved upon the sphere—a paramateric diagram.

The beauty of paramateric diagrams as a means of preserving information is one of elegant economy. Everything necessary for a building is set forth in a single diagram, in which all dimensions, proportions, and geometrical constructions may be found by those who know how to do it. Paramateric diagrams are a traditional way of describing architecture, quite different from the better-known "plan and elevation" method. Plan and elevation are based upon cubic geometry that divides space at right angles to one another with the axes x, y, and z. All modern architecture, industrial design, and engineering are described in terms of these three axes, whether graphically or electronically. Paramateric diagrams are a different form of understanding, an analogous language rather than a literal depiction of space. They are a glimpse into the holistic skills of the ancients, enabling the architect to bring the virtues of order, eurythmy, and symmetry into physical form.

43

Specific Geometric Forms

The Foursquare Holy City

The geometric division of towns and cities into four quarters (hence the word *quarter* for a district) goes back to the Etruscan Discipline. The city of Rome was known as *Roma Quadrata*, though its actual form was not the "holy city plan," which is a city oriented foursquare to the cardinal directions and divided into four by two interesting main streets, the north–south *Cardo* and the east–west *Decumanus*. Many ancient cities dating from Roman times retain this plan at their core. Fourfold divisions of countries, especially islands, are also an ancient geomantic tradition. The island of Bornholm in the Baltic is divided into four distinct regions, or quarters; so are Iceland and Ireland. The four provinces of Ireland—Leinster, Munster, Connacht, and Ulster—are the most ancient conserved example of this ritual division.

The four sides of a foursquare structure face the cardinal directions. The north and south faces are at right angles to the Cardo, while the east and west faces stand at right angles to the Decumanus. The north and south faces thus run east–west and the east and west faces run north–south. The corners of the square are directed toward the intercardinal points, northeast, southeast, southwest, and northwest. The square ground plan orientated in this way immediately produces an eightfold division of space. Each of the four walls of the square faces its corresponding cardinal direction, dividing the *templum* into four quarters whose dividing lines run to the intercardinal points.

The ancient Irish Otherworld is also divisible into four. As the Scottish poet Fiona Macleod (pen name of William Sharp, 1855–1905) recounts:

> There are four cities that no mortal eye has seen but that the soul knows; these are Gorias, that is in the east; and Finias, that is in the south; and Murias, that is in the west; and Falias, that is in the north. And the symbol of Falias is the stone of death, which is crowned with pale fire. And the symbol of Gorias is the dividing sword. And the symbol of Finias is a spear. And the symbol of Murias is a hollow that is filled with water and fading light. (quoted in Blamires 2013, 103)

The symbols traditionally associated with the provinces of Ireland, and the four otherworldly cities are related to the four suits of the Tarot, which themselves have elemental connotations. Structures such as this—integrating time, space, and the possibilities of happening—are the spiritual essence of traditional European society, in which no part is isolated from any other part.

The Sevenfold: Rosicrucian Allusions

Seven-sided structures are rare in architecture, sacred and profane. Although the Druid's Cord provides an approximate means of dividing a circle into seven,* and other methods were used, the technique

---

*On the construction use and of the Druid's Cord, see chapter 45, "Tools and Techniques."

appears not to have been published until 1655 by Carlo Ranaldini (1615–1693). But in any case, accurate sevenfold construction on an architectural scale was uncommon until the seventeenth century. The Christian Basilica of Our Lady of Scherpenheuvel in Belgium was designed in 1606 by Wenceslas Cobergher (1560–1634). Founded on July 2, 1609, the Feast of the Visitation, it is a seven-sided church set in a heptagonal *hortus conclusus*, which itself is inside a seven-sided town with heptagonal defensive ramparts. It was built on the site of a sacred Oak tree that bore a miraculous image of the Virgin Mary. Another seventeenth-century heptagon, built in 1622, is the mausoleum of Prinz Ernst von Schaumberg (1569–1622) at Stadthagen, Lower Saxony, Germany. The architect was Giovanni Maria Nosseni (1544–1620). The fortifications of the town of Coevorden in the Netherlands, constructed in 1672, were, like Scherpenheuvel, heptagonal.

Seven-sided defenses of Coevorden, Netherlands

This period when seven-sided sacred buildings were constructed is the time when a significant magical current emerged in Europe in Rosicrucianism. In the *Fama Fraternitatis* (1614), the first Rosicrucians taught of the discovery of the miraculous tomb of Christian Rosenkreuz, a seven-sided vault whose sides were symbolic of the seven planets. According to the *Fama Fraternitatis*, the vault had an inscription made by Rosenkreuz, describing it as "the compendium of the Universe I made in my lifetime to be my tomb." Each side measured eight feet high and five feet wide, and represented one of the seven planets, with the entrance on the side dedicated to Venus. In the late nineteenth and early twentieth centuries, temples of the Order of the Golden Dawn followed this symbolism, using a seven-sided "vault of the adepts" for a particular grade initiation, emblematically re-creating the legendary tomb of Christian Rosenkreuz. The Osiris Temple in Weston-super-Mare in southwestern England used a temporary structure set up in the cellar of an inn.

Unexpectedly, two stations on the London Underground rail system are heptagonal structures that allude to this Rosicrucian vault. Designed by Charles Holden (1875–1960), they are at Hounslow West and Ealing Common, both built in 1931. Each has seven seven-sided lamps that illuminate the interior. And, as mentioned earlier (chap. 22), Holden's 1929 headquarters of the London Underground at 55 Broadway was designed by him as a Temple of the Winds, with symbolic carvings of the personified winds on the outside of the seventh floor, and sculptures signifying Day and Night on the south and north sides, respectively.

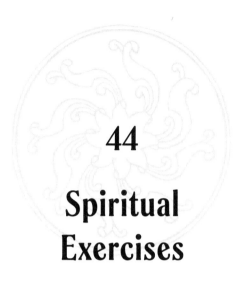

44

Spiritual Exercises

*Become thyself, in order to know the
Cosmos and the gods.*
—Delphic Oracle

Spiritual Exercises

The Way of the Eight Winds recommends the spiritual exercises I outlined in my books *Practical Magic in the Northern Tradition* (1989) and *Pagan Magic of the Northern Tradition* (2015). They are composed of five basic elements applicable to many spiritual pathways. The prerequisite for such exercises is *purity of intention*: that the power one has or seeks to acquire will be used only for one's personal needs, not for subverting the free will of other people, but for the benefit of all. Generally, these exercises should be undertaken only in a state of purification, and a state of physical cleanliness, involving ablutions and the wearing of clean clothes. As with all things important in life, spiritual exercises should be approached carefully and step by step, for spiritual states are not attained easily.

298 Makings

Cover of an original German publication for the Way of the Eight Winds

Meditation

1. *Sitting in a definite posture.* The body must be in a relaxed yet alert position. There are two ways of sitting. One is with crossed legs, as can be seen in ancient representations such as the horned figure (identified as the antlered god, Cernunnos) on the Gundestrup Cauldron. This is sometimes called the *Keltensitz* ("Celts' seated posture") in German, although it is known from all the northern European countries. The second posture is sitting with the legs beneath the body, as if kneeling.
2. *Regulation of breathing.* This involves quiet, deep, regular breathing. When the breath is under control, a state of serenity is readily accomplished. One aspect of *önd*, the breath, is our immediately controllable part of the universal spirit of the Cosmos.
3. *Banishment of unwanted thoughts.* This is perhaps the most difficult part. Firstly, attention is withdrawn from external objects and other distractions. The eyes are closed, and any mental images that appear there must be suppressed. Bodily sensations will fade and become almost unnoticed. When the first three elements have been mastered, then the body and mind is prepared for the final two, which are concentration/visualization and the utterance or call.
4. *Concentration.* Banishment of unwanted thoughts can be accomplished either by rendering the mind blank or by concentrating the mind upon some definite thing. The visualization of something centrally relevant to the spiritual pathway is usual. It may be something of personal importance to the practitioner, such as the Cosmic Axis or a particular attribute of a deity, or a symbolic form such as a rune. One should find one's most expressive symbol and dwell upon it until it becomes a core part of their consciousness.
5. *The Utterance or Call.* The sacramental energy present in specific words that may reflect the primal speech is understood in

all the world's sacred practices. Northern tradition *galdr* (verbal magic), Buddhist mantras, and similar formulaic calls access particular energies for the practitioner. The call expresses a particular aspect of sacred reality with which the practitioner has the most affinity.

When the exercise is finished, whatever it is, there should be a reawakening, a reentry into the "familar reality" of the everyday world. This is done in the reverse order of the stages described above, consciously enabling each part of the mind and body in turn to resume their everyday function. One will feel revitalized after the exercise.

Seers' Journeys

Seers' journeys can take one of two forms: journeying inways, as in pathworkings; or as a physical pilgrimage to a place of mantic power. The inward seer's journey is a visualization of a voyage through the terrains of one's inner landscape. This can be in the form of the re-creation of a mythical, legendary, or archetypal journey, imagining (in the literal sense of visualizing images) the hero's journey such as Hermod's ride to the underworld or the Arthurian knights seeking the Holy Grail. The reenactment of such a mythic journey, whether in the mind or in the physical world, produces experiences and insights that otherwise are unavailable.

The physical seer's journey can take two forms: either traveling a prescribed route in a proper frame of mind or wandering until one comes across a place of mantic power. This can be the urban wandering described above, or exploring a heretofore unknown wild area until one comes across a special place where one can commune with or contact eldritch powers, or which is congenial to spiritual exercises. In a pilgrimage, one progresses along particular paths, trackways, and roads to a particular objective: a place of mantic power, such as a holy well, mountain, or sacred shrine. Pilgrims pass through significant wayside places that provide their own experiences, which culminate in the arrival at the final objective. However, arrival at the final objective—as in a direct car journey or dropping in by helicopter without passing along the way—is not the object of the exercise. "It is better to travel hopefully than to arrive," as Robert Louis Stevenson wisely observed, and a German saying used in the Way of the Eight Winds is *"Der Weg ist das Ziel"*—The way is the objective.

An Example Pathworking of the Way of the Eight Winds (1990)

Many mythological tales involve journeys in stages. The protagonists visit certain places where they must perform deeds or ask questions in order to progress to the next one. The places themselves express certain general principles and the questers or pilgrims must overcome them to progress. The following pathworking of the Way of the Eight Winds comes from an ancient Welsh poem, *Preiddeu Annwn* (The Spoils of Annwn), which recounts how King Arthur and his men embark on a ship entering the underworldly realm and visit seven forts or cities in turn before achieving their goal, to steal the magical cauldron of Pen Annwn. Many men are lost at each stage of the journey, and finally, only seven return. These seven cities recall the seven turns of the classical labyrinth and the seven stages of initiation.

Although Arthur's journey is by ship, the seven cities are symbolic of any pilgrimage journey or grades of initiation. The Way of the Eight Winds presents these visualizations as follows:

I. First is Caer Achren (or Ochren)—the City of the Trees. This signifies the earth, the forest through which the pilgrim travels to gain entrance to further lands and symbolic cities.

II. Caer Manawyddan—the City of the Sea God. This is the watery

state of transition, where one must give up the things one has brought so far.
III. Caer Goludd—the City of Riches. Here the delights of life are apparent, and the pilgrim must be wary of being detained here and never progressing further.
IV. Caer Rigor—the City of Frustration. This is where one feels one has failed; one is turned away, and internal realization is needed for the pilgrim to reach the next stage.
V. Caer Feddwydd—the City of Celebration. This signifies the fulfillment of the riches gained in City III, Caer Goludd, for those who could get beyond it.
VI. Caer Pedruven—the Four-Sided City. Here one gains a revelation of understanding, of wholeness and completion.
VII. Caer Sidhe (Sidd or Wydr)—the City of Glass. This is the center, the innermost realm, where all things can be seen.

When one traces the turns of the classical labyrinth, one can find the character of the cities at the successive turns.

Runic Exercises

The Way of the Eight Winds also uses runic exercises, which require a conversant knowledge of the twenty-four runes of the Elder Futhark.

First, make twenty-four cards, each with one of the runes drawn upon it. Learn to see and recognize runes, first on the cards, then to distinguish them when they appear among other things. Runes may appear in the shapes of anything one sees; in the branches of trees; in shadows; in the shapes of other things.

The exercise consists in going out and looking for the twenty-four runes in order. This can be done while walking about, for example, or by looking out of the window on a bus journey. Some runes will be easy to see, but when you don't see one, that is a blockage—meditate on that rune and the meaning it has to you.

Spiritual Exercises 303

Wheel of the Elder Futhark runes

Rites and Ceremonies

Although the present age is rife with invented ceremonies and commemorations of events and personages of particular political significance, these differ from traditional ones in that they are arbitrary. Traditional rites and ceremonies are performed for specific purposes, such as the consecration or inauguration of a building or other structure. They are performed at the proper auspicious time, determined by

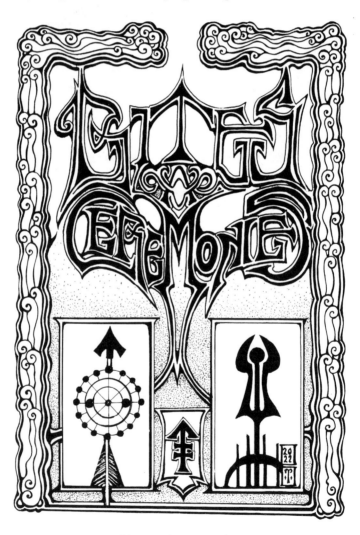

Rites and ceremonies

electional astrology or chronomancy. The rites take an appropriate form that emphasizes the nature and purpose of the thing being inaugurated. These rites are symbolic, structured through a system of correspondences that embodies the qualities required in the new thing whose full existence begins at this point. As an ancient Egyptian maxim from the *Instruction of Ankhsheshonq* papyrus (third century BCE) relates: "The builders build houses, the musicians inaugurate them."

Those who participate in the rites and ceremonies are not just spectators, as in modern ribbon cuttings by celebrities, but play their part in the event. It is important to perform proper rites and ceremonies at the inauguration of any spiritual project. Surviving folk traditions and written records give precise details of these techniques. The recognition of a place of mantic power does not require an elaborate ritual. A biodegradable offering of flowers (not wax candles—they should be removed after use) is sufficient. The re-establishment of places of ancient sanctity and the recognition of other, new ones is an important means of restoring our recognition of the once-sacred nature of the world.

Labyrinth fire ceremony in Baden-bei-Wien, Austria, on April 24, 1994

45

Tools and Techniques

The *Druid's Cord* or *Snor*

The *Druid's Cord* is a string or rope with twelve knots equally spaced, making thirteen equal units. In the East Anglian tradition, this measuring cord is called a *Snor* and the marker-knots are *snotches*. Druid's Cords can be of any length, so they can be a way of using different measures, depending on distance between knots, so long as they are equally spaced. But the cord is not primarily a form of measurement, but a proportionate geometrical tool.

The primary function of a Druid's Cord is the production of angles on the ground, as in laying out a garden or building plot. The cord can be used to construct triangles, all sides being whole numbers. For a right angle, the Pythagorean triangle of sides 3, 4, and 5 is used. For an approximation of the seventh part of a circle, a triangle of 5, 4, 4. Nineteen different triangles with whole-unit sides can be made with the Druid's Cord, producing forty different angles at the vertices. It is possible that this basic tool was used in antiquity to lay out stone circles and enclosures, ancient Egyptian structures, Norse triangular sacred plots, labyrinths on the ground, and medieval "mystic plots" for ritual use. The Druid's Cord also facilitates various other

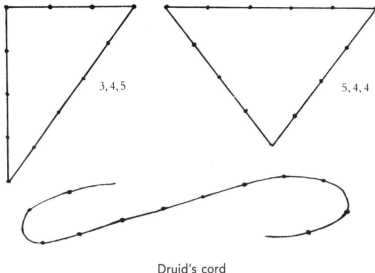

Druid's cord

shapes to be laid out (Morgan 1990, 109–13; Pennick and Gout 2004, 52–55, 111).

Making a Druid's Cord

One must consider for what the cord is to be used. If it is for laying out a sacred space outdoors, and various angles are required, a convenient length is thirteen feet. There are two methods of making a Druid's Cord.

The first method is to measure off a cord into thirteen equal sections using a ruler or tape measure, and then to tie knots at equal intervals along it. There are no knots at either end. The length of each section should be no more than a foot, or the cord will be longer than thirteen feet and unwieldy.

The second method involves measuring the cord off in a traditional way. For the purposes of this example, I assume intervals of around a foot. Take a cord longer than thirteen feet and estimate a convenient length from the end for the first knot. Then loop the cord from the first knot back to the end and tie another knot that distance from the first one. There will now be two knots the same distance apart as the distance between the end of the cord and the first knot. Continue this process measuring along the cord by looping back until twelve knots have been tied. Finally, loop back the remaining cord to the second-from-last knot and cut it off to length. There will now be a cord with twelve knots and thirteen sections. In laying out a ritual or sacred space on open ground, one will also need pegs around which the cord will run to mark out the space.

Measure in Magic

Taking someone's measure is considered to give the measurer power over that person. It is associated with death because the coffin-maker always needed to measure the dead person's body to make a coffin the right size for burial. If an evil person should have one's measure, then one was doomed.

But measurement was also an element of traditional healing. An accusation of measurement witchcraft from northern England is preserved in a Durham *Book of Depositions* from the year 1565 to 1573 (vol. 21 of the Publications of the Surtees Society). The alleged witch was Jennet Pereson, who was accused of using witchcraft in "measuring belts to preserve folks from the fairies," and taking payments to heal people "taken with the fairy." She was said to have sent for south-running water to heal a sick child whom they believed had been taken with the fairy and thus fallen ill. Her anti-fairy magic was condemned as witchcraft (Henderson 1866, 140–41). Three hundred years later in Wales, Marie Trevelyan recorded measurement used as a form of medical diagnosis (1909, 317):

> Old women who were skilful in making herb-tea, ointments, and decoctions of all kinds, professed to tell for certain if a person was consumptive. This was by measuring the body. They took a string and measured the patient from head to feet, then from tip to tip of

the outspread arms. If the person's length was less than his breadth, he was consumptive; if the width from shoulder to shoulder was narrower than from the throat to the waist, there was little hope of cure. The proper measure was made of yarn.

This practice appears to be based upon a belief that the ideal proportions of the human body are concomitant with health.

There are analogous ways of using things that have been calibrated against known measures. An example is Ouncle Weights, whose last official use was in Scotland. These were large stones, usually taken from the seashore, checked for weight against known weights and then used unaltered as weights on scales. Although they may have been odd numbers, they had a practical use in times when calibrated official weights were unavailable (Warrack 1911, 392).

Natural Measure and Mete-Wands

Natural Measure is a holistic system of great antiquity that is still of use today in handicrafts as well as restoration or reconstruction of premodern artifacts and buildings. The Way of the Eight Winds recommends it as more appropriate in these cases than decimal or metric measurements. Mete-wands (measuring sticks) should be made using these traditional units. The present author used his own, made in the Runestaff Crafts workshop, to lay out permanent labyrinths and other geomantic structures.

Natural Measure is an ancient system with its known origins in the Iron Age and used well into the medieval period. It continues today as the basis of the mile and its traditional submultiples, still in use in the United Kingdom (semi-officially) and the United States. The mile is a multiple of the ancient measure known as the northern foot, which measures 13.2 inches (335.3 mm). This northern foot is the basis of an ingeniously interlinked system of land measures, being the base unit of the rod, the rood, the acre, the furlong, and the mile. The northern foot has a

4:3 relationship to the natural foot (or Welsh foot), which are both submultiples of the rod (otherwise perch or pole) (16 feet, 6 inches; 5.0292 meters). The northern foot is one-fifteenth of a rod and the natural foot, one-twentieth. Both northern and natural feet are subdivided into palms or shafthands (Scots *shathmont* or *shaftmon*), 3.3 inches (83.8 mm). Three palms or shafthands make one natural foot and four make a northern foot. Each shafthand is further subdivided into three thumbs of 1.1 inches (27.9 mm), and each thumb is divided into three barleycorns of 0.37 inches (9.3 mm). So, the natural foot measures 9 thumbs (27 barleycorns) and the northern foot, 12 thumbs (36 barleycorns).

Measurements used in handicrafts and building construction extend these measures using an 8:3 pattern. An ell (cubit) is 2 northern feet long (8 shafthands); a fathom consists of 3 ells or 6 northern feet (24 shafthands); a rod is 2½ fathoms or 15 northern feet or 20 natural feet (60 shafthands). One furlong is 40 rods, which equals 600 northern feet or 800 natural feet or one-eighth of a mile. (In the eighteenth century, for surveying purposes, the furlong was subdivided into ten units called chains.) The mile measures 8 furlongs or 320 rods, which is 4,800 northern feet or 6,400 natural feet. Sometimes in England, a longer mile was reckoned, 10 furlongs in length. This is the country mile or Derbyshire mile, equal to 6,000 northern feet or 8,000 natural feet.

Measure of areas is derived from squares based on the rod (perch

NATURAL MEASURE

THE NATURAL FOOT IS DIVIDED INTO 27 BARLEYCORNS

AND, AS THREE BARLEYCORNS MAKE A THUMB, 9 THUMBS

AND, AS THREE THUMBS MAKE A SHAFTHAND, 3 SHAFTHANDS

THREE SHAFTHANDS MAKE A NATURAL FOOT

FOUR SHAFTHANDS MAKE A NORTHERN (SAXON) FOOT

or pole) of 15 northern feet. A rood of land measures one rod wide by one furlong in length, which is 15 × 600 northern feet or 20 × 800 natural feet. Its area is thus 9,000 square northern feet or 16,000 square natural feet. Four roods make an acre, measuring 60 × 600 northern feet or 80 × 800 natural feet. A ferlingate or *ferdelh* is one square furlong, 600 × 600 northern feet or 800 × 800 natural feet. Four ferlingata make one townyard or virgate, a quarter of a square mile or 1,200 × 1,200 northern feet. Four virgata make one hide of land, half of a square mile or 2,400 × 2,400 northern feet. The famous Hyde Park in London, England, is a relic of this traditional land measure, and the customary four quarters of medieval towns reflect the townyard of four ferlingata. From 1785, when the United States was surveyed for settlement, the mile was taken as the unit for the grid with which it was laid out. It was divided into sections of land that were then subdivided into four square quarters of 160 acres with sides half a mile long, the old English townyard. These quarters were again subdivided into 40-acre quarter-quarter parcels, the old English ferlingate. The landscape of the United States is the largest surveyed example of natural measure.

Traditional land measure is thus a completely integrated system. The present foot commonly used is not the northern one, though the northern foot is embedded in the measured landscape. It is a compromise originating in 1305 in the *Statute for Measuring Land* (33 Edw. I, Stat. 6, A.D. 1305), part of the reforms of King Edward I of England (1239–1307; reigned 1272–1307). Until then, different parts of the king's realm had different measures in use. In former Anglo-Saxon areas, the northern foot was used, but the natural foot was used in predominantly Celtic parts. Versions of the Roman foot were used by builders along with the Norman foot and the Greek common foot. The *Statute for Measuring Land* abolished these local variants and set up a standard foot that remains so today. Land-measure units from the rod upward remained the same but were redefined in the new system. The rod was now 16 feet 6 inches in the new measure, which subdivided the new foot into 12 inches and abolished the old subdivisions. This made the new foot (304.8 mm), a ratio of 10:11 with the old northern foot, which is the reason that the mile is an odd figure of 5,280 feet. Edward I's statute introduced one new measure. Three of the new feet became the meter-yard (yard, 914.4 mm) to which later mete-wands conformed. This was subdivided into 16 units, the nail of 2¼ inches, used in Britain until the twentieth century in cloth measure. Four nails of cloth measure made one quarter; three quarters made one Flemish ell. Four quarters made one yard, and five quarters made one English ell. Another measure related to the yard is the hand used to measure the height of horses: one hand being 4 inches, one-ninth of a yard. Thus, the new system of 1305 did not destroy the ancient measures but refigured them in an ingenious new way that accommodated the previous ones.

Mete-Wands

The traditional wood for a mete-wand is either oak or hazel. It is essential that the wood be arrow-straight. A simple mete-wand can be made from a straight stick, cut to the required length, generally an ell in traditional natural measure. Or it can be a flat piece of wood like a ruler. Either way, it can be marked into subdivisions, either by measurement with a ruler or tape measure, or by using a string the same length as the rod, looped back to find halfway and then redoubled to make quarters and doubled again to make eighths. In my traditional craft works produced by Runestaff Crafts from 1984 onward, I used a mete-wand with traditional measure for determining the dimensions of my artifacts.

Orientation

In the Catholic tradition, the center line (axis) of churches was aligned toward the point on the horizon where the sun rises on the day of the saint to which it was dedicated. Thus, a church dedicated to Saint George would align to sunrise on April 23, and so on. The line was laid out by direct observation and taken when the whole sun's disc was in view. Details of the ritual of church orientation were published by the Scottish freemason W. A. Laurie in his book *The History of Free Masonry and the Grand Lodge of Scotland* (1859, 414):

> On the evening previous, the Patrons, Ecclesiastics, and Masons assembled, and spent the night in devotional exercises; one being placed to watch the rising of the sun, gave notice when his rays appeared above the horizon. When fully in view, the Master Mason sent out a man with a rod, which he ranged in line between the altar and the sun, and thus fixed the line of orientation.

Church of St. Cecilia

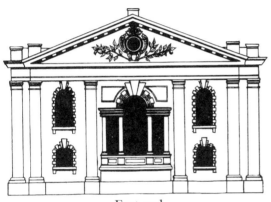

East end

West end

Orientation—east and west ends of a church dedicated to Saint Cecilia, designed by Nigel Pennick according to London principles, 2009. Not yet built.

Opposing Limbs of the Sun

A technique used in ancient India, Egypt, and Europe to determine a terrestrial north–south line uses "opposing limbs of the sun."

A method to make a line running due north–south using a magnetic compass finds only an approximation of terrestrial north because the magnetic poles do not coincide with the terrestrial poles. In addition, the magnetic field of the Earth is in continuous change, so the

The construction of sundials is related to the art of orientation. Portable sundial made by Nigel Pennick in 1999 for the latitude of the Schwarzwald, south Germany.

positions of the magnetic poles are always moving. Drawing a line halfway between the apparent rising and setting points of the sun gives a very good means of determining true north–south. This method of "opposing limbs of the sun" needs open, level ground with no obstructions such as trees or buildings that would block observation of the sun on the horizon. It also requires clear weather that allows observation of both events. The observer must be present during both sunrise and sunset, which, on a long summer's day can be a long time, depending on latitude. Sighting using a measuring rod the lower edge of the sun's disc in the morning, and the same height in the afternoon, is more practical and reduces the time necessary.

These positions are marked on the circle, and a line drawn between them. Bisecting this line gives the meridional line, terrestrial north–south. Particular measurements are not needed because this is a geometrical method. The east–west line can then be determined by making a right angle from the meridional line. A traditional way to determine a right angle is to use three rods of different lengths. This works on ratio, not absolute size; any convenient units will suffice, though of course the Way of the Eight Winds recommends natural measure as aesthetically appropriate. Rods of three, four, and five units long are brought together to form a Pythagorean triangle, which has a right angle.

A Practical Modern Example of Ancient Orientation

This technique is very ancient, probably dating from megalithic times, but it was continued in practical use by surveyors into modern times. Needing perfect accuracy to drive their tunnels in the proper place through the three-dimensional environment beneath the city streets, tube railway (subway) surveyors at the end of the nineteenth century always worked from first principles. The tunnel builders made their own surveys between mark points, which they fixed themselves by direct observation. In August 1898 civil engineers commenced the building of the Baker Street and Waterloo underground railway (now the Bakerloo Line of Transport for London), a deep tube line far beneath the streets. Not relying on existing maps, the chief surveyor, Francis E. Wentworth-Shields (1869–1959), conducted solar observations to determine his own meridian (true north–south line) north of the River Thames in Regent's Park. The true meridian was determined by observing the sun at the same elevation in the morning and afternoon with a theodolite and, after making the necessary corrections for changes in declination, bisecting the angle to obtain the meridian. The same technique was then repeated south of the Thames. From these two points, a survey connecting the two points was made at night through the streets, and shafts sunk to commence the tunneling. The principles used in ancient times were successful, and the Bakerloo tunnels were driven with pinpoint accuracy.

Labyrinths

Virtutis omnis est in actione laus.
(The glory of all virtue is in its performance.)
—SEVENTEENTH-CENTURY MOTTO

The classical (Cretan) labyrinth is unicursal with seven circuits that correspond symbolically with the seven planetary spheres that surround the Earth in traditional cosmology. In Christian mythology, seven steps support God's Throne of Majesty, as in the Basilica of San Michele Maggiore in Pavia, Italy, where a mosaic labyrinth that once depicted the Minotaur was set into a Throne of Majesty with seven steps. The seven cities in Arthurian myth also reflect the labyrinth.

As a pilgrimage or meditative pathway, the seven-turn labyrinth is a remarkable experience. When one enters, one walks close to the center point, which is the goal. But immediately, the first turn brings one far away, almost back to the beginning, where the next turn, amid the pathways, turns the walker back on a circuit even farther from the center. This comes close to the entrance at the next turn, which brings one

Way of the Eight Winds temporary floral labyrinth laid out by Nigel Pennick near Cologne, Germany, 2003.

into the outer circuit, as far from the center as possible. Having gone right round the outer circuit, one comes again near the entrance. From here, the circuit then takes one close to the center again. But the expectation of reaching the center is dashed as the path once more turns away on another circuit. This comes again close to the center, but again, one is turned away, skirting around the center yet not reaching it. But this is a short circuit, which, after one more turn, suddenly, and unexpectedly brings the pilgrim to the center. This is a challenge to the walkers' perseverance.

During my labyrinth workshop at the *Art in Action* festival at Waterperry House in Oxfordshire in 1987, I observed many adults became perplexed when walking through my brick classical labyrinth, clearly disheartened by the turns intended to deceive one into believing the next one was the center. Many stormed out, embarrassed and cross, making excuses and stating it was all silly, believing they had made a mistake, and failed to reach the center. They had not made any mistake

Labyrinth designed by Nigel Pennick in 1999 as a commission to celebrate the millennium at Pluckley (Kent, England). Original design with through passage to be used as one of the entrances to the churchyard. Unfortunately, not built.

in following the paths, but rather had experienced the frustration inherent in the design. This was exactly what the labyrinth was intended to do. However, it also demonstrated many modern people's lack of faith in themselves and inability to persevere in unfamiliar cicumstances.

Making Labyrinths

Traditionally, outdoor labyrinths were laid out using natural pebbles or boulders, or they were cut into turf with a spade. Materials for temporary labyrinths should be easily removable, or nonintrusive and biodegradable. I used biodegradable sawdust for the labyrinths I constructed at the Strawberry Fair in Cambridge for a number of years. Other materials I have used have included flowers, pinecones, and bark from felled trees. When making a labyrinth, one must consider the size it will be, and the time needed to build it. A labyrinth of stones I built on a beach in Ireland in 1988 with three others took three hours, as we were gathering stones as we went along. As the outer rings grew, it required us to walk farther and farther away to find suitable stones. Working like this is a spiritual exercise in its own right, requiring fortitude and endurance to complete the task.

Constructional method for the classical labyrinth

The classical labyrinth is based on a pattern of nine dots forming a cross. The distance between the dots defines the widths of the paths of the finished labyrinth. Laid out in the shape of an X, a cross is drawn through the central dot, between the arms of the X. Next, four angles are drawn whose apices are the inner four dots. From the end of these angles, parallel loops are drawn to the next corresponding dot, and once the final ends are joined up, we have a labyrinth.

It is not necessary to have a gridded plan drawn out unless one is building a permanent labyrinth to a particular design. To make the classical design, first lay out a cross of the chosen materials on the ground. Make sure that this center is far enough away from other things to enable a whole labyrinth to be completed. Once a cross has been made, decide on how wide the paths should be. The wider the path, the more materials will be needed for the labyrinth.

Constructing a classical labyrinth from wood blocks during a Way of the Eight Winds workshop by Nigel Pennick at Baden-bei-Wien, Austria, 1994.

Lay out the four *L*-shaped corners in the four angles of the cross as far away from it as the width of the path. Then connect the end of one of the *L* shapes to the top of the cross with a loop of material. This creates the center. Further loops are laid at path-widths from those already on the ground until finally the last end is connected up. A Baltic-type design begins with two interleaved pieces shaped like the letter *C* (or a *Jera* rune), and from these looping begins. One must decide where the ends of two of the four lines will be and this is more complex than a classical labyrinth, which "works out" from the way it is built.

ᛉ *Geomantic Walking*

Geomantic Walking is a quest for knowledge and understanding of unseen forces within the urban or rural environment. We pass through an unknown space, yet simultaneously cultivate curiosity and awareness of the psychic effects of its geomantic ambience.

This almost intangible feeling is the overall effect of the interaction over time between the physical structure, historic usages and events, and the current relationship and relations of individuals to that particular ambience.

Physically walking through an urban environment, one can experience an awareness of places that conceal hidden mysteries engendering a sensation of wonder and the miraculous. One may experience a feeling of transcendent awe in things and places that at a first cursory glance might appear mundane. Only by adventuring do we have a chance to enter into the vast and strange realms of the unknown. Perhaps beneath the polluted crust of everyday reality we may, in a receptive frame of mind, encounter shining the magic light.

Among the many factors that affect our reaction to where we find ourselves are time of day (the angle and brightness of light), the weather (seasonable or otherwise), and local air (and pollution) flows. The adverse effects of tall buildings erected ungeomantically at unsuitable places has been discussed elsewhere (see chap. 23). At any given time, the direction and strength of the wind may not appear of particular importance. Weather forecasts can be obtained easily, and only professional meteorologists, those who sail yachts, fly kites, or pilot aircraft, may pay much attention to the wind. Wind turbines automatically accommodate themselves to the wind conditions, as did traditional windmills in their final days. However, the time-honored understanding of the wind comes from millennia of observations on how humans are affected. Certain systems of divination will not work on windy days, and sensitive people can be "distempered" by strong winds and put out of action.

Although in many towns and villages weathervanes and weathercocks are present on buildings, few people ever take any notice of them. At best, they are considered ornamental relics of past times. However, they are of great value today in Geomantic Walking, for it is important when one visits a place to take note of the wind direction indicated by a vane. On most medieval churches one can determine the direction of the wind from the relation between the vane's direction and the orientated church.

The interaction between us as individuals and our surroundings is the essence of our being. Like the ever-changing and fluid flux of flowing air that we call the winds, our surroundings alter continually. As living beings, we are adapted to accommodate these changes. But often we do not notice them and take our natural adjustments for granted. Our consciousness generates the perception that we are separate individuals, which makes it difficult for some to realize that we are but integral parts of the continuum of existence. Yet it is possible to become aware, and that is a fundamental objective of the Way of the Eight Winds: *In One is All*.

"It is better to travel hopefully than to arrive." Robert Louis Stevenson motto on a sundial designed by the "new art" architect Herbert George Ibberson, at Hunstanton (Norfolk, England), 1908.

PART V
Metaphorical Texts

What we perceive to be discrete things are in reality those minute parts of an interconnected continuum that we select and name. We walk between darkness and light, and strive, if we are wise enough, to achieve balance and harmony in our ephemeral existence between birth and death.

46

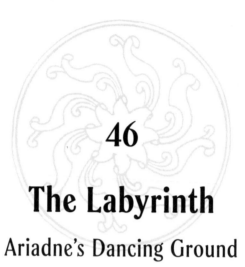

The Labyrinth
Ariadne's Dancing Ground

The Grecians rais'd an everlasting Monument
to their Genius's in the Labyrinth of Crete
built by Dedalus.
—ROBERT MORRIS,
LECTURES ON ARCHITECTURE (1734)

Because of its Greek origins, the Theseus-Minotaur legend of the labyrinth is best known. Compared with other labyrinth myths, it is aberrant, relegating the female role to the outside. Most labyrinth myths place the woman or goddess at the center, admitting the right man to be her lover. There, she is at the center of things. In the Greek myth, Ariadne is almost incidental. Although she gives Theseus the red thread that leads him to the center of the labyrinth, it is not she who is present there, but a male monster that he must slay. Having slain the monster and liberated the intended sacrifices, Theseus flees Crete, taking Ariadne with him. But, after performing the celebratory Crane Dance on Delos, Ariadne is left behind, seemingly abandoned because she is no longer of use to the hero.

On Delos, Ariadne led the Crane Dance—a labyrinthine spiral dance performed with a limp-like step said to imitate the love-dance of the Crane. Ariandne, whose title (recorded in a Linear B tablet from Knossos) was probably "Mistress of the Labyrinth," coming from the matristic culture of Crete, was the natural leader of the dance of the Goddess. According to legend, a dancing place was built at Knossos for Ariadne. Clearly, this was a labyrinth. The labyrinth of Knossos was built by Daedalus on the orders of the tyrannical King Minos. Daedalus is depicted as a metalworking technician who later escaped by Sardinia by flying. This legend seems to record a period when the former matristic culture was being overtaken by patriarchy; then the pattern of the Crane Dance, remembered by the Mistress of the Labyrinth, was made in physical form by a male technician. But perhaps, as Ariadne's title suggests, they were built by men for women to use in the rites of the Goddess. Outside the context of the living tradition, the activities of spirit that only humans can bring to a place, through the oral, gestural, and ritual dynamics of the song-dance, the physical form of the labyrinth is but a reminder of a great living richness.

But so long as the Anima Loci was honored, then the spirit of the place was maintained and enhanced. However, should any misuse take place, such as suggested by the Minotaur and the Wayland legends, then a harmful onlay would ensue. Essentially, the physical labyrinth is a static form of expression, but when made with regard to the Anima Loci it becomes ensouled matter as the living incarnation of spirit. It transforms into physical form the ephemeral path of the Crane Dance, as a material manifestation of the spiritual world.

In ancient central Europe, the crane was an archaic soul-bird of the Goddess, and in the Celtic tradition, cranes are sacred birds of mystery. Their feathered skins were used in soul-flight and as "medicine bags" to hold Oghams and other mysteries of Bardism. Also, the Siberian Ostyaks, among whom shamanism was long preserved, danced a version

The Lapwing Dance is the British equivalent of the Crane Dance. Lapwing dancing the labyrinth on a painted glass panel commissioned by artist Helen Field and made by Nigel Pennick in 2003.

of the Crane Dance, wearing crane skins. Until the nineteenth century, or perhaps later, the related "Lapwing Step" or *Schwäbischer Paß* was danced by shoemakers in the turf labyrinth at Stolp (now Słupsk, Poland) in Pomerania. In Manx mythology, three cranes stand at the entrance to the underworld, guarded by the deity Mider. They call to passersby to keep away, lest they be dragged from this life.

47

Wayland's House

In recent years, the labyrinth has enjoyed a wide recognition. Expanding beyond the bounds of church architects and local folk tradition, it has entered contemporary life and postmodern society. This renewed understanding of the labyrinth has come with a gradual dawning of the recognition that ancient Indigenous tradition, after all, is not the worthless, superseded stuff of benighted dolts and savages (as propagated for many years by devotees of industrial state modernism). When the labyrinths and labyrinth myths of ancient Crete and ancient Scandinavia were reexamined in this light, they were found to be not merely of interest, but of vital importance to human consciousness.

The legend of Wayland, analyzed here in the light of the teachings of the Way of the Eight Winds, shows us important things about our technological civilization. Wayland's story describes the results of the use of the intellect to the detriment of body and soul. Where humanity is present, hopefully we can be mindful of using mechanical technique without becoming dehumanized. But without this humane quality, we threaten our own souls and the material continuance of life itself.

In the unimaginable plurality of the Cosmos, there are the natural things we know: these are those things that our systems of awareness, perception, and consciousness can deal with. But there are also

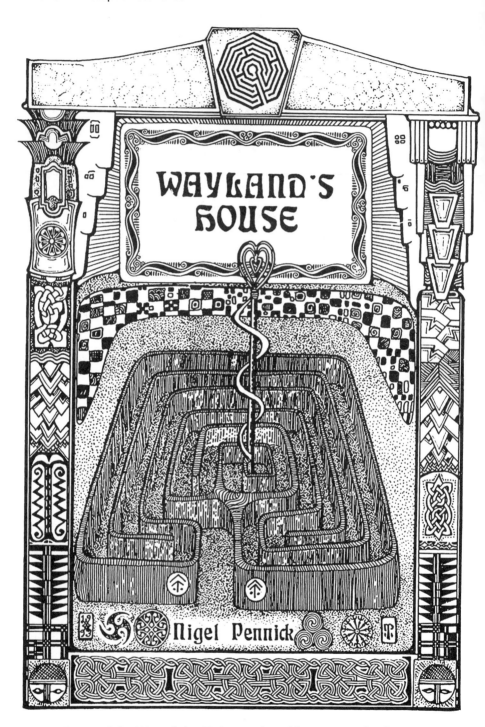

Cover of the Way of the Eight Winds publication *Wayland's House*

unknowable things that are equally natural. Elements of these can be glimpsed when we recognize the boundaries that are inherent in our perceptive faculties, and endeavor to understand them and their implications. Only then can we fully acknowledge our own position in the Cosmos, as conscious living beings that are not separated, but one with all life.

The Oral Tradition—Points of View

This work explores the legend of the metalworker known in England as Wayland (also known as Wieland and Völund). This legend is an allegory of technicianship relevant today. Traditionally, myths have different meanings to different people; they are flexible, multivalent descriptions of various aspects of transvolution. A myth has many "functions," symbolizing great depths of meaning that develop dynamically in relation to the circumstances in which it is retold. Unfortunately, modernity has promoted the opposite: the commonplace assumption that anything has a function—*one* function—that is *the* function. But this literalism, which is the root of all fundamentalist intolerance, is contrary to the direct experience of the pluralistic multiplicity of existence.

Like all ancient mythology, the legend of Wayland was an orally transmitted epic or story-complex whose episodes were re-created by storytellers, poetesses, and poets at appropriate instances. These tales were versions of "the story" from their point of view; different storytellers told alternative viewpoints of the story-complex according to the necessities and requirements of teller and participators ("audience"). Perhaps millennia passed from the coming-into-being of the story complex and the time it was written down.

The ancient Bardic tradition of the Celts, for example, forbade writing things down—it dulled the memory and removed the dynamic re-creation of the myth each time it was retold. But later, under the influence of so-called Religions of the Book that literalistically revere the word, only written material was considered of value by those in power. The fixity of the written word, in important ways contrary to the flow of manred in the Cosmos that is Nature's way, led inevitably to the impoverishment of mythology. When any story was written down, it was the specific oral version circulating among the men who recorded it.

Writing at a period when patriarchal religion was in the ascendancy, the male priests and monks who committed the stories to writing invested them with their own worldview, to the exclusion of others. Pluralism was killed. Other versions were either unknown to the writers, or were ignored or censored according to their prejudices, dogmas, and doctrines. In general, the viewpoint of women was ignored or suppressed. Later, with universal education based on the same belief system, the fixed written version of the legend was assumed without question to be the correct one.

Now the written version, essentially a fragmental selection of a multivalent whole, was taken as the standard of correctness and authenticity by which the alternative oral versions that still circulated should be judged. Appropriate knowledge as a force for transformation was thereby truncated, forced into a specific mould, and forged in an inflexible, unchanging form that reinforced the status quo of knowledge. It still has the negative effect of producing in the individual an inability to change life in a meaningful way, preventing direct human experience of a larger realm. Intuition, imagination, memory, vision, foresight became secondary to studying the authorized text. Universal education, sponsored by the state with national curricula intended to promote certain worldviews, drove down alternative viewpoints, including the orally transmitted storytelling that once was the core culture of society.

The Tragedy of Wayland

In the guise of swans, the valkyries, Odin's female "choosers of the slain" would make flights in swan form from Asgard to Middle Earth. When they spied a suitable stream for bathing, they would throw off their swan-skins and bathe in human form. Any mortal man who surprised them in the water could prevent them from leaving again if he stole their swan-plumage. Once, three valkyries, Alvit, Olrun, and Svanhvit, were swimming in the waters where they were surprised by three brothers, Wayland, Egil, and Slagfinn, who stole their swan-skins. Possession of the swan-skins gave the three men magical power over the valkyries, whom they forced to be their wives. But after nine years, the men's spell was spent, and the valkyries, assuming swan-form, escaped.

Slagfinn and Egil left home and journeyed northward in search of the escaped valkyries. Wayland, knowing the pursuit to be futile, stayed at home to pursue his craft as smith. He made 700 new rings as copies of the ring that Alvit had given him and bound them together like a garland. But, one night, returning from hunting, he noticed that Alvit's ring had disappeared. He saw this as a sign that Alvit would return. That night, he was surprised in his sleep and made prisoner by the Swedish king, Nidud, who used Wayland's own magic sword to mutilate his leg so that he could not walk. Captive and lamed, Wayland was taken to an island where he was compelled to make weapons for the king. There, Wayland built a labyrinth.*

Wayland still had the swan-skin that he had stolen from Alvit, and with it he was able (like the other labyrinth-man Daedalus) to escape from the island by air. But instead of escaping, he decided on a terrible revenge for his abduction and mutilation. One day, Nidud brought back the magic sword he had stolen from Wayland for him to repair. Wayland forged a replica of the sword which he gave to the king in place of the magically empowered original. Shortly afterward, Wayland enticed Nidud's sons into the labyrinth, where he killed them with his magic sword. Then he dismembered them and made drinking vessels from their skulls and jewels from their eyes and teeth. Then he sent these as gifts to King Nidud, his queen, and Princess Bodvild. They did not suspect the macabre origin of the gifts, believing their sons to have been lost at sea.

---

*The Icelandic name for a labyrinth or maze is *völundarhús*, "Wayland's House."

Later, Bodvild, who had taken one of Wayland's magical rings made of Rhine gold, brought it to Wayland to be repaired. Then he gave her a sleeping potion without her knowledge, and when she was asleep, he raped her. Then, donning Alvit's swan-skin, Wayland flew out of the labyrinth and away from the island to Nidud's palace. There, he stood upon the roof, taunting the king with what he had done to his family. The king summoned Wayland's brother, Egil, and ordered him to shoot him with an arrow. Egil, not wishing to kill his brother, shot at a bag under Wayland's arm. The arrow pierced the bag and blood—that of Nidud's sons, spurted out as Wayland flew away, unharmed. Wayland flew from Sweden to Elfland, where he continued to make weapons.

The Technician Who Profanes the World

At every stage of his story, Wayland profanes the mysteries. He captures and enslaves a valkyrie; he makes weapons for a corrupt master; he profanes Norse labyrinth magic before flying away in stolen magical attire to continue making weapons into the future in Elfland. As such, technique accommodates itself to good or evil purposes alike. Wayland, despite being compelled by the tyrant Nidud to work as a slave, is like those twentieth-century scientists who willingly developed nuclear weapons, and today gleefully tamper with the genetics of life, unable or unwilling to distinguish their love of technique from the effects of that technique. They are wilfully unaware of the inevitable outcome of their work. Shortsightedly, they celebrate technique while setting it at the service of corrupt authority.

Wayland, profaner of sacred taboos, is depicted as practitioner of a technology that is essentially against Nature. But this is not without cost. His wound, here inflicted by Nidud to enslave him, can be seen as symbolizing industrial injuries. Because the human being is a microcosm of the world, Wayland's injury is reflected in the outer world as pollution, and the destruction wrought by weaponry. Industrial pollution is not a new problem—it is only that today it is on an unprecedentedly devastating scale. In his famed Renaissance book on mining, *De Re Metallica*, published in 1556, Georgius Agricola (1494–1555) wrote that in ancient Italy, mining had been forbidden. For although the metals would be useful, the destruction wrought by their extraction and processing could never be compensated for by the useful products. This Pagan view of ecology contrasts markedly with the disastrous implications of contemporary fragmental fixations upon technique without regard to its immediate or long-term effect upon the environment. Techniques invented supposedly to improve the circumstances of human life have become elevated to the quasi-divine status of "research," commanding enormous resources.

Wayland's injury also indicated the disastrous effects of the technological emphasis upon the intellect at the expense of the sensual body. Continual use of technology deprives the amoral Wayland of his humanity, just as Nidud deprives him of his freedom. The dehumanized technician, as in all servants of state power, is viewed fragmentally by the rulers of society as no more than a useful agglomeration of useful characteristics that can be exploited when needed, then reassembled in another form, or thrown away when no longer useful. This is a parasitic lifestyle, where one being preys on another. Technologically, it is reflected in the current fragmental dismantling of the genetic material of life in the tellingly titled "genetic engineering." This desecrational technology has reduced the human to the level of a parasite, in which every part that is not "useful" degenerates and is removed, leaving just the genetic information for reproduction: sentience, consciousness, and soul are negated and obliterated.

The captive Wayland does not need to be able to walk to be a smith: he is permitted no activities save those of his function as a slave. He is defined only by the needs of the state (the king), which take precedence over his personal needs. He is mutilated, deprived of autonomous movement, losing his self-love. In his captivity he displays the authoritarian notion that the human being is a product. This is realized terrifyingly today in both modern totalitarian states and consumer society, in which the rules are laid down permanently and forcibly from above, not autonomously as and when needed by those who use them. It is inherent in the state to classify people according to nationality, race, class, religion, age, and gender, characteristics that pay no attention to individuality.

Wayland's story is a metaphor: he has the chance to use his technique to escape, but instead, he takes terrible revenge on the king by killing his sons and raping his daughter. In the amoral, taboo-breaking technician, his rebellious death drive is reinforced to the detriment of his life force. The destructive tendencies present in the human being, the aggressive aspect of our animal evolution, are refined into a peculiarly human form of destructiveness, informed by intelligence and learning. Wayland thereby awaits his opportunity to destroy the king's posterity rather than escaping immediately.

48

The Wayfarer's Legacy

Through an empty land of abandoned field enclosures and plots where cottages once stood, overgrown with wildflowers and trees, inhabited only by birds and feral animals, a spiritual traveler was passing. Amid the abundant wasteland, the wayfarer was confronted suddenly by an ostentum of an eldritch beast that seemed to beckon toward a certain spot illuminated by a magic light. This manifestation of the numinous was so striking that the wayfarer felt compelled to mark and honor the place lest the spirit depart never to return.

Now and again such events occurred during the age of the Wasting of the Land of Logres, when the Island of Britain was devastated and depopulated after the fall of the Roman Empire. Occasionally, a sacred building would be constructed on the place where a wayfarer had experienced the ostentum, a building that had everything to do with "here." The numen was enshrined and honored according to its peculiar local virtues and attributes. But not before long, an ideology from another landscape in a distant land was imported and onlaid over the particular unique numinosity of the place. Gradually, this numinosity was driven down by repeated imported rituals which had totally different intentions. The local was overridden by a monocultural claim of universality that nevertheless retained the unmistakable stamp of its outlandish origin.

Centralized orders from theocratic authorities in far-off lands drove down local numinosities in order that a standardized doctrine be enforced. Doctrine, being subject to hierarchical power struggles, is mutable. Schisms and reformations imposed from afar worked to further this alienating process until nothing remained of the eldritch numinosity experienced by the ancient wayfarer that had caused the original shrine to be brought into being. The place became gast, spiritually dead, for finally the indwelling spirit had been driven away. War, revolution, invasion, and pestilence finally destroyed what remained. The land was depopulated once more. The ruins stood abandoned, overgrown with trees, inhabited by new kinds of birds and wild animals, for the original ones had long since been exterminated.

EPILOGOS

Confluence

At present, we are amid the ruins of the project of modernism, which nevertheless still remains a faith for many. Back at the beginning of the ninth century of the Roman era, the middle of the first century CE, the Pythagorean sage Apollonius of Tyana taught that "things that violate nature can hardly come to be; and they anyhow quickly pass to destruction, even if they do come to existence" (Conybeare 1912, I:65). And as Thomas Aquinas wrote over a millennium later, "to hold creatures cheap is to slight divine power" (Gilby 1951, 129). But the perennial validity of the sages' spiritual teachings is ignored. The process of destruction rolls on, seemingly unstoppable. Yet the primal forces of creation do not change, and the cavalier destruction of the environment has consequences that anyone who is not hoodwinked by ideology can see. When things turn out badly—as they must if we do not turn away from the present destructive culture, living as if Nature does not matter—then this nemesis will not be the conscious revenge of Mother Nature, nor the wrath of God acting to punish wrongdoers, but the consequence of a certain way of behaving: an avoidable consequence. But it is no less catastrophic. Even when there is a triumph of avoidance—a victory of propaganda over veracity in human affairs—then it will only be a short while in cosmic terms before the truth will out. For it is useless to attempt to fool Nature.

A tragic loss of human empathy accompanies times of trouble when the arts are suppressed as unnecessary because of an urgent threat to survival. Without the presence of art, human emotions that could be shared and uplifted by artistic means now have no outlet but to descend into negativity and destructivity, which are then harnessed and directed by those with ideological agendas to gain power over others. Kindness, altruism, tolerance, and humaneness, expressed in the arts, are viewed as mere weaknesses by these fanatics who care nothing for anything but their beliefs. In the absence of any artistic outlets, existing art becomes devalued and ideological vandalism becomes possible. It is always accompanied by intimidation and often by terror. Ideological vandalism feeds on the fragility of civil society, seeking opportunities to overthrow existing ways and to take power. If the activists succeed, the nonactivist majority become exiles in their own land, a place no longer recognizable because everything they knew and loved has been erased. This cynical manipulation of people is far from a free society of pluralistic tolerance for all. No good ever comes of it, for they are the enemies of the human spirit. We accede to their demands at our peril. When culture is destroyed, then so is humanity.

The only way to be true to one's existence and the common good is by a constant referral back to real, lived experience. The Spiritual Arts and Crafts are a metaphor for our being-in-the-world, and one means of living real experience, because the Spiritual Arts and Crafts are just one segment of the wider symbolic order that is the Cosmos and life on Earth. For the individual, the life of the Spiritual Arts and Crafts only reaches an end when death brings cessation. Until then, the road goes ever on. Two old maxims—one English, one German—bring this to its present conclusion: "It is better to travel hopefully than to arrive," and *"Der Weg ist das Ziel"* ("The Path is the Goal"). We are *dewars* of the Earth, whether we recognize it or not. Dewars who fail to fulfill their spiritual duty will allow or cause the ancestral property that is in their care to be destroyed. All that our forbears have done to maintain culture and life on Earth can be thrown away in a short while if carelessness rather than responsibility is the ruling ethos. The principles of respect for the materials of creation, for the environment and for our fellow human beings that are implicit in the Way of the Eight Winds are in the spirit of the dewar who cares not just for family heirlooms, but the heirloom that belongs to and sustains us all—the Earth on which we live.

During my lifetime, I have seen Nature disappearing, my local countryside being rapidly urbanized, trees felled, hedgerows rooted out, and a catastrophic decline in the numbers and variety of birds and insects. In writing of my ancestral "Old West Surrey," I am telling of a lost land, the traditional culture of rural Old England driven down by modernity as certainly and as thoroughly as other Indigenous cultures in other lands were obliterated by external powers. In the 1980s the noted Suffolk horseman Neil Lanham said: "Tradition hangs by a thread."

In my teachings of the Way of the Eight Winds, I have attempted to maintain and continue this venerable holistic tradition and communicate it to others. There are a few who still live here today, those who know how to live in the land, not just off the land. We live in ever-changing conditions, but it is the essence, not the form, that is significant. Conscious reference to true principles enables us to live as nearly as possible in accordance with the ways of Nature. The forms in which the spirit appears must inevitably change with time. But so long as the essence is not utterly lost, so long as there are those aware that image is not reality, tradition will continue, even though nurtured by a small minority of people. Some may think that we are indeed "at the end of the day," that all of this is doomed, on the edge of extinction in a new darkening age of global catastrophe. But we must always keep in mind that the owl of Minerva only takes flight at dusk.

Symbolic drawing of Irminsul and Cosmic Eggs from
Pennick's Endsville Symbolicon (2023)

APPENDIX 1

Number Symbolism

Pythagoras taught that number was the first principle of all things. Pythagorean principles saw numbers as the source of geometrical figures.

1. The *Monad*. A single point; the essential, primal, indivisible beginning and source of all numbers, perfection, and goodness.
2. The *Dyad*. Departure from unity, doubling, loss of singleness, excess, and the beginning of imperfection in duality. The line joining two points.
3. The *Triad*. The restoration of harmony through the triangular balance of forces; the plane surface.
4. The *Tetrad*. Foursquare stability in the square and the cross. The first feminine square, 2 × 2.
5. The *Pentad*. The pentagram; uniting the first female number, 2, with the first male, 3, in mystic union. The origin of the Golden Section.
6. The *Hexad*. The first perfect number. Six is the perfect number because it reflects Nature in that it is composed of nothing but its own parts. Six is the sum of 1 + 2 + 3, and the product of the multiplication of the first feminine and masculine numbers, 2 × 3. In square measure, it is the area of the 3, 4, 5 triangle and the division

of the circumference of a circle by its own radius. Geometrically, it is the hexagon.

7. The *Heptad*. This is the virgin number, for 7 has neither factors nor is a product.
8. The *Octad*. This is the first cube, product of 2 × 2 × 2.
9. The *Nonad*. This is the first masculine square, 3 × 3.
10. The *Decad*. This contains all the archetypal numbers, 1 + 2 + 3 + 4, as the *Tetractys*.

27 is the first masculine, 3 × 3 × 3.
28 is the second perfect number 1 + 2 + 3 + 4 + 5 + 6 + 7.
35 is the sum of the first feminine and the fist masculine cube, 8 + 27.
36 is the product of the first square numbers 4 × 9; the sum of the first three cubes 1 + 8 + 27; and, as the sum of the first eight numbers, 1 + 2 + 3 + 4 + 5 + 6 + 7 + 8, and the square of the first perfect number, 6 × 6, it is the third perfect number.

APPENDIX 2

Musical Ratios

Musical ratios are part of Pythagorean wisdom. The following three ratios were considered harmonious:

8:16; 2:1—Octave, Diapason
4:6; 2:3—Fifth, Diapente
9:12; 3:4—Fourth, Diatessaron
1:2:3—Octave and a fifth
1:2:4—Double octave

The noted Renaissance architectural theorist Leon Battista Alberti (1404–1472) wrote in *The Ten Books of Architecture* (IX, V):

I am every Day more and more convinced of the Truth of Pythagoras's Saying, that Nature is certain to act consistently.... I conclude that the same Numbers, by means of which the Agreement of Sounds affects our Ears with Delight, are the very same which please our Eyes and our Mind. (Alberti 1986, 196–97)

APPENDIX 3

The Tides of the Day

The eight tides of the day as observed in Old England (with their Anglo-Saxon names),* described in the twenty-four-hour clock system, are as follows:

Morntide (*morgentīd*), from 4:30 to 7:30
Daytide (*dægmǣl*, "day-mark") or Undernoon, 7:30 to 10:30.
  This is the first tide of the Day.
Midday or Noontide (*middæg, nōntīd*), 10:30 to 13:30
Undorne or Afternoon (*ofernōn*), 13:30 to 16:30
Eventide (*ǣfentīd*), 16:30 to 19:30
Nighttide (*niht*), 19:30 to 21:30
Midnight (*midniht*), 21:30 to 1:30
Uht (*ūht*), 1:30 to 4:30

The directions played an integral part in traditional ways of life. The traditional reckoning of solar time was used in northern Europe until the arrival of cheap clocks and the imposition of standardized

---

*For corresponding names in related Germanic traditions, see the author's *Creating Places of Power* (2022), 130–32.

344

mean time, first by railway companies, then by governments. The Greenwich Meridian, surveyed in 1851 and adopted worldwide in 1884, was the signal for time zones to be imposed across most of the globe, generally extending individually across 15 degrees of longitude, and so they remain.

Glossary

ad quadratum: geometrical scheme based upon the square and subdivisions of the square, the octagram and the sixteenfold.

ad triangulum: geometrical scheme based upon the equilateral triangle and its development, the hexagram.

agrimensor (pl. *agrimensores*): member of the Roman guild of surveyors, who used the spiritual principles of the *Disciplina Etrusca*, the Etruscan Discipline.

airt: one of the eight directions; a family; one of the divisions of eight runes (Scots; Old Norse *ætt*).

álfrek: a place that is spiritually dead (Old Norse).

Arts and Crafts movement: denotes the artifacts of a material culture founded in London in 1888 that acknowledges, uses and celebrates its knowledge, traditions, skills, and spiritual understanding of how to do things appropriately and well.

bautastein (pl. *bautasteinar*): an uninscribed standing stone denoting a Pagan sacred enclosure in Scandinavia (Norwegian, from Old Norse *bautasteinn*).

bibliomancy: divination of a phrase or text by the random opening of a book.

Blitz: the destruction of British cities by aerial bombardment by the *Luftwaffe* (German Air Force) in World War II (1939–1945) (from German *Blitzkrieg*, "lightning war"; ironically, a form of warfare invented by a British military officer, J. F. C. Fuller [1878–1966], in 1918).

cardinal directions: north, east, south, and west; between each are the intercardinal directions (q.v.).

Coade stone: an artificial stone developed by Eleanor Coade (1733–1821) in London in 1769; also known as Lithodipyra.

Compagnonnage: the initiated organization of French craftspeople's guilds.

Cosmic Egg: symbol of the coming-into-being of the Cosmos; the emanation of the material world, renewal and regeneration, and rebirth.

Devoir: a particular branch of French craftspeople's guilds.

Devil's Plantation: a piece of uncultivated ground at the corner of a field or road, like a No Man's Land, belonging to the otherworld. Also (in Scotland) Gudeman's Croft, the Old Guidman's Ground, the Halyman's Rig, the Halieman's Ley, the Black Faulie, Clootie's Croft and (in England) Gallitrap, the Devil's Holt, and the Cocked Hat. *See* No Man's Land.

dewar: a hereditary keeper of a spiritual heirloom or numinous place. *See* harrowwarden.

disciplina: customary and time-tested modes and traditions of doing things (Latin). *See* Etruscan Discipline.

dowser: a person who uses a rod or pendulum to detect invisible things, such as underground water, objects in the ground, supposed emergies in the earth, and bodily functions.

electional astrology: working out the optimal inceptional horoscope for a project in advance and founding the venture at that moment (punctual time).

Empyrean, the: the uttermost sphere in European traditional cosmology.

enhazelled field: a place of ritual or combat delineated by a series of hazel posts around the perimeter.

Erdstrahlen: Earth radiation or rays from the ground postulated by German dowsers (German).

Etruscan Discipline: The ancient Etruscan *disciplina* of divination for the foundation and geomantic layout of temples, houses, and towns; the basis for the later Western and central European *Location*.

eurhythmy: the integrated interrelationship of all proportions within a structure or performance.

ex-voto: an artifact offered in thanks to a divine being who has granted a boon or an answer to prayer.

fane: a Pagan sanctuary.

farthest beacon: a distant landmark used in lining-up the first rig in plowing and shepherds' sundials.

feng shui: "wind and water," Chinese geomancy.

foundation: the act of marking the beginning of a building, by laying a stone with rites and ceremonies. Traditionally, the material foundations are called the *grounds*. Also used to describe the "founding event" of a religion, guild, or nation.

Host, the: a consecrated wafer used in the Catholic sacrament of the Holy Communion.

gast: a piece of ground bound magically to be unproductive; a piece of land from which all the spirits have been banished (East Anglian).

gematria: the art of numerology, deriving numbers from names and words in Hebrew and Greek (via Aramaic from Greek *geometria*).

genius loci: the "spirit of the place," honored in various ways as a literal spirit, as a discernable quality, or both (Latin).

geomancy: (1) divinatory technique using earth, stones, beans, nuts, etc., to make figures that are read for their meaning.; (2) the art of location of buildings, etc., holistically in recognition of the site and the prevailing conditions, physical and spiritual, as in the Etruscan Discipline, European *Location*, Indian *Vastuvidya*, Malagasy *Vintana*, Burmese *Yattara*, Chinese feng shui, etc.

guild: cooperative organization of craftspeople.

grounds: physical foundations of a building or the fundamental basis of a principle.

harrowwarden: guardian of a holy place (Old English *heargweard*).

Helikon: diagram noted by Ptolemy and associated with Sebastiano Serlio, division of the square to produce whole-number ratios.

icon: (1) a sacred image that is a spiritual emodiment of the power or personification depicted; (2) a striking image in modernism that is held to embody the character shown or the *Zeitgeist*.

inceptional horoscope: The horoscope of a project at its beginning (see electional astrology).

intercardinal directions: the directions lying at forty-five degrees to the cardinal ones—northeast, southeast, southwest, and northeast.

landwisdom: knowledge of the nature and custom of the country.

legendarium: the overall body of stories, legends, tales, poems, traditions, songs, and writings about any partuicular thing or place, without a judgment of veracity according to the precepts of historical research.

leuga (*baneluca*): sacred boundary around a sanctuary (Anglo-Norman; cf. French *banlieu*).

locus: a particular place (Latin).

main: indwelling empowerment that emanates from the spiritual nature of a being or body (cf. "might and main").

mana: all-pervading energy in the Melanesian and Polynesian traditions. Adopted in the nineteenth century by Western anthropologists and then applied as a general principle in mantic and magical contexts.

manred: the "flowing particles," metaphor for the flux of all things in the Welsh Bardo-Druidic spiritual tradition.

mete-wand: a measuring-stick.

modernism: a theory of art and life based wholly upon materialist values, characterized by industrial production, with deliberate rejection of tradition.

Moirai: the three female Fates in Greek religion, personifications of the tripartite states of being: past, present and future—Clotho, Lachesis, and Atropos (Ancient Greek).

No Man's Land: (1) a triangle of ground at a *trifinium*, belonging to no individual, but to the spirit world. Closely related to the Devil's Plantation (q.v.), etc.; (2) the contested territory between the trenches in trench warfare. *See* trifinium.

Norn (pl. *Nornir*): Northern Tradition version of the Fates: Urd, Verdandi, and Skuld: past, present, and future. *See* Moirai.

Nowl: the polar North Star, the Lode Star, *Polaris*.

omphalos: the "Navel of the World," spiritual center point, often depicted as an egg-stone (Ancient Greek).

orientation: the direction of something toward the east.

ørlög: the history of something; all the concatenation of events that have led up to the coming-into-being of the particular thing or person in question.

ostentum: something that appears or is noticed suddenly, with a meaning immediately apparent to the beholder.

pentagram: a five-pointed, equal-sided star.

psychogeography: the study of specific effects of a geographical environment on the (conscious or unconscious) emotions and behaviors of individuals.

relic: a fragment of human body—such as a skull, bones, or blood—from a person regarded as holy enshrined as an object of worship in a church; a continuation of an earlier cult of the ancestors.

reserved sacrament: a consecrated Host (q.v.) not consumed in a Holy Communion ritual but kept as a sacred presence in a tabernacle in a church.

rig: a straight line, as in plowing or sighting on an object.

rune: (1) a cryptic or magical sigil, carved, painted, written, or recited; (2) character of the ancient Germanic alphabet legendarily gained by Odin through shamanic ritual.

Snor: otherwise called the "Druid's Cord." A a string or rope with twelve knots equally spaced, making thirteen equal units (East Anglia). *See* snotch.

snotch: marker-knots on a Snor (East Anglia).

sociocide: where a whole community and its entire culture is wiped out, only differing from genocide in that the people continue to live, dislocated and empty. Architect Aldo van Eyck defined sociocide in an interview with William Rothuizen in the *Haagse Post* newspaper (the Hague, Netherlands, 14 December 1974), giving as an example the destruction of the Kattenberg neighbourhood in that city: "the difference from genocide is that the people stay alive, though everything else is gone . . . all intersocial relationships vanish and the people are left sad and uprooted."

sprowl: innate energy or spiritual substance, akin to spirament, pneuma, etc. (East Anglia).

stafgarð: ancient Scandinavian sacred ground, literally "fenced enclosures" (Old Norse *stafgarðr*).

Taj al Maluk: Malaysian geomancy (*Tajalmaluk* in Indonesia).

transvolution: the process of the way things happen; change through time that does not necessarily involve evolution or progress.

trifinium: the triangular junction of three paths or roads (Latin).

trollknut: knotted string from Scandinavian folk magic, either interpreted as a "troll-knot," apotropaic against trolls and other harmful entities, or more generally as a "magic knot" (Swedish).

trouvaille: A found object that has significance to the finder (French).

Vastuvidya: Indian geomancy (Sanskrit).

vé: triangular sacred enclosure in Pagan Scandinavia (Old Norse).

vébönd: fence around a *vé*, denoting the extent of the holy ground (Old Norse). *See* vé.

Web of Wyrd: the interwoven fabric of things, places, events, actions, and persons that make up our world as we experience it (Old English *wyrd*).

Will O' the Wisp: Supposed sprite (spirit) carrying a light that leads wayfarers astray in fenland darkness. Goes under other names including Jinny Burnt-Tail and Willywisp.

Wyrd: that which comes to happen (Old English).

Zeitgeist: theoretical "spirit of the age," the claim that certain things are more appropriate to "the time" than others; often used as a recommendation and justification for certain manifestations of modernism (German).

Bibliography and Sources for Further Study

Note: This bibliography contains works that were relevant to the genesis and teachings of the Way of the Eight Winds; wider works, older and more recent, that deal with the subject matter of this book; and relevant works by the current author.

Abercrombie, Patrick. 1933. *Town and Country Planning*. London: Thornton Butterworth.
Ackroyd, Peter. 1990. *Dickens*. London: Vintage.
———. 2000. *London: The Biography*. London: Chatto and Windus.
Agrippa, Henry Cornelius. 2021 [1533]. *Three Books of Occult Philosophy*. Translated by Eric Purdue. 3 vols. Rochester, VT: Inner Traditions.
Alberti, Leon Battista. 1986. *The Ten Books of Architecture: The 1755 Leoni Edition*. Translated by James Leoni. New York: Dover.
Ambelain, Robert. 1940. *La Géomancie Magique*. Paris: Niclaus.
Anawalt, Patricia Rieff. 2014. *Shamanic Regalia in the Far North*. London: Thames and Hudson.
Anderson, Benedict. 1991. *Imagined Communities: Reflections on the Origin and Spread of Nationalism*. London and New York: Verso.
Anglickienė, Laima. 2013. *Slavic Folklore: Didactical Guidelines*. Kaunas: Vytautas Magnus University.
Aspelin, J. H., Haye Hamkens, Siegfried Sieber, and Friedrich Mössinger. 1982. *Trojaburgen*. Translated by Michael Behrend and Debbie Saward.

Thundersley and Bar Hill, UK: Institute of Geomantic Research and the Caerdroia Project.
Aubrey, John. 1857. *Miscellanies Upon Various Subjects*. Fourth edition. London: Smith.
Aurelius, Marcus. 2006. *Meditations*. Translated by Martin Hammond. London: Penguin.
Aveni, A., and G. Romano. 1994. "Orientation and Etruscan Ritual." *Antiquity* 68: 545–63.
Ayres, James. 1977. *British Folk Art*. London: Thames and Hudson.
Babington, Churchill, ed. 1869. *Polychronicon, Ranulph Higden monachi Cestrensis; together with the English Translations of John Trevisa and of an Unknown Writer of the Fifteenth Century*, vol. II. London: Longmans, Green.
Bächtold-Stäubli, Hanns, ed. 1927–1942. *Handwörterbuch des Deutschen Aberglaubens*. 9 vols. Berlin: Koehler und Amelang.
Backhouse, Halcyon, ed. 1992. *Meister Eckhart*. London: Stoddard and Houghton.
Baillie Scott, Mackay Hugh. 1906. *Houses and Gardens*. London: Newnes. (Chapter 17: "The Soul of the House.")
Baker, Phil. 2003. "Secret City: Psychogeography and the End of London." In *London from Punk to Blair*, edited by Joe Kerr and Andrew Gibson. London: Reaktion.
Banks, M. M. 1935. "Tangled Thread Mazes." *Folk-Lore* 46: 78–80.
Baring-Gould, Sabine, and John Fisher. 1907–1913. *The Lives of the British Saints*. 4 vols. London: Honourable Society of Cymmrodorion.
Barker, A. T. 2021. *The Mahatma Letters to A. P. Sinnett from the Mahatmas M. and K. H., Transcribed, Compiled, and with an Introduction by A. T. Barker*. Pasadena, CA: Theosophical University Press.
Barrett, Francis. 2007 [1801]. *The Magus, or Celestial Intelligencer*. Stroud, UK: Nonsuch.
Barrett, William. 1926. *Deathbed Visions*. London: Methuen.
Basford, Kathleen. 1978. *The Green Man*. Ipswich, UK: Brewer.
Bass, Joseph A. 1999. *Famous Trees of Robin Hood's Forest*. Newark, UK: Albatross.
Bauman, Zygmunt. 1988. *Modernity and Ambivalence*. Ithaca, NY: Cornell University Press.
Begg, Ean. 1985. *The Cult of the Black Virgin*. London: Penguin.
Behrend, Michael. 1975. *The Landscape Geometry of Southern Britain*. Bar Hill, UK: Institute of Geomantic Research.

Benson, Robert Hugh. 1906. *The Light Invisible*. London: Pitman and Sons.
Bersuire, Pierre. 1489. *Reportorium morale*. Edited by Johannes Beckenhaub. Nuremberg: Koberger.
Besant, Annie, and C. W. Leadbeater. 1901. *Thought-Forms*. London: Theosophical Publishing House.
Bettis, J. D., ed. 1969. *The Phenomenology of Religion*. New York: Harper and Row.
Betz, Hans Dieter, ed. 1986. *The Greek Magical Papyri in Translation including the Demotic Spells*. Chicago: University of Chicago Press.
Bevan, Robert. 2006. *The Destruction of Memory: Architecture at War*. London: Reaktion.
Billingsley, John. 1980. "Anarchaeology." *Northern Earth Mysteries* 9 (October): 3–6.
Bills, Mark. 2010. *Watts Chapel: A Guide to the Symbols of Mary Watts' Arts and Crafts Masterpiece*. London: Wilson.
Blackmore, Susan J. 2017. *Seeing Myself: The New Science of Out-of-the-Body Experiences*. London: Robinson.
Blain, Jenny, and Robert J. Wallis. 2002. "A Living Landscape? Pagans, Archaeology, and Spirits in the Land." *3rd Stone: Archaeology, Folklore, and Myth—The Magazine for the New Antiquarian* 43 (Summer): 20–27.
Blamires, Steve. 2013. *The Little Book of the Great Enchantment*. Cheltenham, UK: Skylight.
Blind, Karl. N.d. "Wodan, the Wild Huntsman." *The Gentleman's Magazine* n.s. 25: 32.
Blount, Godfrey. 1905. *The Science of Symbols: Setting Forth the True Reason for Symbolism and Ritual*. London: Fifield.
———. 1910. *Arbor Vitæ: On the Nature and Development of Imaginative Design*. London: Fifield.
Bortoft, Henri. 1996. *The Wholeness of Nature—Goethe's Way toward a Science of Conscious Participation in Nature*. Hudson, NY: Lindisfarne.
Bouché-Leclerq, Auguste. 1975 [1879–1882]. *Histoire de la divination dans l'antiquité*. 2 vols. New York: Arno.
Bragdon, Claude. 1913. *Projective Ornament*. Rochester, NY: Manas.
Braudel, Fernand. 1981 *The Structures of Everyday Life*. Translated by Siân Reynolds. New York: Harper and Row.
Breton, André. 1937. *L'Amour Fou*. Paris: Gallimard.

———. 1974. *Manifestos of Surrealism*. Translated by Richard Seaver and Helen R. Lane. Ann Arbor: University of Michigan Press.
Briggs, Katharine. 1977. *A Dictionary of Fairies: Hobgoblins, Brownies, Bogies and Other Supernatural Creatures*. Harmondsworth: Penguin.
Broadbent, Geoffrey. 1977. "A Plain Man's Guide to the Theory of Signs in Architecture." *Architectural Design* 7–8: 474–82.
Broadwood, Lucy E., and J. A. Fuller Maitland. 1893. *English County Songs*. London and New York: Leadenhall.
Broomhall, F. H. 1991. *The Longest Fence in the World: A History of the No. 1 Rabbit Proof Fence from its Beginning until Recent Times*. Perth: Hesperian.
Brown, Calum G. 2001. *The Death of Christian Britain*. London: Routledge.
Brown, P. D. 2022. *Thirteen Moons: Reflections on the Heathen Lunar Year*. North Augusta, SC: Gilded Books.
Browne, Thomas. 1909–1914 [1642]. *Religio Medici*. New York: Collier and Son.
———. 1927 [1635]. *Pseudodoxia (Works)*. Edinburgh: Grant.
Buckley, Joshua. 2004. "Keeping Up the Day: Joshua Buckley Interviews Nigel Pennick." *Rûna* 15: 2–5; 16: 7–10.
Bulwer-Lytton, Edward. 1871. *The Coming Race*. Edinburgh and London: Blackwood and Sons.
Burdick, Lewis Dayton. 1901. *Foundation Rites with Some Kindred Ceremonies: A Contribution to the Study of Beliefs, Customs, and Legends Connected with Buildings, Locations, Landmarks, etc*. New York: Abbey.
Burgess, Michael W. 1978. "Crossroad and Roadside Burials." *Lantern* 24: 6–8.
———. 1979. "Early East Anglian Antiquarians, I: Alfred Watkins and the Theory of Ley Lines." *Lantern* 25: 6–9.
Caine, Mary. 1978. *The Glastonbury Zodiac: Key to the Mysteries of Britain*. Torquay, UK: Grael Communications.
Carpenter, Edward. 1912. *The Art of Creation: Essays on the Self and Its Powers*. London: Allen and Unwin.
Carr-Gomm, Philip, and Richard Heygate. 2010. *The Book of English Magic*. London: Murray.
Cellarius, Andreas. 1660. *Harmonia Macrocosmica*. Amsterdam: Janssonius.
Chambers, William. 1773. *A Dissertation on Oriental Gardening*. Second expanded edition. London: Griffin.
Chapman, Rod. 2007. *Seven: An Idiosyncratic Look at the Number Seven*. North Elmham, UK: 7Star.

Charpentier, Louis. 1972. *The Mysteries of Chartres Cathedral*. Translated by Ronald Fraser. New York: Avon.

Charters, Samuel. 1973. *Robert Johnson*. New York: Oak.

Chippindale, Christopher. 1987. *Stonehenge Complete*. London: Thames and Hudson.

Chippindale, Christopher, Paul Devereux, Rhys Jones, and Tim Sebastian, eds. 1990. *Who Owns Stonehenge?* London: Batsford.

Coleridge, Samuel Taylor. 1920. *Biographia literaria, Chapters 1–4, 14–22*. Edited by George Sampson. Cambridge: Cambridge University Press.

Coles, Alex, ed. 2000. *Site-Specificity: The Ethnographic Turn*, vol. 4. London: Black Dog.

Colquhoun, Ithell. 1957. *The Living Stones*. London: Owen.

Conybeare, F. C., ed. and trans. *Philostratus: The Life of Apollonius of Tyana*. 2 vols. London: Heinemann, 1912.

Cook, Martin Godfrey. 2015. *Edward Prior: Arts and Crafts Architect*. Marlborough: Crowood.

Corbin, Alain. 1994. *Village Bells: Sound and Meaning in the Nineteenth-century French Countryside*. Translated by Martin Thom. New York: Columbia University Press.

Crawford, Alan. 1985. *C. R. Ashbee: Architect, Designer and Romantic Socialist*. New Haven: Yale University Press.

Crawford, J. C. 1969. *History of the State Vermin Barrier Fences (formerly known as "Rabbit-proof Fences")*. Perth: Department of Agriculture and Food, Western Australia.

Crooke, W. 1909. "Burial of Suicides at Crossroads." *Folk-Lore* 20: 88–89.

Cumont, Franz. 1919. "Mithra ou Serapis Kosmokrator." *Comptes Rendus des séances de l'Academie des Inscriptions et Belles-Lettres*: 322.

Curnow, Trevor. 2004. *The Oracles of the Ancient World*. London: Duckworth.

Dalí, Salvador. 1935. *La Conquète de l'Irrationel*. Paris: Surréalistes.

Danser, Simon. 2005. *The Myths of Reality*. Wymeswold, UK: Alternative Albion.

Davidhsson, Ólafur. 1903. "Isländischer Zauberzeichen und Zauberbücher." *Zeitschrift des Vereins für Volkskunde* 13: 150–67.

Davies, Owen. 2003. *Cunning Folk: Popular Magic in English History*. London: Hambledon.

Dávila, Nicolás Gómez. 2023. *The Authentic Reactionary: Selected Scholia* of Nicolás Gómez Dávila. Translated and edited by Ramon Elani. North Augusta, SC: Arcana Europa.

Debord, Guy. 1992. *The Society of the Spectacle*. London: Rebel.

Demetrius. 1932. *On Style*. Translated by W. Rhys Roberts. In *Aristotle, the Poetics; Longinus on the Sublime; Demetrius on Style*, translated by W. Hamilton Fyfe and W. Rhys Roberts. London: Heinemann.

Denham, Michael Aislabie. 1892–1895. *The Denham Tracts*. 2 vols. London: Folk-Lore Society.

De Santillana, Giorgio, and Hertha von Dechend. 1969. *Hamlet's Mill: An Essay Investigating the Origin of Human Knowledge and its Transmission Through Myth*. Boston: Gambit.

Devereux, Paul. 1982. *Earth Lights: Towards an Understanding of the Unidentified Flying Object Enigma*. Wellingborough, UK: Turnstone.

———. 2002. "The Secret History of Corpse Ways." *3rd Stone* 41 (Winter 2001/2002): 7–11.

Devereux, Paul, and Ian Thomson. 1987. *The Ley Guide: The Mystery of Aligned Ancient Sites*. Llanfyllin, UK: Empress.

Dewey, John. 1922. "Realism without Monism or Dualism." *The Journal of Philosophy* 19: 13.

Dutt, W. A. 1926. *The Ancient Mark Stones of East Anglia*. Lowestoft, UK: Flood and Sons.

Dyggve, Ejnar. 1954. "Gorm's Temple and Harald's Stone Church at Jelling." *Acta Archaeologica* 25: 221–41.

Eitel, Ernest John. 1873. *Feng-Shui, or the Rudiments of Natural Science in China*. London: Trübner.

Eksteins, Modris. 1989. *The Rites of Spring: The Great War and the Birth of the Modern Age*. Boston: Houghton Mifflin.

Ekwall, Eilert. 1980. *The Concise Oxford Dictionary of English Place-Names*. Fourth edition. Oxford: Clarendon.

Eliade, Mircea. 1959. *The Sacred and the Profane*. New York: Harcourt, Brace, Jovanovich.

Ellis-Davidson, Hilda. 1993. *The Lost Beliefs of Northern Europe*. London: Routledge.

Endell, August. 1902. "Originalität und Tradition." *Deutsche Kunst und Dekoration* 9 (1901–1902): 289–96.

Epictetus. 2008. *Discourses and Selected Writings*. Edited and translated by Robert Dobbin. London: Penguin.

Erdmann, Martin. 1883. *Zur Kunde der hellenische Städtgrundungen.* Straßburg: Heitz.
Ericson, E. E. 1936. "Burial at the Cross-Roads." *Folk-Lore* 47: 374–75.
Ernst, Max. 1929. *La Femme 100 Têtes.* Paris: Carrefour.
Evans Wentz, W. Y. 1911. *The Fairy Faith in Celtic Countries.* Oxford: Oxford University Press.
Faber, Richard. 1983. *The Brave Courtier: Sir William Temple.* London: Faber and Faber.
Falk, Ann-Britt. 2006. "My Home is My Castle: Protection against Evil in Medieval Times." In *Old Norse Religion in Long-Term Perspectives: Origins, Changes, and Interactions,* edited by Anders Andrén, Kristina Jennbert, and Catharina Raudvere. Lund: Nordic Academic Press. Pp. 200–205.
Farrar, Janet, and Stewart Farrar. 1981. *Eight Sabbats for Witches.* London: Hale.
Feuchtwang, Stephan. 1974. *An Anthropological Analysis of Chinese Geomancy.* Vientiane, Laos: Vithagna.
Fevre, Ralph W. 2000. *The Demoralization of Western Culture: Social Theory and the Dilemmas of Modern Living.* London and New York: Continuum.
Fontenrose, Joseph. 1971. *The Ritual Theory of Myth.* Berkeley: University of California Press.
Forrest, Robert. 1976. "The Mathematical Case against Ley Lines and Related Topics." *Journal of Geomancy* 1.1 (October): 10–15.
Fortune, Dion. 1933. "Ceremonial Magic Unveiled." *The Occult Review* 57 (January): 13–24.
Fowler, David. 2013. *Scarborough Snippets.* Scarborough, UK. Farthings.
Franklin, Anna. 2002. *The Illustrated Encyclopedia of Fairies.* London: Vega.
Garrard, Bruce, and David Rossiter. 1980. *The Arrow: The Founding of the New Cathedral at Salisbury.* Salisbury, UK: N.p.
Gellner, E. 1992. *Postmodernism, Reason and Religion.* London: Routledge.
Geoffrey of Monmouth. *The History of the Kings of Britain.* Translated by Lewis Thorpe. London: Penguin, 1966.
Gerard of Cremona. 1978 [1655]. "Astronomical Geomancy." In *The Fourth Book of Occult Philosophy,* by Henry Cornelius Agrippa. London: Askin.
Gerner, Manfred. 1983. *Farbiges Fachwerk.* Stuttgart: Deutsche Verlags-Anstalt.

———. 2003. *Formen, Schmuck und Symbolik in Fachwerkbau*. Stuttgart: Fraunhofer Informationszentrum Raum und Bau.
Gilby, Thomas, ed. and trans. 1951. *St. Thomas Aquinas: Philosophical Texts*. London: Cumberlege / Oxford University Press.
Godwin, Joscelyn. 1987. *Music, Mysticism and Magic: A Sourcebook*. London: Arkana.
Golding, John. 2000. *Paths to the Absolute: Mondrian, Malevitch, Kandinsky, Pollock, Newman, Rothko and Still*. London: Thames and Hudson.
Golvers, Noël. 1994. "De recuiteringstocht van M. Martini, S.J. door de Lage Landen in 1654 over Geomantische Kompassen, Chinese verzamelingen, lichtbeelden en R. P. Wilhelm van Aelst, S.J." *De Zeventiende Eeuw* 10: 331–50.
Gordon, Elizabeth Oke. 1914. *Prehistoric London: Its Mounds and Circles*. London: Covenant.
Gouk, Penelope. 1988. *The Ivory Sundials of Nuremberg 1500–1700*. Cambridge: Whipple Museum.
Gould, Veronica Franklin. 1998. *Mary Seton Watts (1849–1938): Unsung Heroine of the Arts and Crafts*. Compton: Watts Gallery.
Graham, Daniel. 1988. "Symmetry in the Empedoclean Cycle." *The Classical Quarterly* 38.2: 297–312.
Graves, Tom. 1978. *Needles of Stone*. London: Turnstone.
Green, C. 1968. *Out-of-the-Body Experiences*. Oxford: Institute of Psychophysical Research.
Green, Dennis Howard. 1998. *Language and History in the Early Germanic World*. Cambridge: Cambridge University Press.
Grist, Tony, and Aileen Grist. 2000. *The Illustrated Guide to Witchcraft: The Secrets of Wicca and Paganism Revealed*. Newton Abbot: Godsfield.
Groves, Derham, 1991. *Feng-Shui and Western Building Ceremonies*. Singapore and Lutterworth: Brash/Tynron.
———. 2011. "Some Similarities between the Feng-Shui of Chinese Joss-Houses in Australia and Postmodern Architecture." *Grainger Studies: An Interdisciplinary Journal* 1: 55–73.
Guenon, René. 1945. *Le Règne de la Quantité et les Signes des Temps*. Paris: Gallimard.
———. 2009. *The Essential René Guenon*. Edited by John Herlihy. Bloomington, IN: World Wisdom.

Guidon. 2011 [1670]. *Magic Secrets and Counter-Charms*. Hinckley, UK: Society of Esoteric Endeavour.

Habermas, Jürgen. 1987. *The Philosophical Discourse of Modernity*. London: Polity.

Hall, Alaric. 2007. *Elves in Anglo-Saxon England: Matters of Belief, Health, Gender and Identity*. Woodbridge, UK: Boydell.

Halliwell, James Orchard. 1874. *Dictionary of Archaic and Provincian Words*. London: Smith.

Hambling, David. "Weatherwatch: How to Catch the Wind in a Trap of Stone." *The Guardian*. 28 June 2013.

Hancox, Joy. 1992. *The Byrom Collection*. London: Cape.

Hanson, Richard Patrick Crosland. 1985. "The Transformation of Pagan Temples into Churches in the Early Christian Centuries." In *Studies in Christian Antiquity*, edited by Richard Patrick Crosland Hanson. Edinburgh: T. and T. Clark.

Harland, John, and T. T. Wilkinson. 1867. *Lancashire Folk-Lore*. London: Warne.

Harley, Laurence S. 1953. "Alignments of Ancient Sites in Essex: New Judgement on 'The Old Straight Track.'" *The Essex Naturalist* 29: 63–76.

Harte, Jeremy. 1999. *Research in Geomancy 1990–1994: Readings in Sacred Space*. Wymeswold, UK: Heart of Albion.

Hasenfratz, Hans-Peter. 2011. *Barbarian Rites: The Spiritual World of the Vikings and the Germanic Tribes*. Translated by Michael Moynihan. Rochester, VT: Inner Traditions.

Haverfeld, Francis. 1913. *Ancient Town Planning*. Oxford: Clarendon.

Heanley, Rev. R. M. 1902. "The Vikings: Traces of their Folklore in Marshland.' *Saga Book of the Viking Club* 3: 35–62.

Hegel, G. W. F. 1977. *Phenomenology of Spirit*. Translated by A. V. Miller. Oxford: Oxford University Press.

Heidegger, Martin. 1927. *Sein und Zeit*. Halle: Niemeyer.

———. 1967. *What Is a Thing?* Chicago: Regnery.

———. 1977. *The Question Concerning Technology and Other Essays*. Translated by William Lovett. New York: Harper and Row.

———. 1987. *Being and Time*. Translated by John Macquarrie and Edward Robinson. London: Blackwell.

Heilbronn, J. L. 1999. *The Sun in the Church: Cathedrals as Solar Observatories*. Cambridge, MA, and London: Harvard University Press.

Henderson, William. 1866. *Notes on the Folk-Lore of the Northern Counties of England and the Borders*. London: Longmans, Green.
Herrick, Robert. 1902 [1648]. *The Poems of Robert Herrick*. London: Richards.
Herzog, Ze'ev. 1999. "Deconstructing the Walls of Jericho." *Ha'aretz Magazine* (Oct. 29): 1–9.
Heselton, Philip. 1991. *The Elements of Earth Mysteries*. Shaftesbury and Rockport, UK: Element.
Hibbert, Francis Aidan. 1891. *The Influence and Development of English Gilds*. Cambridge: Cambridge University Press.
Hildburgh, W. L. 1944. "Indeterminabilty and Confusion as Apotropaic Elements in Italy and Spain." *Folk-Lore* 55. 4 (Dec.): 133–49.
Hodson, Geoffrey. 1925. *Fairies at Work and Play*. London: Theosophical Publishing House.
Hoggard, Brian. 2004. "The Archaeology of Counter-Witchcraft and Popular Magic." In *Beyond the Witch Trials: Witchcraft and Magic in Enlightenment Europe*, edited by Owen Davies and William De Blécourt. Manchester: Manchester University Press.
———. 2019. *Magical House Protection: The Archaeology of Counter-Witchcraft*. New York and Oxford: Berghahn.
Hole, Christina. 1977. "Protective Symbols in the Home." In *Symbols of Power*, edited by H. R. Ellis-Davidson. London: Folklore Society. Pp. 121–30.
Howlett, England. 1899. "Sacrificial Foundations." In *Ecclesiastical Curiosities*, edited by William Andrews. London: Andrews. Pp. 30–45.
Hubbard, Elbert. 1916. *The Philosophy of Elbert Hubbard*. Edited by John T. Hoyle. Fabriano: Roycrofters.
Hufford, David J. 1995. "Beings Without Bodies: An Experience-Centered Theory of the Belief in Spirits." In *Out of the Ordinary: Folklore and the Supernatural*, edited by Barbara Walker. Logan: Utah State University Press. Pp. 11–45.
Hultkrantz, Åke. 1961. *The Supernatural Owners of Nature*. Stockholm: Almqvist and Wiksell.
Jacobsen-Widding, Anita. 1979. *Red-White-Black as a Mode of Thought: A Study of Triadic Classification by Colours in the Ritual Symbolism and Cognitive Thought of the Peoples of the Lower Congo*. Uppsala Studies in Cultural Anthropology I. Stockholm: Almqvist and Wiksell.

Inwood, Brad, trans. 1992. *The Poem of Empedocles*. Toronto: University of Toronto.
Jekyll, Gertrude. 1904. *Old West Surrey*. London: Longmans, Green.
Johnson, Marjorie T. 2014. *Seeing Fairies: From the Lost Archives of the Fairy Investigation Society, Authentic Reports of Fairies in Modern Times*. Charlottesville, VA: Anomalist.
Johnston, Walter. 1912. *Byways in British Archaeology*. Cambridge: Cambridge University Press.
Jones, Francis. 1954. *The Holy Wells of Wales*. Cardiff: University of Wales.
Jones, Graham. 2007. *Saints in the Landscape: Heaven and Earth in Religious Dedications*. London: Tempus.
Jones, Prudence 1982. *Eight and Nine: Sacred Numbers of Sun and Moon in the Pagan North*. Bar Hill: Fenris-Wolf.
———. 1990. "Celestial and Terrestrial Orientation." In *History and Astrology*, edited by Annabella Kitson. London: Unwin Hyman.
Jones, Prudence, and Nigel Pennick. 1995. *A History of Pagan Europe*. London: Routledge.
Jung, Carl G. 1972. *Synchronicity: An Acausal Connecting Principle*. London: Routledge and Kegan Paul.
Kandinsky, Wassily. 1912. *Über das Geistige in der Kunst*. Munich: Piper.
Kearns, Rev. J. F. 2001. *Silpa Sastra*. Cambridge, UK: Institute of Experimental Geomancy.
Kittredge, George Lyman. *Witchcraft in Old and New England*. Cambridge, MA: Harvard University Press.
Koop, Kenneth. 1946. *The Earliest Survey of Britain*. Cairo, Egypt: N.p.
Kowald, Margaret. 2022. *Beyond the Fence: Darling Downs—Moreton Rabbit Board, 1892–2022*. Warwick, Queensland, Australia: Darling Downs—Moreton Rabbit Board.
Kraft, John. 1985. *The Goddess in the Labyrinth*. Åbo: Åbo Akademi.
———. 1986. "The Magic Labyrinth." *Caerdroia* 19: 14–19.
Lakoff, George, and Mark Johnson. 1980. *Metaphors We Live By*. Chicago: Chicago University Press.
Larson, Laurence Marcellus. 1912. *Canute the Great, 995 (circ)–1035, and the Rise of Danish Imperialism during the Viking Age*. New York: Putnam's Sons.
Laurie, William Alexander. 1859. *The History of Free Masonry and the Grand Lodge of Scotland*. Edinburgh: Seton and Mackenzie.

Lauweriks, Johannes Ludovicus. 1919. "Het Titanische in de Kunst." *Wendingen* 2.4: 5.

Leadbeater, C. W. 1900. *The Astral Plane: Its Scenery, Inhabitants and Phenomena*. London: Theosophical Publishing Co.

———. 1909. "The Influence of Surroundings." *The Theosophist* 30.10 (July): 474–82.

Le Braz, Anatole. 1982. *La Légende de la mort chez les Bretons armoricains*. Marseille: Lafitte.

Leather, Ella Mary. 1914. "Foundation Sacrifice." *Folk-Lore* 24: 110.

Lecouteux, Claude. 2012. *The Secret History of Poltergeists and Haunted Houses: From Pagan Folklore to Modern Manifestations*. Translated by Jon E. Graham. Rochester, VT: Inner Traditions.

———. 2013. *The Tradition of Household Spirits: Ancestral Lore and Practices*. Translated by Jon E. Graham. Rochester, VT: Inner Traditions.

———. 2015. *Demons and Spirits of the Land: Ancestral Lore and Practices*. Translated by Jon E. Graham. Rochester, VT: Inner Traditions.

———. 2018. *The Hidden History of Elves and Dwarfs: Avatars of Invisible Realms*. Translated by Jon E. Graham. Rochester, VT: Inner Traditions.

Lee, Frederick George, ed. 1875. *Glimpses of the Supernatural*. 2 vols. London: King.

Lethaby, William Richard. 1891. *Architecture, Mysticism and Myth*. New York: Macmillan.

———. 1911. *Architecture: An Introduction to the History and Theory of the Art of Building*. London: Williams and Norgate.

———. 1913. "Art and Workmanship." *The Imprint* 1: 1–3.

Lethbridge, T. C. 1957. *Gogmagog: The Buried Gods*. London: Routledge and Kegan Paul.

Lethbridge, T. C., et al. 1974. *Gog Magog: The Discovery and Subsequent Destruction of a Great British Antiquity*. Cambridge: Land of Cokaygne.

Lichtheim, Miriam. 1980. *Ancient Egyptian Literature III: The Late Period*. Berkeley: University of California Press.

Lindig, Erika. 1987. *Hausgeister: Die Vorstellung übernatürlicher Schützer und Helfer in der deutschen Sagenüberlieferung*. Frankfurt and Bern: Lang.

Link, Johan Heinrich Friedrich. 1834. *Die Urwelt und das Alterthum, erläutert durch die Naturkunde*. 2nd edition. Berlin: Dummler.

Lip, Evelyn. *Chinese Geomancy*. 1979. Singapore: Times Books International.

Little, Greg, and Andrew Collins. 2022. *Origins of the Gods: Qesem Cave, Skinwalkers, and Contact with Transdimensional Intelligences.* Rochester, VT: Bear and Co.

Livingstone, Karen, Max Donnelly, and Linda Parry. 2016. *C. F. A. Voysey: Arts and Crafts Designer.* London: Victoria and Albert Museum.

Lockyer, Norman. 1906. *Stonehenge and Other British Stone Monuments Astronomically Considered.* London: Macmillan.

Lorenz, Konrad. 1989. *The Waning of Humaneness.* London: Unwin.

Lovett, Edward. 1925. *Magic in Modern London.* Croydon: Croydon Advertiser.

Lyle, Emily B. 1990. *Archaic Cosmos: Polarity, Space and Time.* Edinburgh: Polygon.

MacFarlane, Robert. 2003. *Mountains of the Mind: A History of a Fascination.* London: Granta.

Machen, Arthur. 1922. *Far Off Things.* London: Secker.

———. 1923. *The London Adventure, or The Art of Wandering.* London: Secker.

Machen, Arthur, and A. E. Waite. 2003 [1905]. *The House of the Hidden Light: Manifested and Set Forth in Certain Letters Communicated from a Lodge of the Adepts.* Edited by R. A. Gilbert. Coverdale, UK: Tartarus.

MacKail, John William. 1899. *The Life of William Morris.* 2 vols. London: Longmans, Green.

MacLeod, Sharon Paice. 2018. *Celtic Cosmology and the Otherworld: Mythic Origins, Sovereignty and Liminality.* Jefferson, NC: McFarland.

MacManus, Dermot. 1959. *The Middle Kingdom: The Faerie World of Ireland.* Gerrard's Cross, UK: Smythe.

Mair, Craig. 1988. *Mercat Cross and Tolbooth.* Edinburgh: Donald.

Mallarmé, Stéphane. 1917 [1897]. *Un coup de dés jamais n'abolira le hasard.* Paris: La Nouvelle Revue Français / Gallimard.

Mallien, Lara, and Johannes Heimrath, eds. 2008. *Was ist Geomantie? Die neue Beziehung zu unseren Heimatplaneten.* Klein-Jasedow, Germany: Drachen.

Mallien, Lara, and Johannes Heimrath, eds. 2009. *Genius Loci: Der Geist von Orten und Landschaften in Geomantie und Architektur.* Klein-Jasedow: Drachen.

Malraux, André. 1954. *The Voices of Silence.* London: Secker and Warburg.

Maltwood, K. E. 1964. *A Guide to Glastonbury's Temple of the Stars: Their*

Giant Effigies Described from Air Views, Maps and from "The High History of the Holy Grail." London: Clarke.

Mannhardt, Wilhelm. 1875. *Wald- und Feldkulte I: Der Baumkultus der Germanen und Ihrer Nachbarstämme.* Berlin: Borntraeger

Martin, Stephen A., ed. 2001. *Archibald Knox.* London: Artmedia.

Mason, Hugo. 2001. *All Saints' Church, Brockhampton, Herefordshire.* Brockhampton: Brockhampton Parochial Church Council.

Matless, David. 1993. "Appropriate Geography: Patrick Abercrombie and the Energy of the World." *Journal of Design History* 6.3 (September): 167–78.

Matthews, John, and Caroline Wise, eds. 2016. *The Secret Lore of London.* London: Coronet.

Maudsley, Henry. 1939. *Natural Causes and Supernatural Seemings.* London: Watts.

McFadzean, Patrick. 1985. *Astrological Geomancy: An Introduction.* York, UK: Northern Earth Mysteries.

———. 1999. *Vastu Vidya: Studies in Indian Geomancy.* Cambridge, UK: Institute of Experimental Geomancy.

McNeill, F. Marian. 1957–1968. *The Silver Bough.* 4 vols. Glasgow: MacLellan.

Mermet, Alexis. 1959. *Principles and Practice of Radiesthesia: A Textbook for Practitioners and Students.* Translated by Mark Clement. London: Stuart.

Merrifield, Ralph. 1988. *The Archaeology of Ritual and Magic.* New York: New Amsterdam.

Michell, John. 1967. *The Flying Saucer Vision.* London: Sidgwick and Jackson.

———. 1969. *The View Over Atlantis.* London: Garnstone.

———. 1975. *The Earth Spirit: Its Ways, Shrines and Mysteries.* London: Thames and Hudson.

———. 1981. *Ancient Metrology: The Dimensions of Stonehenge and of the Whole World as therein Symbolised.* Bristol: Pentacle.

———. 1983. *The New View over Atlantis.* London: Thames and Hudson.

———. 1986. *Stonehenge: Its History, Meaning, Festival, Police Riot '85, and Future Prospects.* London: Radical Traditionalist Papers.

———. 2005. *Confessions of a Radical Traditionalist.* Edited by Joscelyn Godwin. Waterbury Center, VT: Dominion.

———. 2009. *The Sacred Center: The Ancient Art of Locating Sanctuaries*. Rochester, VT: Inner Traditions.

Montaigne, Michel de. 1948. *The Complete Works of Montaigne: Essays—Travel Journal—Letters*. Translated by Donald M. Frame. Stanford: Stanford University Press.

Morris, Robert. 1734. *Lectures on Architecture Consisting of Rules Founded upon Harmonick and Arithmetical Proportion in Building*. London: Brindley.

Morris, William, et al. 1893. *Arts and Crafts Essays*. London: Rivington, Percival.

Morton, James. 2018. *The Hidden Lives of London Streets*. London: Robinson.

Mössinger, Friedrich. 1938. "Maibaum, Dorflinde, Weihnachtsbaum." *Germanien* 10: 145–55.

———. 1938. "Die Dorflinde als Weltbaum." *Germanien* 10 (1938): 388–96.

———. 1940. "Baumtanz und Trojaburg." *Germanien* 12 (1940): 282–89.

Mössinger, Friedrich, and Siegfried Sieber. 1978. *Troytowns in Germany*. Translated by Michael Behrend. Bar Hill, UK: Institute of Geomantic Research.

Mowl, Tim, and Brian Earnshaw. 1988. *John Wood: Architect of Obsession*. Bath: Millstream.

Narby, Jeremy, and Francis Huxley, eds. 2001. *Shamans Through Time: 500 Years on the Path to Knowledge*. London: Thames and Hudson.

Nauman, St. Elmo, Jr. 2021. *Exorcism Through the Ages*. New York: Open Road Integrated Media.

Newman, Leslie. 1940. "Notes on Some Rural and Trade Initiation Ceremonies in the Eastern Counties." *Folk-Lore* 51.3: 32–42.

Nichomachus of Gerasa. 1994. Translated by Flora R. Levin. *The Manual of Harmonics*. Grand Rapids, MI: Phanes.

Nissen, Heinrich. 1906–1910. *Orientation—Studien zur Geschichte der Religion*. 3 vols. Berlin: Weidmann.

Notebaart, Jannis C. 1972. *Windmühlen*. The Hague: Mouton.

O'Brien, Denis. 1967. "Empedocles' Cosmic Cycle." *The Classical Quarterly* 17.1: 29–40.

O'Brien, Flann. 1993. "The Myles na gCopaleen Catechism of Cliché." In *The Best of Myles: A Selection from "Cruiskeen Lawn."* London: Flamingo. Pp. 201–27.

Pakenham, Thomas. 2001. *Meetings with Remarkable Trees*. London: Cassell.

Pálsson, Herman, and Paul Edwards, trans. 1972. *The Book of Settlements: Landnámabók*. Winnipeg: University of Manitoba Press.

Parisinou, Eva. 2000. *The Light of the Gods: The Role of Light in Archaic and Classical Greek Cult*. London: Duckworth.

Parsons, Melinda Boyd. 1987. "The 'Golden Dawn,' Synaesthesia, and 'Psychic Automatism' in the Art of Pamela Colman Smith." In *The Spiritual Image in Modern Art*, compiled by Kathleen J. Regier. Wheaton, IL: Theosophical Publishing House.

Pennick, Nigel. 1970. "Geomancy." In *The Other Britain*, supplement to *Cambridge Voice* 16, series 2, no. 4, p. 16.

———. 1972. "Organic Metaphysics: A Study of the Work of D'Arcy Thompson." *Arcana* (December): 4–23.

———. 1974a. *Caerdroia: Ancient Turf, Stone and Pavement Mazes*. Trumpington, UK: Megalithic Visions.

———. 1974b. *The Mysteries of King's College Chapel*. Cambridge: Land of Cokaygne.

———. 1976a. *Ancient Hill-Figures of England*. Bar Hill, UK: Institute of Geomantic Research.

———. 1976b. "Glastonbury Abbey." In *Glastonbury: Ancient Avalon, New Jerusalem*. Edited by Anthony Roberts. London: Zodiac House. Pp. 54–61.

———. 1978a. "Ley and Solar Lines around Stonehenge." *Picwinnard* 8.

———. 1978b. "Pioneer Researchers in Geomancy." *Stonehenge Viewpoint* 9.1.

———. 1979a. *The Ancient Science of Geomancy: Man in Harmony with the Earth*. London: Thames and Hudson.

———. 1979b. *The Cambridgeshire Ley Project: List of Leys Claimed by Alfred Watkins (1932)*. Bar Hill, UK: Institute of Geomantic Research.

———. 1980. *Sacred Geometry: Symbolism and Purpose in Religious Structures*. Wellingborough, UK: Aquarian Press.

———, ed. 1982. *British Geomantic Pioneers, 1570–1932*. Bar Hill, UK: Institute of Geomantic Research.

———. 1985a. *The Cosmic Axis*. Bar Hill, UK: Runestaff.

———. 1985b. "Geomantic Reflections." *Practical Geomancy* 1.1 (Winter): 13–14.

———. 1986. *Einst war uns die Erde heilig*. Waldeck-Dehringhausen, Germany: Hübner.

———. 1987a. *Earth Harmony*. London: Rider.

———. 1987b. *Landscape Lines, Leys and Limits in Old England*. Bar Hill, UK: Runestaff–Old England.

———. 1987c. "The Subterranean Kingdom I: Secret Rites in Secret Places." *Exploring The Supernatural* 1.12: 49–53.

———. 1987d. "The Subterranean Kingdom. Part Two: Darkness and Light." *Exploring The Supernatural* 1.13: 33–37.

———. 1989a. *Practical Magic in the Northern Tradition*. Wellingborough, UK: Thorsons.

———. 1989b. "The Zürich Lindenhof Alignment." *The Ley Hunter* 109: 16–17.

———. 1990. *Mazes and Labyrinths*. London: Hale.

———. 1993a. *Anima Loci*. Bar Hill, UK: Nideck / The Way of the Eight Winds.

———. 1993b. "Earth Lines and Dowsing." *Journal of the British Society of Dowsers*, vol. 35: 204–7.

———. 1993c. *Visions of the Goddess*. Cambridge, UK: Nideck / The Way of the Eight Winds.

———. 1993d. *Wayland's House*. Bar Hill, UK: Nideck / The Way of the Eight Winds.

———. 1995. *Secrets of East Anglian Magic*. London: Hale.

———. 1996. *Celtic Sacred Landscapes*. London and New York: Thames and Hudson.

———. 1997. *Leylines*. London: Wiedenfeld and Nicolson.

———. 1997. *The Celtic Saints: An Illustrated and Authoritative Guide to these Extraordinary Men and Women*. London: Thorsons.

———. 1997. *The Celtic Cross: An Illustrated History and Celebration*. London: Blandford.

———. 2001. *The Three Fates*. Cambridge, UK: Library of the European Tradition.

———. 2002. "The Religion of Northern Europe." In *The Times World Religions*, edited by Martin Palmer. London: Times. Pp. 44–51.

———. 2002. *Masterworks: Arts and Crafts of Traditional Buildings in Northern Europe*. Wymeswold, UK: Heart of Albion.

———. 2003a. "Postmoderne Monumente." *Hagia Chora* 17: 109.

———. 2003b. *Ursprünge der Weissagung: Von Orakeln, heiligen Zahlen und magischen Quadraten*. Düsseldorf: Patmos.

———. 2004a. *Cambridge: Spirit of Place.* Bar Hill, UK: Old England House.
———. 2004b. "Heathen Holy Places in Northern Europe: A Cultural Overview." *Tyr: Myth—Culture—Tradition* 2: 139–49.
———. 2004c. *Makings.* Bar Hill, UK: Old England House.
———. 2005a. *The Bloomsbury Wonder.* Cambridge, UK: Sacred Land.
———. 2005b. *The Mysteries of St. Martin's: Sacred Geometry and the Symmetry of Order.* Cambridge: Sacred Land.
———. 2005c. *The Sacred Art of Geometry: Temples of the Phoenix.* Bar Hill, UK: Spiritual Arts and Crafts.
———. 2005d. *The Spiritual Arts and Crafts.* Bar Hill, UK: Spiritual Arts and Crafts.
———. 2005e. "Vom Fortbestehen alter Grenzen." *Hagia Chora* 20: 103.
———. 2010. "Pines on the Horizon, or, Seeing What We Want to See." *Silver Wheel Annual* 2: 97–101.
———. 2011. *The Toadman.* Hinckley: Society of Esoteric Endeavour.
———. 2013. "The Ensouled World." In *Silver Wheel* 4: 138–44.
———. 2015. *Pagan Magic of the Northern Tradition: Customs, Rites, and Ceremonies.* Rochester, VT: Destiny Books.
———. 2018. "Northern Cosmology: The World Tree and Irminsul." In *Tyr: Myth—Culture—Tradition* 5 (2018): 104–20.
———. 2019. *The Eldritch World.* North Augusta, SC: Arcana Europa.
———. 2022. *Creating Places of Power: Geomancy, Builders' Rites, and Electional Astrology in the Hermetic Tradition.* Rochester, VT: Inner Traditions.
———. 2023. *Wyrd Times: Memoirs of a Pagan Renaissance Man.* North Augusta, SC: Arcana Europa.
Pennick, Nigel, and Robert Lord. 1977. *Terrestrial Zodiacs in Britain.* Bar Hill, UK: Institute of Geomantic Research.
Pennick, Nigel, and Paul Devereux. 1989. *Lines on the Landscape: Leys and Other Linear Enigmas.* London: Hale.
Pennick, Nigel, and Helen Field. 2003. *A Book of Beasts.* Milverton, UK: Capall Bann.
Pennick, Nigel, and Marinus Gout. 2004. *Sacrale Geometrie: Verborgen Lijnen in de Bouwkunst.* The Hague: Synthese.
Petitpierre, Dom Robert, ed. 1972: *Exorcism: The Report of a Commission Convened by the Bishop of Exeter.* London: Society for Promoting Christian Knowledge.

———. 1976. *Exorcising Devils*. London: Hale.
Poseck, Helena von. 1979 [1905]. *Feng-Shui and the Chinese House*. Bar Hill, UK: Institute of Geomantic Research. [Originally published as "How John Chinaman Builds His House" in *The East of Asia Magazine*.]
Puvhel, Martin. 1976. "The Mystery of the Cross-Road." *Folklore* 87.2: 167–77.
Rackham, Oliver. 1986. *The History of the Countryside*. London: Dent.
Raglan, Lady. 1939. "The "Green Man" in Church Architecture." *Folk-Lore* 50: 45–57.
Randall, Arthur. 1966. *Sixty Years a Fenman*. Edited by Enid Porter. London: Routledge and Kegan Paul.
Rayson, George. 1865. "East Anglian Folk-Lore I: Weather Proverbs." *The East Anglian, or, Notes and Queries on Subjects Connected with the Counties of Suffolk, Cambridgeshire, Essex and Norfolk*: 1.
Rees, R. Wilkins. 1898. "Ghost Laying." In *The Church Treasury of History, Custom, Folk-Lore etc.*, edited by William Andrews. London: Andrews. Pp. 240–70.
Reichenbach, Baron C. 1926. *Letters on Od and Magnetism*. London: Hutchinson.
Reiser, Oliver L. 1974. *This Holyest Erthe: The Glastonbury Zodiac and King Arthur's Camelot*. London: Perennial.
Regier, Kathleen J., ed. *The Spiritual Image in Modern Art*. Wheaton, IL: Theosophical Publishing House.
Reuter, Otto Sigfrid. 1934. *Germanische Himmelskunde*. Jena: Köhler and Amelang.
———. 1985. *Sky Lore of the North*. Translated by Michael Behrend. Bar Hill, UK: Runestaff.
Roberts, Anthony. 1974. *Atlantean Traditions in Ancient Britain*. Llanfynydd: Unicorn.
———. 1981. *Geomancy: A Synthonal Re-appraisal*. Westhay, UK: Privately published.
Robb, Graham. 2020. *The Debatable Lands: The Lost World Between Scotland and England*. London: Picador.
Rose, Herbert Jennings. 1935. "*Numen inest*: 'Animism' in Greek and Roman Religion." *Harvard Theological Review* 28.4: 237–57.
Ross, Cathy. 2003. *Twenties London: A City in the Jazz Age*. London: Museum of London / Wilson.

Ross, Cathy, and Oliver Bennett. 2015. *Designing Utopia: John Hargrave and the Kibbo Kift.* London and New York: Wilson.
Rossbach, Sarah. 1984. *Feng-Shui: The Chinese Art of Placement.* London: Rider.
Rudge, E. A. 1952. "The Statistical Evidence for a Conglomerate Alignment in Essex." *The Essex Naturalist* 29: 178–86.
Rudge, E. A., and E. L. Rudge. 1952. "The Conglomerate Track." *The Essex Naturalist* 29: 17–31.
Saint-Yves d'Alveydre, Joseph Alexandre. 1903. *L'Archéomètrie.* Paris: Dourbon-Aîné.
Sartori, Paul. 1898. "Ueber das Bauopfer." *Zeitschrift für Ethnologie* 30: 1–54.
Schuré, Édouard. 1889. *Les grands initiés: Esquisse de l'histoire secrète des religions.* Paris: Perrin.
Screeton, Paul. 1974. *Quicksilver Heritage: The Mystic Leys—their Legacy of Ancient Wisdom.* Wellingborough, UK: Thorsons.
———. 1978. *The Lambton Worm and Other Northumbrian Dragon Legends.* London: Zodiac House.
Sennett, Richard. 1998. *The Corrosion of Character: The Personal Consequences of Work in the New Capitalism.* New York: Norton.
Seymour, St. John D. 1913. *Irish Witchcraft and Demonology.* Dublin: Hodges, Figgis.
Sieber, Siegfried. 1936. "Ein Trojaburg in Pommern." *Germanien* 8: 83–86.
Sinclair, Ian. 1998. *Lud Heat & Suicide Bridge.* London: Granta.
———. 2002. *London Orbital.* London: Granta.
Skinner, Stephen. 1982. *The Living Earth Manual of Feng-Shui.* London: Routledge and Kegan Paul.
Solnit, Rebecca. 2001. *Wanderlust: A History of Walking.* London: Verso.
Spence, Lewis. 1920. *An Encyclopædia of Occultism.* London: Routledge.
———. 1937. *Legendary London: Early London in Tradition and History.* London: Hale.
———. 1947. *Myth and Ritual in Dance, Game, and Rhyme.* London: Watts.
Speth, G. W. 1894. *Builders' Rites and Ceremonies.* Margate: Keeble's Gazette.
Squire, Charles. 1905. *The Mythology of the British Islands: An Introduction to Celtic Myth, Legend, Poetry and Romance.* London: Blackie and Sons.
Stansky, Peter. 1989. *William Morris, C. R. Ashbee, and the Arts and Crafts.* London: Nine Elms.

Stone, Alby. 1998. *Straight Track, Crooked Road: Leys, Spirit Paths, and Shamanism.* Wymeswold, UK: Heart of Albion.

Sykes, Wirt. 1880. *British Goblins: Welsh Folk-Lore, Fairy Mythology, Legends and Traditions.* London: Sampson Low, Marsden, Searle and Rivington.

Taussig, Michael. 1993. *Mimesis and Alterity: A Particular History of the Senses.* London: Routledge.

Temple, William. 1908 [1685]. *Upon the Gardens of Epicurus, with Other XVIIIth Century Garden Essays.* London: Chatto and Windus.

Teudt, Wilhelm. 1931. *Germanische Heligtümer.* Jena: Diederichs.

Theophilus. 1979. *On Divers Arts.* Translated by John G. Hawthorne and Cyril Stanley Smith. New York: Dover.

Thijn, Joseph Albert Alberdinck. 1859. *De Helige Linie: Proeve over de oostwardische richting van kerk en autaar als hoofbeginsel der kerklijke bouwkunst.* Amsterdam: Langenhuysen.

Thomas, Val. 2019. *Of Chalk and Flint: A Way of Norfolk Magic.* London: Troy.

Thorndyke, Lynn. 1964. "Imagination and Magic: Force of Imagination on the Human Body and of Magic on the Human Mind." In *Mélanges Eugène Tisserant 7.* Vatican City: Biblioteca Vaticana. Pp. 353–58.

Thorsson, Edred. 1992. *Northern Magic: Mysteries of the Norse, Germans and English.* St. Paul, MN: Llewellyn.

Tilley, Christopher. 1994. *A Phenomenology of Landscape: Places, Paths and Monuments.* Oxford: Berg.

Tolley, Clive. 1995. "The Mill in Norse and Finnish Mythology." *Saga-Book* 24: 63–82.

Tominaga, Yoshihide, and Mohammedreza Shirzadi. 2021. "Wind Tunnel Measurements of Three-Dimensional Turbulent Flow Structures Around a Building Group: Impact of High-Rise Buildings on Pedestrian Wind Environment." *Building and Environment* 206: 1–15.

Trevelyan, Marie. 1909. *Folk-Lore and Folk-Stories of Wales.* London: Stock.

Trubshaw, Bob. 1995. "The Metaphors and Rituals of Place and Time: An Introduction to Liminality." *Mercian Mysteries* 22: 1–8.

Turner, Victor. 1973. "The Center out There: Pilgrim's Goal." *History of Religions* 12.3: 191–230.

Tuzin, D. 1984. "Miraculous Voices: The Auditory Experience of Numinous Objects." *Current Anthropology* 25.5: 579–96.

Tyack, George S. 1899. "Mazes." In *Ecclesiastical Curiosities*, edited by William Andrews. London: Andrews. Pp. 186–205.

Tzara, Tristan. 1931. *L'Homme approximatif.* Paris: Fourcade.

Váňa, Zdeněk. 1992. *Mythologie und Götterwelt der slawischen Völker.* Stuttgart: Urachhaus.

Vaneigem, Raoul. 1975. *The Revolution of Everyday Life.* Translated by John Fullerton and Paul Sieveking. London: Practical Paradise.

Walditch, Beatrice. 2014. *Listening to the Stones: Living in a Magical World I.* Avebury, UK: Heart of Albion.

———. 2015. *Knowing Your Guardians: Living in a Magical World II.* Avebury, UK: Heart of Albion.

Walenkamp, H. J. M. 1905. "Voor-historische Wijsheid." *Archictectura* 12: 333–36, 376–85; 13: 185–88.

Walshe, Maurice O'C., ed. and trans. 1979–1987. *The Complete Mystical Writings of Meister Eckhart.* 3 vols. New York: Crossroad.

Warrack, Alexander. 1988 [1911]. *The Scots Dialect Dictionary.* Poole: New Orchard.

Watkins, Alfred 1922. *Early British Trackways.* Hereford and London: Watkins Meter Company / Simpkin, Marshall, Hamilton, Kent.

———. 1925. *The Old Straight Track.* London: Methuen.

———. 1927. *The Ley Hunter's Manual.* Hereford and London: Watkins Meter Company / Simpkin, Marshall.

———. 1932. *Archaic Tracks Round Cambridge.* London: Simpkin, Marshall.

Watts, Mary Seton. 1904. *The Word in the Pattern.* London: Ward.

Werbner, Richard. 1989. *Ritual Passage, Sacred Journey.* Manchester: Manchester University Press.

Westcott, W. Wynn [pseud. Sapere Aude], ed. 1895. *The Chaldæan Oracles of Zoroaster.* London: Theosophical Publishing Co.

Whelan, Richard, ed. 2000. *Stieglitz on Photography: His Selected Essays and Notes.* New York: Aperture.

Wilde, Lady [Jane Francesca Speranza]. 1887. *Ancient Legends, Mystic Charms, and Superstitions of Ireland.* 2 vols. Boston: Ticknor.

Williams Ab Ithel, John, ed. 1862–1874. *Barddas; or, a Collection of Original Documents, Illustrative of the Theology, Wisdom, and Usages of the Bardo-Druidic System of the Isle of Britain.* 2 vols. Llandovery and London: Roderic/Quaritch.

Williams-Ellis, Clough. 1928. *England and the Octopus.* London: Bles.

Wirth, Herman. 1934. *Die Heilige Urschrift der Menschheit*. 9 vols. Leipzig: Koehler and Amelang.

Woodcock, Peter. 2000. *This Enchanted Isle: The Neo-Romantic Vision from William Blake to the New Visionaries*. Glastonbury, UK: Gothic Image.

Yeats, Frances A. 1966. *The Art of Memory*. London: Routledge and Kegan Paul.

Zaborsky, Oskar von. 1936. *Urväter-Erbe in deutscher Volkskunst*. Leipzig: Koehler and Amelang.

Index

Note: Page numbers in *italics* refer to illustrations.

Abercrombie, Patrick, 202
Abred, 241
Ab Uno, *33*
Adam, 122
Addison, Joseph, 201
Adler, Alfred, 23, 161
Aer, 105
Æther, 89, 105, 163, 194
Agricola, Georgius, 333
agrimensores, 44
Agrippa, H. C., 13, 34
Air, 105
airts, 127
Alberti, Leon Battista, 50, 343
alchemy, and two worlds, 85
álfrek, 181
 of Anima Loci, 163–68
Alvit, 331
ambience, 8
Anaxagoras, 34
Anaximander, 94
ancient wisdom, the recovery of, 27–31
Andronicus of Cyrrhus, 136
Anima Loci, 159–68, *160*, *162*
 defined, 159
 principles, 161–68
 processes, *166*
Ankou, 245
Annwn, 241
Apollonius of Tyana, 337
Aquinas, Thomas, 278, 337
archaeology, and violation of sacred
  spaces, 225–28
archangels, 119
Archée, 194
Ariadne, 324–26
Aristotle, 93
Arnarson, Ingulf, 179
"Arsé-Versé," 268
Ars Magna of London, 5–6, 9, *10*
art, 277–83
Artemis, 161
Arthur, King, 301–2
Art of Line, 285–86
Arts and Crafts, Spiritual, 202,
  276–83, 338
Arts and Crafts movement, 277–78
"As above, so below," 34, 100, *240*
Asenby labyrinth, 262
astrology, electional, 157–58

375

Atropos, 108–9
Aurelian, 61–62
Aurora Pallantias, 124
Austin, John, 260
authenticity, history of, 43–50
Axis Mundi, 103–7

Bacon, John the Elder, 238
ba gua geomantic mirror, *200*, 246
Bakerloo Line of Transport, 315–16
banfáithi, 236
Barbari, Jacopo de', 286
barbwire, 207–11, *210*
Barnard, Charles, 207
Barrie, J. M., 224
Bazel, Karel de, *21*, 281
being present, 167–68
beings, taxonomy of, 173–75
Bennett, Francis J., 252
Benson, Robert Hugh, 196–97
Bergson, Henri, 35
Berlin Wall, 213
Bersuire, Pierre, 62
Beverley stages of sanctity, 216–18
"Big Bang," 82–84
Birmingham districts, 8–9
Black, William Henry, 254
Blake, William, 33, 57
Bloomsbury Wonder, The, 3
blues, as healer, 93
Bodvild, 331–32
body, human, 85–89
   fourfold perception of, 87
   as reflection of the Cosmos, 89
boldness, 42
"borderline cases," 215
borderlines, crossing, 205–18
Boreas, 134, 137
Botolph, Saint, 67

boundaries
   boundary marker, London, *206*
   crossing, 205–18
   defensive boundary in Wales, *212*
   described, 205–6
   industrial, 207–11
   sacred, 215–18
   seven kinds of, 205
   streets as, 214–15
Brabant, 214
Bragdon, Claude, 279
Braque, Georges, 26
breathing (for meditation), 299
Breton, André, 5–6
Breugel, Pieter the Elder, 223
British national borders, 206–7
Broadwood, Lucy, 271
Browne, Thomas, 34
Bulwer-Lytton, Edward, 194
Buyan, Island of, 134, *135*
Byrom, John, 290

Caecias, 137
calendars, 54
Calvary Mountains, 233
Cambridge ley lines, *256*
Cambridge University, *59*
Camillo, Guilio Delminio, 286
cardinal directions, 119–25
Cardinal Virtues, and cardinal
   directions, 119
Cardo, 259, 293
Carroll, Lewis, 224
cause and effect, 36–38
Cecilia, St., *63*
Celtic tradition, 329–30
ceremonies, 304–5, *304–5*
Ceugant, 241

Chambers, William, 201–2, 204
chance, defined, 53
charcoal burners, *188*
Charpentier, Louis, 195
chicken wire, 207–8, *208*
Chinook, 143
Christianity, 34, 59, 62, 146, 177, 179, 233
Church of St. Cecilia, *313*
Cicero, 43
Claudius Ptolemy, 289
Clement, St., 60
closs, 245
Clotho, 108–9
Cockaigne, Land of, 12, 223–24
Cockaygne Press, 12–13, *13*
Cockney speech, 30
Coevorden defenses, *295*
Coleridge, Samuel Taylor, 22, 279
compass rose, 140
Completion, 40
concentration (for meditation), 246
concrete, 74
Cornell, Joseph, 6
Cosmic Axis, 239–42
 defined, 239
Cosmic Egg, 82–84, *83*, *84*, *340*
Cosmic principles, 79
Cosmos
 Cosmic Order, 108
 as cyclic, 100
 Norton diagram of, *107*
 and the One, 33–34
 principles of, 35–36
crane, 325–26
Crane Dance, 324–26
Creation theories, 82, 95, 98–100
 Jewish, 87
cross, *88*

crossroads, 55, *55*, 257–60
 and divination, 260
 symbolism of, 257, 260
Crystallization, 40
currents, 236–38
cylchau, 241

Daedalus, 261, 325
Dag-sign, 268
Dames, Michael, 252
Daoism, 64
Debord, Guy, 8
Decumanus, 259, 293
Delphi, omphalos at, 102–3
Delphic Oracle, 297
Denham, Michael Aislabie, 173–75
derilans, 66
Derry, 186
De Stijl, 286
Devil's Arrow, *231*
dewar, 168, 338–39
Diablo, 143
Dindsenchas, 171
directions, four, 119–25
dís, defined, 178
Dísablót, 178
divination, 53–56
 purpose of, 54
Divine Immanence, 169–71, *170*
Divinity, human personifications of, 57–64
Dobbie Stones, 180
dowsing, 195–96
Druids, and transmigration, 177–78
Druid's Cord, 294, 306–8
 defined, 306
 making a, 307–8, *307*
dryads, 172–73

dualism, 62–64
duende, 195
Duke, Edward, 251–52

Earth
  center of the, 101–2
  defined, 89
  divisions of, 115–18
  flat Earth theory, 101–2
  our place on, 113–18
  and the Sun, 126
earth energies, 193–98
Eckhart, Meister, 279–80
eddies, 236–38
Egil, 331
eight tides of the day, 126–31, *129*, *344–45*
  Germanic version, *131*
  names of, 128
eight winds, 134–39, *136*
Eitel, Ernst Johann, 200
Elder Futhark runes, 302, *303*
eldritch world, the, 75–77, *76*
  entry into, 76–77
elements, four, 80–84, *81*, 89
Elgar, Edward, 30
Emerson, Ralph Waldo, 279
empathy, loss of, 338
Empedocles of Acragas, 82
"English Garden" design, 202
enhazelled ground, 181–83
ensoulment, 229
Epictetus, 40
Er, 103–5
Erdstrahlen, 196, 245
Eresburg, 241–42
Eshu, 257–58
Eternal Tradition, the, 39–42
Etesian, 143

Etruscan Discipline, 44, 105, 114–18, 122, 293
Eurus, 134, 137
Exorcism report, 197–98
experience, four aspects of, 26
Expression and development, 40
Externsteine, 234

Fair-Gortha, 220
fairies, 4
fairy tracks, 244–46
Father Thames, 238
feng shui, 194–95, 199–204
  in the West, 199–200
festivals, 153
  religious, 154–55
fiat lux, 98
Fielding, H., 171
Five Precepts, 280
flow, 194
focusing-in, 51
Föhn, 143
foot, northern, 309–10
Force, the, 196
form, 279–80
"form follows function," 281
fortitude, 122
Fortitudo, 122
Fortune, Dion, 193
Fountain of Youth, 223
Four Corners of the Heavens, 113–14, *115*
four directions, 119–25, 128
  goddesses of the, *120*
four elements, 80–84, *81*, 89
four humors, 90–93
  defined, 90
  and winds, *92*
foursquare holy city, 293–94

four winds, 132–42
  origins of, 132–33
  refined into eight winds, 134–39
Frideswide, 189
fundamentalism, xi
Fusui temple, Peasholm Park, *203*

Gabblerout, 221
Gaillard, "Slim," 31
Gardner, Gerald, 155
gargoyles, 272–73, *272*
gast, 181
gates, 215–16
gateways, as transition points, 259
genetic engineering, 333
genius loci, 65–66, 159, 171, *177*
Geoffrey of Monmouth, 247
geomancy, 11–17, 157
  defined, 9
  described, 230
  and *Exorcism* report, 197–98
  geomantic protection, 267–73
  geomantic walking, 320–22
  physical elements of, 230–38
  vist to Hilton, *15*
geomantic compass, Japanese, *204*
geometry, sacred. *See* sacred geometry
Gibbons, Orlando, 285
Gibbs, James, 288
goði, 178–79
God-nails, 283
gods, 57–64
golden section, 271
Goldsmith, Oliver, 71
Grahame, Kenneth, 189
Great Wall of China, 211
green industrial revolution, 46–47
"Green Man," 189
guardians, 66

guilds, Five Precepts of, 280
Gwyllion, 221
Gwynvyd, 241

Hablik, Wenzel, 277
Hadewijch, 233
Halyman's Rig, 181
hamadryads, 172–73
hammer, 282–83, *282*
Hephaistos, 59
harmonics, *286*, *287*
harrowardens, 66
Hawk, the, 143
health, and the four humors, 92
Heanley, R. M., 221
Heelstone, 250
Heimat, 178
Helikon, 289–90, *289*
Helios, 60–62
Hennebique, François, 74
herm, 259
Hermes, 59
Hermes Trismegistus, 34, 100
Herrick, Robert, 40
Hesperus, 124
hex signs, 268
Higden, Ranulph, 148
Highland Clearances, 70
hills, 235–36
history, 43
Holden, Charles, 140, 296
Homer, 161
Hooker, John Lee, 93
hours, 127
House of the Rising Sun, 122–24, *123*
Hubbard, Elbert, 196
humors, four, 90–93
Hundertwasser, Friedensreich, 68

Hunters' Hall, 190
Hytersprites, 180

idis, defined, 178
imagination, the power of, 22–23
Immanence, Divine, 169–71
Inception, 40
indeterminate, taxonomy of the, 173–75
industrialization, 73
"In one is all," 32–33, *36*, 100, 322
Institute of Geomantic Research, 12, *14*
Inwood, William, 140
Irish Otherworld, 294
Irminsul, 242, *242*, *340*
Iron Curtain, 212–13
"It is better to travel hopefully than to arrive," 301, *322*, 338
Iustitia, 121

jazz language, 31
Jerusalem, 34
Jesus, 62, 122
Johnson, Robert, 258
Johnston, Duncan Alexander, 252
Jonson, Ben, v
Joyce, James, 192
Judeo-Christian tradition, 34, 64
Justice, 121

keeping up the day, 153, 155
King's Circus, 251
"king's highway," 247
KISS, 25
Koop, K. H., 254

labyrinths, 261–66, *264*, *265*, *305*, 316–20, *319*, 327
  classical, 316, 318–20
  defined, 261
  labyrinth workshop, 1987, 317–18
  making, 318–20, *320*
  millennium at Pluckley commission, *318*
  principles of, 263–64
  Strawberry Fair labyrinth, *16*
  Theseus-Minotaur legend, 324–26
  and the Way of the Eight Winds, 16–17
Lachesis, 108–9
Landnábók, 171–72
Land of Cockaigne, 12, 223–24
landscape, and spirituality, 176–78
landscape gardening, 72
Landsker Line, 207
land wights, 171–72
Lanham, Neil, 339
Lapwing Step, 326, *326*
Last Chance Saloon, the, 215
Laurie, W. A., 313
Lauweriks, J. L. M., 23, 262
"laws" of nature, 36–38
Leadbeater, C. W., 7, 193, 195
Leibniz, Gottfried Wilhelm, 49
leshy, 189
Lethaby, William Richard, 101–2, 202, 230, 258, 279
"Let there be light," 41
Lewis, C. S., 224
ley lines, 254, *256*
Lichfield Cathedral, *240*
Lipari, 133–34
literalism, 23–26, 29–30, 161
Llevantades, 143
Lockyer, Norman, 155, *156*
  on Stonehenge, 252–54
locus amoenus, 222–24
locus terribilis, 65, 219–22
  defined, 219
  what to do in, 221–22

London, the spirit of, 5–11
London Underground, heptagonal
  stations of, 296
lo pan, 199
Lorca, Federico García, 195
Los Angeles, 67
lost speech, 28
Lucan, 186
Lucifer, 124
Lugh, 259
Luilekkerland, 224
Lux, 41, 98

Machen, Arthur, 5, 11, 22, 35, 235
Macleod, Fiona, 294
Macrocosm, 100
magic, measure in, 308–12
Magical Papyri, 95
Maitland, J. A. Fuller, 271
Mallarmé, Stéphane, 49
Malraux, André, 9
mana, 194
manred, 48, 236
Matless, David, 203
Maypole, 187, *243*
measure
  land measure, 309–12
  in magic, 308–12
  traditional, 285–86
meditation, 299–300
Meridies, 122, 124
Mermet, Alexis, 195–96
metalwork, 261–62
metaphors for the ineffable, 194–98
mete-wands, 312
mezuzah, 267, *267*
Michael, Saint, 232–33
Microcosm, 100
mile, 309

mining, 333
Minotaur, 324–26
Mistral, 143
modernity, 45–47, *45*
modernization, 69–70
monetarist view of the world, 167
moot hills, 235–36
More, Thomas, 224
Morganwg, Iolo, 240
Morning Star, 124
Morris, Robert, 324
Morris, William, 48
Mortimer, Robert, 197
"Moses' Book of the Great Name," 97
mountains
  holiness of, 230–33
  tutelary deities of, 232–33
mulberry, 119
music, 27–28, 287
  healing power of, 93
  musical ratios, 343
Music of the Spheres, 287
Myrddin Wyllt, 190
myth, functions of, 329

Nameless Art, 11
names, 65–68
Nash, John, 214
Natural Measure, 309–11, *310*
Nature
  disappearance of, 339
  diversity of, xi–xiii
Naval Hospital gate, *216*
nemetona, 186
New York City, 67
Nicholas, Saint, 60
Nichols, Ross, 155, 254–55
Nicholson, John, 11
Nichomachus of Gerasa, 94

Nidud, King, 331
No Man's Land, 222
Nornir, 109, *110*
North Star, 106
Nosseni, Giovanni Maria, 295
Notos, 134, 137
Nox, 124–25
number symbolism, 341–42

obryn, 241
Occam's razor, 24
Occidens, 122, 124
Odin, 59, 179, 259
odyle, 194
Offa's Dyke, 206
Ogdoas, 94–97
Old Curiosity Shop, the, *7*
Olrum, 331
omphalos, 62, 101–2
    at Aachen, *103*
    and crossroads, 258
    at Delphi, 102–3, *102*
    at Uisnech, 248
önd, *166*, 280
    defined, 163
One, and all, 32–33
onlay, of Anima Loci, 163, 164
opposing limbs of the sun orientation, 314–15
orgone, 194
Oriens, 122
orientation (of buildings, etc.), 312–16
    opposing limbs of the sun, 314–15
ørlög, 52, 165
    defined, 52n*
    and history, 69–74
    for the individual, 69
    sanctification of, 164

Orpheus, 82–84
oskorei, 245
Ouncle Weights, 309

Paganism, year in, 155
paradise, 222–24
paramateric diagrams, 290–92, *291*
paths, 242–46
patience, 276
patriarchy, 49
Pennick, Nigel (author)
    early influences of, 1–5
    end of his traveling, 17–18
    maternal grandmother of, 4
    near-death experiences of, 4, 17–18
pentagram, 268, *271*
Percht, Frau, *58*
Pereson, Jennet, 308
Perilous Spaces, what to do in, 221–22
Perseus, 246
place
    our place on Earth, 113–18
    and sense of being, 65
place-names, 65–68
places, numinous places in the land, 192–98
places of spirit, 176–83
"plan and elevation" diagrams, 292
planetary spheres, 94–97, *96*
Plato, 103–5
Pliny the Elder, 121
Plymouth city center, 203–4
Polaris, 106
Polybius, 92
Pope, Alexander, 72
Poseidon, 59
post-onlay sites, 165
prana, 194
primal speech, 27–31

principles, 35–36
Priscus, Lucinius Tarquinius, 173
probability, 53
progression, stages of, 40–42
proportion, and ratio, 285–88
protection, geomantic, 267–73
  for religious buildings, 271–72
prudence, 119–21
Prudentia, 119
psychogeography, 8
purity of intention, 297
Pythagoras, 81, 94
  and music, 287, 343

qi, 195
Quhaip, 273

railways, 214
Ranaldini, Carlo, 295
ratio, and proportion, 285–88
reality, and science, 23
Red Lion Passage, *6*
Red Mount Chapel, *235*
Regent Street, 214
Reich, Wilhelm, 194
religions, essence of, xi
Remora, 121
rhinoceros, etymology of, 192–93
Richard III, 228
rites, 304–5
rivers, 236
roads, 247–49
  Irish, 248
  Swedish, 248
Robin Hood, 189
"Rock of Ages," 234
rocks, numinous, 234–35
rod (measure), 311–12
Rodin, Auguste, 279

Rome, city plan of, 293
Rosenkreuz, Christian, tomb of, 296
Rosicrucianism, and seven-sided
  structures, 294–96
Rosmerta, 59
royal roads, 247–49
Rudolf of Fulda, 242
runes, 302–3
  protective, *269*
runic exercises, 302–3
Ruskin, John, 276

sacred geometry, 284–92
sacredness, 169–75
  violation by archaeology, 225–28
Saffron Walden Town Maze, 265–66, *266*
Saint Odile well, *237*
Saint Swithun's Day, 150
Salisbury, 255–56
sanctification, 163–64
Sansnom, 190
Schaumberg, Ernst von, 295
Schlaraffenland, 224
Schwarzwald forest, *185*
science, and reality, 23
seasons, 128, 153–58
Sea Witches, 147–48
"Seek Paradise," 19
seers' journeys, 300–301
Septentrio, 122, 124–25
Serlio, Sebastiano, 289
"serpent power," 195
seven-sided structures, 294–96
Sextus Empiricus, 241
Sextus Propertius, 42
Shakespeare, William, 30
shrine of the Black Madonna, *217*
Sidwell, St., *61*

Sion, Llewellyn, 240
sitting (for meditation), 299
skills, traditional, 73–74
skills and wisdom, ancient, 73–74, 277–83. See also Spiritual Arts and Crafts
Skiron, 137
Skirrid, 232
skyscrapers, 149–50
Slagfinn, 331
smågubbar, 262
Smith, Harry W., 184, 204
Society for Symbolic Studies, 12
Solano, 143
Sol Iustitiae, 62
solstices, 128–30
spectacle, 51–52
speech, primal, 27–31
Spindle of Necessity, 104–7
spirit paths, 244–46
spirit-places, 176–83
spirits of the earth, 169–75
  described, 172–73
  taxonomy of the, 173–75
Spiritual Arts and Crafts, 202, 276–83, 338
spiritual exercises, 297–305
Spoils of Annwn, The, 301–2
Stabilization, 40
Stevenson, Robert Louis, 301, *322*
St Martin-in-the-Fields Church, *288*
Stonehenge, 250–56, *251*
  alinements, 255
  astronomical divisions of the year, *253*
storytelling, 329–30
streets, as boundaries, 214–15
Stribog, 133
Sturluson, Snorri, 248

sub-creation, 278
success, 42
Sucellos, 59
Sullivan, Louis, 281
sun, 60–62
sundials, *314*
sun-god, 60–62
Svanhvit, 331
swan-valkyries, 330–32
symbols, 23–26, 29–30
symmetry of order, the, 288
syncretism, 60
Système Hennebique, 74

technicians, who profane the world, 330–34
temenos, 186–87, 215
temperament, defined, 90–92
Temperance, 121
Temperantia, 121
Temple, William, 200–201
Temple of Solomon, *216*
Temple of the Four Winds, *139*, 140
templum, 115
Terry, Quinlan, 140
Tetractys, 81–82
Theon of Smyrna, 287
"The Path is the Goal," 338
Theseus-Minotaur legend, 324–26
"The way is the objective," 301
Thomas the Rhymer, 77
Thor, 282
thoughts, banishing, 299
Three Fates, 108–12
tides, eight, 126–31, 344–45
time, 258
Tolkien, J. R. R., 22, 75, 278
Toplady, Augustus, 234
Tower of the Winds, 118, *133*

"Tower of the Winds," 140
tradition, 43–45, 339
trait, 285
Transition, 40
transmigration of souls, 177–78, 241
Transvolution, 40
trees
 rituals with, 173
 sacredness of, 184–87
 sacred tree, Bavaria, *187*
 as symbols of Cosmic Axis, 184
trench warfare boundaries, *209*
Trevelyan, Marie, 308
Trevisa, John, 148
Tristram, Sir, 190
trouvailles, 6
Tubal Cain, 59
tunnels, 315–16
turf mazes, 263
"Twelve Apostles, The," 271
Tyack, George S., 266

UFOs, 196
unity of all existence, *21*, 34
Utopia, 224
utterance of the call (for meditation), 299–300

Väderhatt, Erik, 147, *147*
Valentine and Orson, 190
valkyries, 330–32
vé, 182
viewpoints, alternative, materialist vs. spiritual, 20–21, 23–26
Vintios, 134
violation of sacred spaces, 225–28
Virgil, 215–16, 225
Vitruvian Man (da Vinci), *86*

Vitruvius, 118, 138–39, *287*
"Vout-o-Reeny," 31
Voysey, C. F. A., 281–82
vril, 194

walking, geomantic, 320–22
walls, as boundaries, 211–13
wandering, 5–8
Watkins, Alfred, 155–57, 254–55
Watson, James Paton, 203–4
wayfarers, legacy of, 335–36
Wayland's house, 327–34, *328*
Wayland the Smith, 261, 327–34
Way of the Eight Winds, the, *xii*
 and Anima Loci, 159–68
 banner, xiii
 and belief, 60
 as continuance of holistic tradition, 339
 cover of German publication, *298*
 example of pathworking, 301–3
 floral labyrinth, *317*
 and geomancy, 74
 meditation in, 299–300
 operating spirit of, 12–14
 origins of, 1–18
 runic exercises, 302–3
 spiritual exercises, 297–305
 as spiritual path, xi–xiv
 and tradition, 43–44
 and traditional understandings, 193
weathercocks, 150–52, *152*
Weber, Max, 46
Web of Wyrd, 108–12
wells, 236–38
Wentworth-Shields, F. E., 316
wheel of time, Icelandic, *130*
Wild Dog Barrier Fence, 208

Wilde, Lady Jane, 220–21
Wild Huntsman, 221
Wild Man, 189
wildwood, 187–91
will, and conformity with Nature, 29
William of Occam, 24
Will O' the Wisp, 221
wind-corners, 149
windmills, 144–45, *145*
winds, in divination and magic, 146–48, *148*
winds, eight, 134–39, *136*
winds, four, 132–42
wind vanes, *141*, 150–52, *151*
Wirth, Herman, 157
wisdom, recovery of ancient, 27–31
witch balls, 246
witch-posts, 268
woivre, 195
Wood, Edgar, 278
Wood, John the Elder, 250–51

Woodwose, 189
world, and Cosmos and human body, 85–89
worldviews, 85–89
  symbolic vs. literalism, 23–26
  world as ensouled, 161
Worm, Ole, 199–200
Wright, Frank Lloyd, 281
wyrd, defined, 111
Wyrd Sisters, 108–12

Yarthkins, 180
year divisions, 153–58
  Pagan, 155–56
yin-yang, 64
Ymir, 99–100
yrias, 244

Zephyros, 134, 137
zodiac, and human body, 91
Zoroaster, 28
Zum Irrgarten, 268, 270